The Individual's Guidebook to

WILLS
AND
ESTATES

Edward M. Melillo, Esq.

THE INDIVIDUAL'S GUIDEBOOK TO WILLS AND ESTATES

1405 SW 6th Avenue • Ocala, Florida 34471 • Phone 352-622-1825 • Fax 352-622-1875

Website: www.atlantic-pub.com • Email: sales@atlantic-pub.com
SAN Number: 268-1250

Library of Congress Cataloging-in-Publication Data

Names: Melillo, Edward M., author.
Title: Your guide to wills and estates / by Edward M. Melillo, Esq.
Description: Ocala : Atlantic Publishing Group, Inc, 2017. | Includes bibliographical references and index.
Identifiers: LCCN 2017046774 (print) | LCCN 2017047296 (ebook) | ISBN 9781620235096 (ebook) | ISBN 9781620235089 (pbk. : alk. paper) | ISBN 1620235080 (alk. paper)
Subjects: LCSH: Estate planning—United States. | Wills—United States. | Probate law and practice—United States. | Executors and administrators—United States.
Classification: LCC KF750 (ebook) | LCC KF750 .M45 2017 (print) | DDC 346.7305/4—dc23
LC record available at https://lccn.loc.gov/2017046774

Printed in the United States

PROJECT MANAGER: Katie Cline
INTERIOR LAYOUT AND JACKET DESIGN: Nicole Sturk

Thank you for taking the complex and changing subject matter of estate planning, and putting it together into an easy-to-follow compilation—very helpful and useful. I hope that many others get the chance to complete their estate plans.

Douglas E. Wilson, J.D., Attorney

Mr. Melillo has taken what can be an uncomfortable topic and has presented it in a clear, motivational, and even entertaining way. I would recommend "The Individual's Guidebook to Wills and Estates" as an essential reference to anyone seeking to better understand the necessary process of preparing a Will. Mr. Melillo writes well, understands how to address the topic in a way laymen can comprehend, and offers excellent examples of the way Wills have—and haven't—worked in history.

Daniel Hanson, Educator and Administrator

Everyone who needs to complete their Last Will and other estate planning documents will find this book a valuable reference tool with easy instructions and sample estate documents. This book will help readers overcome the roadblocks to understanding estate planning and convinces readers to complete their Will and estate documents.

Thuha T. Vuong, DDS, University of Washington

Here's a book on estate planning that everyone can understand. It details how to prepare each section of a Last Will and discusses when a Trust is helpful to include in your estate plan. The author uses real-life examples to help explain legal situations. Sample Wills, Trusts, and Powers of Attorney are included, along with the Last Wills of various past celebrities. The book is a valuable resource tool—one I have recommended to others.

Gina Iandola, Banking Manager

Gotta do it! So you might as well get it done right. This book becomes a nice resource to understand how to wisely get your Last Will done, as well as to know whether a Trust is necessary to have in your estate portfolio. Included in this book are sample Last Wills, Trusts, and a Durable Power of Attorney for Health Care and Financial Management. There are real-life examples and so much more. And all of it is clearly explained. Gotta get it!

John Streidl, M.D.

TABLE OF CONTENTS

INTRODUCTION

THOUGHTS FROM THE AUTHOR ON ORGANIZING YOUR ESTATE

What the caterpillar perceives as the end;
to the butterfly is just the beginning.
Everything that has a beginning has an ending.
Make your peace with that and all will be well.

BUDDHIST SAYING

In the 1990s, it was a surprise to hear, even back then, that a large majority of adult Americans did not possess a valid or updated Will (also called a "Last Will," or "Last Will and Testament"). Various national surveys at the time revealed that between 60 to 75 percent of Americans died without a Last Will.[1] It seemed to be an overwhelmingly high statistic for something so important to have. It is one of those things that you need to get done but keep holding off. And to those who have completed a Will … congratulations for having the discipline and initiative to get it done. But, for complete peace of mind, just remember that the dynamics of a changing world make it necessary to follow up on that Will, and to ask: "How long ago was it prepared? Have my life's circumstances changed since my Last Will was completed? Namely, does it need to be updated?"

---

1. Beyer, G. (1999). Wills, Trusts and Estates, Ch. 2, §2.1, "Reasons Most Individuals Die Intestate." Aspen Law & Business.

There is a garden variety of reasons for not completing or updating a Last Will, one of which is the obvious avoidance of having to plan for one's own mortality. Perhaps you want to make sure everything is correct and includes all the right legal angles to fit your needs. Surely, you need time to think about selecting the right Executor for your estate, someone who must have your back; that is, your complete trust in honestly dealing with your assets and heirs, as well as being able to prudently handle the administration of your estate. Or maybe there are unanswered questions about how you plan to have your assets transferred. Can you sensibly give assets to an heir all at once? Or should you put it in a trust and distribute portions of it over time? It is important to question whether your children will wisely hold onto the inheritance they receive or joyously burn through it. It can be overwhelming to think about, especially with a busy family life and a full-time job, or jobs. Other reasons might include one's lack of assets, the costs as well as the time and effort needed for the preparation, the revelation of private facts, and the intimidation and complexity of completing a Will and other estate documents. Most of all, you probably want time to think things through and plan it perfectly since it is your prized estate that is being given away.

Pragmatically, the notion that you can die or become incapacitated at any time, like in a traffic accident while on the way to the grocery store, should be a compelling enough reason to complete your Last Will and any accompanying estate planning documents. Answers to these questions about preparing a Will and the construction details needed to build your estate are compiled and referenced in this book. Sudden death, coupled with a family to care for, ought to prioritize in the mind of the reasonable person to get that estate plan finished.

Remember that you can always amend or change a Will. And should you become intellectually challenged due to an accident, physical harm, disease, or otherwise, having done your Last Will cements your wishes that overbearing or disinherited heirs will find it very difficult to change in probate court. Also, inserting a no-contest clause in a Last Will or Trust tends to greatly lessen any chance of in-fighting among heirs. See, examples of a no-contest clause under Article 7.3 of the sample Living Trust in

Chapter 3, and under the Last Will of Vickie Lynn Marshall (aka Anna Nicole Smith) in Chapter 6. Various references and tips on the constructs to writing a Will are further explained under Chapter 2.

What do recent surveys show today about the percentage of Americans getting their Wills completed? Have we gotten better over the past 25 years? Computer and internet technology have greatly improved the chances, no doubt. What we have seen in the past quarter century is remarkable. The world has progressed from having little or no computer and internet access to having lightning-fast internet access and computer capability. And smart phones have literally mobilized the world, with instant information at our fingertips. We are no longer stuck with cumbersome typewriters or that pesky white-out ink. Now, in a computerized and mobile world, with information available at a moment's inquiry, tasks are so much easier to get done. Our social networking connects us with others like they were next door. Our questions receive instant answers and real-time feedback. That is today's norm. So, it's very reasonable to assume that we could only have gotten better with estate planning, too.

Recent surveys about estate planning pretty much arrive at the same conclusion. The author chose to present one of the surveys here that presents a nice, broad overview of estate-planning factors, with a substantiated survey that interviewed a full and diverse range of adults. It is summarized below and provides the latest update to the variation of the question, "How many Americans have a solid Will?" After all, if you prepare a Will, you want a good one, one that reads clearly, both legally and grammatically, and not a Will with vague or confusing language.

In June 2016, USLegalWills.com tasked a survey that asked 2,012 adults, aged 18 and older, about their Last Wills. The selected survey was conducted in the United States by Google Consumer Surveys. It has a root square mean error of only 1.4 percent.

Across all age groups, the survey found that only 28.4 percent of Americans had an up-to-date Will. Of those who had completed a Will, 8.6 percent had an out-of-date Will that needed to be amended or changed. It is necessary to do this, for example, when you want to change your personal representative, add or delete beneficiaries, or make a change in the asset allocation. We need to make sure that an out-of-date Will does not make matters worse than having no Will at all. Further:

1. The survey showed that 63 percent of Americans have no valid Will. And including the 8.6 percent of individuals who have an out-of-date Will, a total of 71.6 percent of Americans have either a Will that is not up to date or no Will at all.

2. Even when we focus on Americans over the age of 35, two-thirds don't have an up-to-date Will.

3. Only half of Americans over the age of 65 have up-to-date Wills in place.

4. One in six Americans over the age of 65 have a Will that is out-of-date.

5. Wealthy Americans are no more likely to have written their Will.

6. Wealthy Americans are more likely to have an out-of-date Will.[2]

The facts in the selected survey show less-than-encouraging results. In the 21st century, we haven't gotten any better at getting a Last Will completed. Why? Well, it's hard to say for certain. But we do know that everything starts by affirming the importance and the high priority of getting one's estate planning completed. For instance, in the work place, more companies are encouraging their employees to complete their estate planning documents. Ideally, more communities would be proactive in informing their residents, not just about matters important to the local community, but also about estate planning considerations. For example, attorneys could volunteer to speak at community center seminars and educate residents about the process of estate planning, supplemented with question-and-answer sessions. Community and senior center organizers can contact their local

---

2. (2016, June). Demystifying the Last Will and Testament-Survey of Americans Without Wills. The U.S. Legal Wills Blog: Retrieved September 8, 2017, from https://www.uslegalwills.com/blog/americans-without-wills/

county Bar Association to seek volunteer attorneys to speak at community gatherings.

The USLegalWills.com survey results are dispiriting. So dispiriting, in fact, that this book was created to boldly try to put a dent into those stubborn figures. Congratulations to those who can commit to getting their Last Will and any accompanying estate documents completed, and kudos to those who inform family or friends about the relative ease of organizing a Last Will as part of an estate plan.

If people feel complacent about moving forward, it is generally because they do not know where to begin. No doubt, there are many questions to answer. With this book, the author hopes to provide readers with targeted explanations of any and all questions that are of consideration to preparing a Last Will, as well as whether a Testamentary Trust or a Living Trust is a practical addition to one's estate portfolio. The explanations are easy to understand and formatted in a way the author hopes will encourage readers to tackle and complete their estate planning.

Whether poor or wealthy, young or old, male, female, or transgender, the need to complete one's Will crosses all economic and social barriers. But even men of great wealth, like Howard Hughes, did not possess a valid Last Will. Abraham Lincoln, Jimmy Hendrix, Pablo Picasso, Martin Luther King, Jr., Steve McNair, and even Bob Marley all died without having a Last Will or some sort of a valid estate plan in place.

The real disturbance in the legal cosmos is straight ahead of us, and it is just starting to occur. That matter concerns the transfer of wealth from generation to generation. Over roughly the next 30 years, estimates of wealth transfer conservatively range around $60 trillion![3] That is a lot of wealth to transfer in comparison to the ways and means currently set up (via completed Wills and other estate planning instruments) to handle the vast reservoir of wealth that must flow to the next generation. Considering

---

3. Havens, J. & Schervish, P. (2014, May). National Wealth Transfer and Potential for Philanthropy Technical Report. *Center on Wealth and Philanthropy*, Boston College

the 2016 survey results, many of us are simply just not prepared. And Last Wills are supposed to be the guiding backbone for wealth transfer.

Chapter 2 of the book dissects a Last Will and explains the options to what language can be included. It looks at the basic constructs of a Will. Chapter 2 additionally includes a section with definitions and terminology related to Wills and estate planning. Finally, the chapter discusses whether a trust should be part of one's estate plan, either as a Testamentary Trust included within a Last Will, or in a separate Living Trust.

Chapter 3 includes sample estate documents. They include a simple Last Will, a more complex Last Will with a built-in trust (known as a Testamentary Trust), and a separate Living Trust. These sample documents provide readers with reference ideas and guidance in structuring their own documents. Chapter 3 also provides direction about caring for one's needs, while alive, through Durable Powers of Attorney for Healthcare and Financial Management. A sample Durable Power of Attorney for Healthcare and Financial Management is additionally provided for the reader's reference.

In Chapters 4, 5, and 6, the book presents various actual Last Wills from famous individuals, like Elvis, Tom Clancy, Thomas Jefferson, Alfred Nobel, and other prominent individuals. These Last Wills show real-life examples in which the language can be either smoothly written, like a sheet of music, or vague and confusing, resulting in discord and disagreement among potential heirs.

In Chapter 7, the laws of descent and distribution (i.e., the laws that direct your post-mortem estate if you fail to complete a Will) and the probate and trust laws are specified for each of the 50 states and the District of Columbia (Washington, D.C.). Now, some of the various Last Wills in the book admittedly derive from jurisdictions outside the United States, including Alfred Nobel from Sweden and Princess Diana from England. But in all these Wills, there is a blueprint that all jurisdictions follow. Specifically, the Testator who creates a Will must have sufficient intellectual capacity and be unaffected by undue influence at the time of preparing and signing a

Will. Primarily, the Testator must be of sound mind; he or she must know that a Last Will is being prepared; there exists no duress, from anyone or anything, at the time of preparation and signing; and he or she must understand what assets are being given away and to whom.

With this in mind, it is little wonder why preparing one's estate plan is a vitally important step toward a smooth transition of family wealth. It is too disastrous to see how over 70 percent of Americans who currently either do not have a Last Will completed or have an out-of-date Last Will will attempt to handle the transfers of all the existing wealth to new recipients of the next generation. If there is no Last Will, the Decedent's estate will fall under the laws of descent and distribution in the state where he or she was a resident. Thus, if you fail to make the critical decisions of fiduciary appointments and asset distribution as part of creating a Last Will, the state court will make those decisions without your input.

Here is just one example of a common issue that arises in an estate setting: What are the different consequences of wealth transfer, with a Will and without a Will, in the wealth transfer to a child who might not be so money-wise, or lacks the intellectual capacity to properly manage assets?

Of course, in a Last Will, you can clearly designate how you want your assets handled. For example, the common advice given to a Testator regarding minor children would be to set up a trust within the Will, called a Testamentary Trust, where you can select and appoint a trustee to manage the child's assets. You can further appoint the Guardian in your Will to oversee the "person" of the minor child. But if you die without a Last Will, your estate will be divided up according to state law, which becomes the default rule-making authority over your estate and all your assets.[4] So, say you have an estate with assets, but no Will.[5] If a child of the Decedent is

---

4. Details about how to set up a Will and determine the needs of incorporating a Trust within one's estate portfolio are further explained in Chapter 2.
5. Dying without a Will is dying "intestate." More specifically, intestate succession applies when either: 1) Decedent dies without a Will, 2) Decedent's Will is denied probate due to invalidity, or 3) The Will failed to dispose of all of the estate's properties.

under 18, and there is no surviving parent, the court will likely appoint a guardian for the minor person and a trustee for the minor's trust estate until that minor turns 18. Who knows if a court-appointed guardian or trustee can be fully trusted? You may know those persons whom you trust to handle your assets, but the court is only making an educated guess, based on the arguments presented by your heirs, i.e., those who have a lineal relationship to gain your assets. And typically, if there is a surviving parent, as next of kin, that person will generally take over the management of the person (as guardian), and likely also the estate (as trustee of the assets) of the minor child. However, this is not always a great relief to fall back on because over 50 percent of parents become legally separated or get divorced before a child turns 18. Therefore, the surviving parent might not always be the first choice by the Decedent to take control of his or her assets. This is especially true if the division of assets in the original divorce or separation was a contentious issue. You, in your hypothetical post-mortem state, may see a financial disaster in the wealth transfer if an ex-spouse takes over. But that is the raw reality. The courts simply and objectively rely on fiduciary state laws governing Executors, Guardians, and Trustees, should anyone mismanage or embezzle funds from an estate.

To rock one's conscience further, when your minor child turns 18, all the assets will be given to that child who just became a legal adult — all of it at once. So often, such a young adult spends the newly-gained assets without much discipline. Unfortunately, too, at this young age, these suddenly "wealthy" young adults become the attraction of entrepreneurs and financial con-artists. Essentially, the bag of money you are handing over, without that Will in place, has a big hole in it. The exposed asset trail that it creates will quickly attract the wrong elements who have a mindset to swoop down and take it away.

The true story that parallels this example is when rock singer Kurt Cobain died in 1994. He had no Last Will. Consequently, his minor child was in line to inherit a good portion of his vast multimillion-dollar empire upon turning 18 years of age.[6] We hear estimates that the Cobain estate is worth over $450 million today![7] Every young adult with inherited assets will be at the mercy of their own intellect in protecting their assets. It again stresses the importance of having parents properly plan their estates so that their children are protected from financial sharks and that each estate is safely turned over to the next generation. Kurt Cobain's copyrights, trademarks, likeness, and other rights related to him and his music were separate property rights that were to be divided equally between the spouse and children under Washington law. Thus, Courtney Love received half of the estate and the other half went to Cobain's only known child, Frances Bean Cobain. While Frances was a minor, her mother, Courtney, held the assets in trust until Frances turned 18 years of age. Young Frances was only about 20 months old when her father, Kurt Cobain, died. On her 18th birthday, her net worth ballooned to roughly $200 million. Any person that wealthy would ideally have a team of trusted professionals under their employ to manage such a large fortune.

A lot of that "loose" money flowing out of the big bag of wealth transfer can drain really fast. During the author's college years, for example, a friend, who was 24 years old at the time, inherited a home and a 401k pension from his parents who unexpectedly died in an accident. In less

---

6. Washington State is one of nine "community property" states in the United States. Puerto Rico is also a community property jurisdiction. Community property includes all properties jointly owned by both spouses, whether purchased during the marriage, or an asset otherwise commingled with each spouse's funds. The surviving spouse receives all the community property of the first-to-die spouse, unless the Decedent's half of the community property is otherwise given to someone else through a Last Will. But separate property in an intestate estate is divided up between the surviving spouse and the child or children. So, with Cobain's music and right of publicity considered separate property (where these intangible rights existed prior to his marriage), one-half would go to the surviving spouse, Courtney Love, and the other half to Cobain's only known child, Frances Bean Cobain, when she turned 18 years of age in 2010. During her minor years, her mother, Courtney Love, held her funds in trust. Revised Code of Washington 11.04.015(1)(b).

7. Molon, A. (2014, April 5). Inside Kurt Cobain's $450M Empire. Retrieved May 22, 2018, from https://www.cnbc.com/2014/04/04/kurt-cobain-and-the-big-business-of-dead-celebs.html

than 18 months, the money was drained, and the house was sold to pay for the costs of living a lavish lifestyle. A generation of wealth, drained away, in such a fast and reckless way. This is just one example of some of the nasty consequences that could happen to anyone who lacks a proper Will and estate plan.

So, in the end, without a Will in place, the courts and the lineal heirs who make the best legal arguments to gain your assets will prevail. Again, it is the raw reality. You need to make sure to create a protective umbrella in your estate planning, such as to protect your hypothetical child's inherited assets in the above example, whether it might include a Testamentary Trust or a separate Living Trust. You can especially customize the language, for instance, to direct when the beneficiary can receive funds (for example, in three stages, such at ages 21, 25, and 30),[8] how much they can receive over time, and for what purposes the funds can be used. Draw a framework or outline how you want to see your assets handled and distributed, then talk with a competent legal mind to structure the Last Will and any other estate planning documents. Your true wishes are better guaranteed to be honored through written estate documents. In the end, it will certainly settle the mind to complete a solid Last Will, now, as part of one's estate planning.

Envisioning the convergence zone of wealth transfer and incomplete estate planning is a recipe for lots of heartache. The consequences negatively raise the risks to the estate in ways that will see wealth being drained by expensive litigation, cause the disenfranchisement of family relationships, and incur much wasted time, most of it saddled with anger and frustration. The author hopes that understanding the collisions of intestate wealth transfer

---

8. It is the author's experience, in very simple terms here, that the best way to provide asset transfers to children, especially in wealthier estates, is to transfer assets in stages, generally based on age. Sometimes, it can also be contingent on, say, graduating with a school degree or completing a certain goal. And understand the realities; in the first transfer of assets, say at 21 years of age, the young adult child can be expected to lack the full discipline in managing it, as compared to the second, third, or even fourth round of wealth transfer. So, whether your kind heart gives money away to the child at 21, 25, or even 30 years of age, expect the first transfer to be used up quickly. It is up to you to best gauge how each beneficiary will spend and manage it.

and family relationships will only encourage readers to make it a precious high priority to get their Last Wills and other estate-planning documents completed as soon as practicable.

An estate is generally probated under state court jurisdiction.[9] It will be one's last residence in the county of the state in which he or she resided. Should you die without a Will, aside from the court selecting the Executor of your estate, the expected challenges in probate court will include who is entitled to your assets and in what sums those assets will be distributed. With no direction, the money claims among close and more distant relatives will gear into full bloom. It can feed on itself and can negatively affect what was an otherwise wonderful relationship among heirs over decades past.

So, the discord and disconnect really start from the estate — your estate if you fail to complete a Will. Gauging the current trajectory from the above survey about the significantly large number of unprepared estates arriving into probate courts with no Wills, or bad Wills, we are going to see many head-on contests. The transition of wealth without a Will makes for many uncomfortable, if not nasty, estate matters for heirs to deal with. In the end, the courts will decide estate matters, typically to the detriment of the whole estate, given the amount of additional legal work needed to resolve an estate with no Last Will or a vague and/or ambiguous Last Will. The probate and appellate courts will expect to become even busier, and lawyers handling the additional litigation will likely become richer.

Each Testator can imagine the time wasted and the money lost to legal wrangling as compelling reasons to finally complete an up-to-date Last Will. So, don't have state laws, adversary legal counsel, and uninvited heirs be the default for managing your entire estate, and carving up assets that took a lifetime to accumulate.

---

9. Those individuals under the jurisdiction of the Federal Probate Code, including Native Americans on reservations or other federal lands and indigenous Hawaiians, are exempted. 25 U.S. Code § 2206 - Descent and distribution

It is unlikely that anyone wants to die without having some authority in directing what, and to whom, one wants to give his or her assets and heirlooms. You may think that you are too young to prepare a Last Will, or maybe you don't have enough assets worth distributing. Or, many of us just forget to complete one. The reader can derive a lot by just viewing the sample documents in Chapter 3, and the Last Wills of notable individuals in Chapters 4, 5, and 6.

Over 50 percent of Americans can do very well with their estates by just creating a simple Last Will. And a very large majority of the rest of us can easily incorporate a Testamentary Trust into our Last Will. Reasons to have a trust would be to handle real properties, business succession, or manage the estates of minor children or disabled individuals who may inherit assets. An individual can otherwise place his or her assets in a separate Living Trust, where assets like bank and brokerage accounts and real property may fund the trust. In such case, a Will is also created, which is commonly known as a pour-over Will. That is, whatever assets are not in the Living Trust before death, will "pour over" into the Living Trust upon death. Choices to make about what types of documents and what language to incorporate depend on the financial and business scenarios of each estate. All the sample documents are included under Chapter 3.

The Testator appoints a Personal Representative (also known as an Executor) in a Will. More so, the Testator can customize the set-up and administration of the estate, and select the tasks required to manage it, including the process of distributing one's assets to the designated heirs. Most Testators in their Wills provide for an easy distribution of their assets to their surviving spouse, or otherwise to their children or next of kin, divided equally. A simple Will can even include a tangible personal property list where the Decedent can list certain properties going to certain beneficiaries or have a list detailing bequests of cash amounts to beneficiaries. Beneficiaries can be any reasonable recipient, including individuals, organizations (charitable or otherwise), animals, and government entities.

In every state, territory, and jurisdiction of the United States, including Washington, D.C., there is no minimum adult age limit or wealth index to determine whether it is a good time to complete one's Last Will. Furthermore, after you complete your Last Will, it is wise to revisit it periodically to consider any amendment(s) to it (known as a "Codicil" to your Last Will), or to complete a new Last Will.

Death is the least planned action in our lives; so, having an existing Last Will already in place is always a wise decision. It comforts the soul to know that one has given direction to how one's assets will be entrusted and distributed. It will also tend to significantly lessen the risks of possible litigation to determine who gets a piece of your asset pie. The goal in proper estate planning is to clearly describe how one's estate assets shall be handled and distributed, including the specific post-mortem care of assets for minor or disabled children by the fiduciary appointments you have designated as guardians or trustees. Accordingly, the smoother the administration and distribution of assets under a Last Will, the less discord, mistrust, infighting, and permanent bad relations will likely occur.

EDWARD M. MELILLO, ESQ.

CHAPTER 1

NOTABLE INDIVIDUALS WHO DIED WITHOUT A LAST WILL

Let every American, every lover of liberty, every well wisher to his posterity, swear by the blood of the Revolution, never to violate in the least particular, the laws of the country; and never to tolerate their violation by others.

ABRAHAM LINCOLN
[EXCERPTED FROM LINCOLN'S LYCEUM ADDRESS OF 1838, SPRINGFIELD, ILLINOIS]

ABRAHAM LINCOLN
February 12, 1809 — April 15, 1865

Abraham Lincoln, the 16th President of the United States of America, was inaugurated to his second term as President of the United States on March 4, 1865. After four trying years, Lincoln brought the Union back together with the defeat of the Confederate Army. Just weeks later, on April 14, 1865, he was shot by John Wilkes Booth while watching a play at Ford's Theater in Washington, D.C. Unfortunately, during intermission, the bodyguard assigned to protect President Lincoln decided to partake in a few drinks with the president's carriage crew at the Star Saloon, which was next door to Ford's Theater. Ironically, the bodyguard dropped into the saloon about the same time that John Wilkes Booth was apparently finishing his drinks at the same tavern before proceeding to Ford's Theater to kill Lincoln. When Booth went to shoot the president, he passed by the empty chair where the bodyguard was supposed to be watching over Lincoln.[10] It is sad to think that Lincoln's bodyguard and Booth may well have seen or passed each other at the bar. The president survived into the next day before succumbing to his fatal wound. Although a lawyer himself, our 16th president, ironically, was our first president to die without a Last Will.

MARTIN LUTHER KING, JR.
January 15, 1929 — April 4, 1968

Injustice anywhere is a threat to justice everywhere.

MARTIN LUTHER KING JR.

Martin Luther King, Jr. was a Baptist preacher who helped lead the American civil rights movement of the 1950s and 1960s. He took a strong but nonviolent stance against institutionalized bigotry and prejudice in the United States. He was a stalwart in the momentum behind the creation of the Civil Rights Act of 1964, which was spearheaded by President John F. Kennedy and ultimately passed by Congress and signed into law by President Lyndon Johnson in 1964.[11] The act effectively ended the Jim Crow laws in the southern states where "separate, but equal" were words

10. Martin, P. (2010, April 7). Lincoln's Missing Bodyguard. Retrieved October 22, 2016, from https://www.smithsonianmag.com/history/lincolns-missing-bodyguard-12932069/
11. Civil Rights Act of 1964, Pub.L. 88-352, 78 Stat. 241 (1964)

created to carve up communities according to race and to hide insidious hatred and prejudice toward black people and other people of color. Despite the passing of laws against racial discrimination, Dr. King continued to preach that the seeds of prejudice will always plant themselves where there is abuse of power in government or an otherwise complacent populace; so, the nonviolent fight against racial discrimination must be fought wherever it grows.[12]

Dr. King was assassinated on April 4, 1968. Despite the constant risks and threats to his life, Dr. King never drafted a Last Will. His surviving wife, Coretta Scott King, inherited his estate, but when she died in 2006, the children auctioned most of Dr. King's memorabilia, generating approximately $32 million. As recently as 2014, litigation ensued among the children over rights to keep or sell Dr. King's Bible and Nobel Peace Prize medal.

HOWARD HUGHES
December 24, 1905 — April 5, 1976

When Howard Hughes died, his purported Last Will was apparently discovered at the headquarters of the Mormon Church in Salt Lake City, Utah. The Will, however, was proved to be a forgery in a Nevada court. After seven years of extended litigation, his estate was eventually divided among his 22 cousins. Aside from paying a large amount in attorney fees, approximately half the estate went to pay federal estate taxes. The heirs split the remaining $2.5 billion. Imagine the savings and goodwill if Mr. Hughes had set up proper estate planning around a Last Will and certain specific trusts to protect and save his assets for charity rather than be exposed to taxes and litigation. In this case, roughly 2 to 3 billion dollars could have been

---

12. Martin Luther King Jr. (2018, January 18). Retrieved April 22, 2018, from https://www.biography.com/people/martin-luther-king-jr-9365086

preserved for higher purposes instead of the funds being consumed by federal estate taxes, and attorneys' fees to clean up the estate.

PABLO PICASSO
October 25, 1881 — April 8, 1973

The great artist Pablo Picasso died in 1973 without a Will at the age of 91. It took six years to litigate and settle his estate among various family members, alleged relatives, and other claimants. The litigation cost the Picasso estate an estimated $30 million in legal and other fees! His assets were eventually divided up among six heirs.

JIMI HENDRIX
November 27, 1942 — September 18, 1970

Jimi Hendrix, born James Marshall Hendrix, died in 1970 at the age of 27. With no Will and no direction to guide the estate, the Jimi Hendrix estate was exploited for years by those around the music legend. Jimi's father, Al Hendrix, eventually inherited the estate. Al sued and fought with record companies, recording studios, and others to regain Jimi's royalty rights. A California attorney was receiving Jimi's royalties on his music for almost 20 years before Al finally regained Jimi's music rights through the courts.[13] Afterwards, Al created multiple trusts, partnerships, and corporations under Jimi's estate, notably Experience Hendrix, L.L.C. based in Seattle. This

---

13. Staff, L. (2017, July 25). The Messy Afterlife of Jimi Hendrix, http://www.legacy.com/news/celebrity-deaths/article/the-messy-afterlife-of-jimi-hendrix

company, working with MCA Records, has generated many millions of dollars in royalties and sales of memorabilia.

When Al Hendrix died in 2002, all hell seemed to break loose. At the time, the Hendrix estate was worth about $80 million, which went almost entirely to Al's adopted daughter, Janie. Al had divorced Jimi's mother in the late 1950s and adopted Janie when he married her mother in 1968. Jimi's biological brother, Leon, alleged that Janie manipulated Al into writing Leon and his children out of his Will. Leon sued to be included in the estate but lost. In 2004, the court sided with Janie Hendrix, who received most all of Jimi's estate assets.[14] The appeals ended in 2007, when the Washington State Supreme Court upheld a 2004 King County Superior Court verdict upholding the validity of Al Hendrix's Will. Really, the infighting started from Jimi's death in 1970. We can only imagine what determinations Jimi would have made about how his estate should have been divided. By 2007, it already cost family members 37 years of anxiety and heartache, not to mention the enormous legal and accounting fees.

But the legal fighting did not end there. In May 2015, the court issued an injunction prohibiting Leon's business ventures from using registered Hendrix trademarks for the advertising or sale of merchandise.

Then, on March 16, 2017, the company owned by Hendrix's estate filed another suit in U.S. District Court for the Southern District of New York against Jimi's brother, Leon, and Andrew Pitsicalis, Leon's business partner. The dispute involved the use of trademarks and copyrights that they allegedly did not own.[15]

A press release from Experience Hendrix, L.L.C. and Authentic Hendrix, L.L.C. states that Leon and Pitsicalis, through their Purple Haze Properties, L.L.C., had "attempted to hijack trademarks and copyrights for their

---

14. Alexander, B. (2004, September 15). Judge Settles Family Feud Over Jimi Hendrix's Estate. The New York Times

15. NCV Newswire. (2017, March 16). Jimi Hendrix Estate Sues Andrew Pitsicalis and Leon Hendrix. *New Cannabis Ventures*

own personal gain." They did this "through the creation, development, manufacturing, promotion, advertising and sale of cannabis, food, wine, alcohol, 'medicines,' electronic products and other goods."[16]

This is the newest round in a battle that began in 2004 when a judge shut Leon Hendrix out of the family business.[17] Since 2008, Leon and Pitsicalis have lost other court cases related to creations of Jimi Hendrix-themed merchandise — most recently in 2016, after Leon's Purple Haze Liqueur unlawfully used the word "Jimi" and a replication of Jimi's signature on its bottle. As in 2015, Pitsicalis was prohibited from using trademarks owned by Jimi's estate; the ruling stated that he could not register the name "Jimi" or "Jimi Jams" due to its connection with the legendary guitarist.

This must be one of the longest estate battles seen raging, really since 1970, adding up to endless legal and accounting fees to litigate the intangible assets of an estate. This is the most classic case in estate planning, where Jimi Hendrix should have created a Last Will, as well as a trust or trusts for his memorabilia and his intangible assets consisting of his music, his name, and his likeness. One wonders if Jimi would have ever wanted to give something to his brother Leon. We will never truly know.

KURT COBAIN
February 20, 1967 — April 5, 1994

Kurt Cobain was an iconic singer in the 1990s and was the king of grunge music with a worldwide following. In 1994, Kurt Cobain died of an apparent self-inflicted gunshot wound at the age of 27. Although Cobain left behind a suicide note, he failed to leave behind a valid Last Will. Cobain's wife, Courtney Love, and their daughter, were the only intestate heirs. In 2010,

16. L.L.C., H. (2017, March 16). Hendrix Sues Serial Infringer Andrew Pitsicalis. Retrieved September 19, 2017, https://www.prnewswire.com/news-releases/hendrix-sues-serial-infringer-andrew-pitsicalis-300424994.html
17. Alexander, B. (2004, September 25). Judge Settles Long Family Feud Over Jimi Hendrix's Estate. Retrieved May 18, 2017, from, https://www.nytimes.com/2004/09/25/us/judge-settles-long-family-feud-over-jimi-hendrixs-estate.html

the existing estate assets, including control of Cobain's Right of Publicity passed from Courtney to his daughter on the day she turned 18, although the mother had already collateralized Cobain's right of publicity for a loan.

BOB MARLEY
February 6, 1945 — May 11, 1981

Bob Marley and the Wailers November 23, 1979 (Los Angeles, California) © Copyrighted photo courtesy of Edward M. Melillo

Bob Marley lost his life to brain cancer at the age of 36 on May 11, 1981 without leaving a Last Will. Marley's Rastafarian faith did not allow any belief in death. So, making a Last Will was not a serious option, although it would have resolved a lot of confusion and the seemingly endless litigation that ensued over his vast estate. Enduring legal battles and family disputes erupted after the reggae star's death. Under Jamaican law, Marley's widow, Rita Marley, received 10 percent of her husband's $30 million estate, and held a life estate in another 45 percent. Marley's 11 known children (three by his wife and eight by other women) were entitled to equal shares in the other 45 percent, as well as a remainder interest in Rita's life estate. Without a Will, legal claims were filed in various jurisdictions, including Jamaica, New York, and London. Claimants in Bob Marley's estate included all of his known children and their mothers, his widow, a number of grandchildren, many long-lost relatives, band members, and business associates. The legal infighting continued in England until 2014, when rights to the Marley estate were finally settled after 33 years of litigation.

STEVE MCNAIR
February 14, 1973 — July 4, 2009

Steve McNair-Superbowl XXXIV
© Copyright NBC Sports

Steve McNair was a star NFL quarterback for 13 years and made it to Super Bowl XXXIV with the Tennessee Titans for the 1999 season. On July 4, 2009, at age 36, McNair was found shot to death in Nashville, Tennessee, the result of a murder-suicide by a dejected young girl-friend. McNair didn't have a Last Will, but he was married at the time of his death. His widow filed for probate and was appointed Administrator of the estate. Without a Will, Tennessee state law took effect over how the estate would be administered because it was his state of residence, or domicile. Under Tennessee law, when a spouse dies without a Will, the surviving spouse is duly entitled to at least one-third of the estate, and the surviving children split the rest.[18] McNair had four sons, two from his current marriage and two from previous relationships.

McNair certainly would have wanted a Last Will, with protective trusts, since he very likely would have given or bequeathed his assets differently than how state law forced the divisions of assets; moreover, there was too much to lose to federal and Tennessee[19] estate taxes. McNair had not established any tax avoidance protections, such as the creation of trusts for estate tax protection. Consequently, his estate likely had enormous estate and inheritance tax liabilities. Ultimately, with the estate being split apart without McNair's direction under a Will, came great pain and heartache to his family members. McNair earned about $90 million during his NFL career, so the value of his gross estate at the time he died was quite considerable in comparison to most others.

---

18. Tn. Stat. Descent and Distribution, Tit. 31, Ch. 2, §104(a)(2) (2017).

19. Tennessee repealed its state estate taxes for Decedents who died on or after January 1, 2016. Steve McNair died in 2009, so his estate had to pay Tennessee estate (inheritance) taxes on all his net assets over $1 million.

One of the great heartbreaks for lacking a Last Will in the McNair estate is that the surviving wife, as the Administrator for the estate, directed Mc-Nair's mother to start paying a monthly rent of $3,000 on the ranch that McNair bought specifically for his mom when he entered the NFL. She had been residing in the residence for 13 years, ever since the time that McNair started playing professional football. Having no ability to pay, his mother was forced to move out. Then, in 2011, the Administrator (and remember, the former daughter-in-law), sued McNair's mother for damages to recover over $54,000 for personal property items, including furniture and appliances, that she removed from the residence. McNair's mother stated that all the personal property items that she took from the house were items she had purchased herself and had accumulated over the years.[20]

The McNair case highlights the reasons to complete a Will. This story brings to light the minimal cost and bare inconvenience of taking a bit of one's time to create a simple Will (see Chapter 3), compared to the enormous costs of the family heartaches and stresses (especially for McNair's mother and his four sons) dealing without a Will to guide the estate.

20. (2013, December 10). Steve McNair and the Perils of Dying Without a Will. Retrieved August 22, 2017, from, www.familyarchivalsolutions.com/steve-mcnair-perils-dying-without-a-will//

CHAPTER 2

Essential Estate Planning — Knowing About Wills and Trusts

I. Understanding the Importance of Creating a Last Will and the Consequences of Dying Without One

As a well spent day brings happy sleep, so life well used
brings happy death.

Leonardo DaVinci

A. This is the Chance to Give Your Estate Away and to Care for Loved Ones — Make it Your Choice

Your Last Will may be the most important document that you ever sign, should you have the opportunity to complete one. Remember that about two-thirds of Americans are expected to die without a Will, and another 5 to 10 percent are expected to die with an out-of-date Will that needed significant revision. This book is dedicated to encouraging the reader to reach that basic goal of completing a solid Last Will, in addition to constructing other documents for an estate portfolio according to one's financial situation (e.g., business succession or having real properties in several different states), or human need (e.g., having to care for minor or disabled children), whether it be for handling matters before death, during periods of incapacity, or otherwise in a post-mortem setting.[21] The creator of a Last Will, i.e., the Testator, directs how the estate will be managed and how assets will be distributed, with specific instructions for determining who will inherit the real estate, money and investments, and personal belongings. In addition to selecting a Personal Representative (also known as an Executor or Administrator) to manage the estate, the Testator also selects the Guardian for any minor children, the Trustee for managing the assets of a child or disabled person, and/or a Caretaker to raise any animals or to oversee and manage property.

B. What Can be the Consequences for Having no Last Will?

In an intestate estate, in which a person dies without a Will, the courts will take over using state law to control the estate, as well as making selections for all the fiduciary positions mentioned above. We can anticipate that dying without a valid Will can cause a lot of confusion and discord. The greater the dissension among the parties, the greater the likelihood of entanglements and issues in the estate. Uncertainty and suspicion will likely change the atmosphere among potential heirs. One can expect family infighting and legal contests to erupt if matters deteriorate. The elasticity of potential infighting is very steep here, with trust and goodwill being the measuring tools. To give an example using fictitious names and a random scenario, let's say that John is one of four children. He goes into the Decedent's home and takes what he wants, without consideration of his three siblings. One of the other siblings sees this and rushes to also selfishly take out other property items. The last two siblings find out and are dismayed and angry. Greed and anger poison the trust and goodwill among the siblings. The free-for-all breaks down the mutual trust, and each person hires legal counsel to sort out the impulsive and inconsiderate actions

---

21. Chapter 3 explains and details the relative need for additional estate-planning documents, including Testamentary Trusts, Living Wills, and Powers of Attorney for Healthcare and Financial Management. Various sample documents for reference are also included in the chapter.

taken. The same actions can occur with vehicles, real estate, businesses, and other properties of the estate.

C. New Meanings and Challenges: Considerations of Cohabitation Without Marriage in an Intestate Estate

Here is another challenging situation that is evolving through the courts in various states when an individual, while cohabitating for a "period of time" with a partner outside of marriage, dies intestate. Example: A surviving spouse shares his separate household with another partner for a number of years before the surviving spouse dies. This couple never officially get married. Does the partnership of the non-married, live-in relationship have value in the surviving spouse's estate? More specifically, can the live-in partner claim a piece of Decedent's estate? Could living together for an extended period of time in the same household be construed as a "marriage-like" relationship? And how long do you have to live together? Some states might interpret such a relationship as a common law marriage. The Washington State Supreme Court, for example, stated that sharing an intimate relationship with another person under the same household outside of marriage over a period of years is characterized as a "meretricious relationship."[22] But the court additionally noted that, historically, property acquired during a meretricious relationship belonged to the person who acquired it."[23] The court made no presumption that such relationship gave rise to any sort of legal rights to the other partner who did not hold legal title to the other partner's property.[24] In the late 1990s, the author represented a Decedent's three children in a probate case after the Decedent died intestate in Snohomish, Washington. He resided in a trailer on a two-acre parcel. He had been living together with another woman for 12 years before he died. They never got married. After he died, the partner continued to reside in the trailer and claimed the personal and real property as belonging to her due to the long relationship of living together. Washington state, under

---

22. Connell v. Francisco, 127 Wn.2d 339, 898 P.2d 831, 835 (1995).
23. Id. at 347.
24. Id. at 339.

its statute (i.e., codified law), has not recognized common law marriage, except when couples come to reside in Washington from other states that do recognize common-law marriage.[25] And in the meretricious relationship above, the Decedent owned, in title, the land and the trailer. The court awarded the Decedent's three children the entire estate. The Decedent's partner had to move out with no claim. At that time, during the 1990s, a person generally had to be officially married under Washington state law to become a legal heir.[26] So, the partner, unfortunately, lost her lawsuit and had to abandon all of the Decedent's assets.

Ironically, about a decade later, the Washington State Supreme Court had a change of heart. It subsequently ruled that continuous cohabitation and living like a married couple brought value to a Decedent's estate, which it termed a "committed intimate relationship."[27] But how long does it take for a relationship to become a value to the estate? The court eventually stated that a cohabitating relationship of seven to eight years can warrant or satisfy the "duration factor" to "...merit a property division much like a marriage of a similar length...."[28] Wow! That was a complete change in law and policy where a live-in partner can now gain a stake in an intestate estate as a legal heir, based on living with the Principal of the estate for a duration of time similar to a married relationship.[29]

---

25. RCW 26.04.020(4)-Prohibited Marriages. This subsection reads:
    A legal union, other than a marriage, between two individuals that was validly formed in another state or jurisdiction and that provides substantially the same rights, benefits, and responsibilities as a marriage, does not prohibit those same two individuals from obtaining a marriage license in Washington.
26. Prior to 2007, the primary exception to being recognized officially as a married person with spousal rights as an heir, short of possessing a marriage certificate or license, was being married under common law. Specifically, if common law were recognized in another state and a cohabitating couple from such state moved to Washington, then their common law relationship would be recognized like a marriage.
27. Olver v. Fowler, 161 Wn.2d 655, 658, 168 P.3d 348 (2007).
28. Long v. Fregeau, 158 Wn.App. 919, 927, 244 P.3d 26 (Div 3 2010).
29. *See,* Marriage of Lindsey, 101 Wn.2d 299, 304, 678 P.2d 328 (1984).

Therefore, the change in outcomes of court decisions over time can and will significantly affect intestate estates, like it did for unmarried, cohabitating couples in Washington state.[30] And over time, more state courts, if not state legislatures, may find continuous intimate relationships of unmarried cohabitants more accepted as marriage-like relationships that can legitimize a division of property rights when a person dies without a Last Will or accompanying estate plan.

Thus, state court decisions, or case law, add further interpretations of law that hold equal legal force parallel to existing state law statutes. Intestate estates effectively dangle in the wind and are blown in different directions over time as determined by changes in case law. Each state has its own case law[31] and legislative (statutes) laws, which all can be confusing to coordinate and understand.

Thus, without a Last Will, the estate is always exposed to the consequences affected and interpreted under case law. The outcomes of intestate estates can change significantly. Take the author's real-life example described above. If the Decedent in that case had died a decade later, his live-in partner would likely have been able to take up to one-half of the estate, while the Decedent's children would have had to settle with taking equal divisions of the other half of the estate. Overall, the classifications of legal heirs in an intestate estate become more unpredictable, uncomfortable, and frustrating to the lineal heirs. This is yet another reason why completing your estate plan is critical to setting your wishes in place before you die. Don't leave your estate unprotected and subject to changing times and unexpected events.

---

30. *See,* "Living in a Committed Intimate Relationship? Planning for Unmarried Couples," *Real Property, Probate & Trust Newsletter,* Washington State Bar Association (Fall 2016).
31. The interpretations of statutes, rules, and constitutional issues by the Courts.

D. What is the Lineal Line of Succession With no Will?

If there is a surviving spouse, he or she is generally entitled to a statutory percentage share of the Decedent's estate; it depends on the state law where the Decedent's jurisdiction lies. The percentage amount varies from state to state, with divisions of property often dependent on whether the Decedent also left separate property (vs. community property), and surviving children or issue.

After the surviving spouse has taken his or her share, the remainder of the estate is distributed in many states in equal shares to the children of the Decedent, including children from other marriages and children from non-marital relationships. If the Decedent has no living children, his or her grandchildren become heirs. If the Decedent has no living grandchildren, his or her great-grandchildren become heirs. Stepchildren will not inherit from their stepparent, and a stepparent will not inherit from the estate of a deceased stepchild. That is because the stepchild already inherits from his or her biological parent or parents. There is an exception that applies if the stepchild is legally adopted by the stepparent; the stepchild will be able to now legally inherit from the stepparent's estate, but generally will no longer be able to legally inherit from their biological parents. Legally, you inherit lineally from one family only, so if you are adopted, your line of inheritance is transferred to the new legal lineage.

If the Decedent has no living spouse or issue, then the decedent's surviving parents commonly become the heirs, and in some states, the Decedent's surviving brothers and sisters will also be deemed heirs and may share equally in the proceeds of the estate with the Decedent's parents. Thus, with no spouse, no children, and no surviving parents, the Decedent's brothers and sisters will inherit the estate in most states. Half-siblings generally inherit the same as full siblings. If the Decedent's brothers and sisters are deceased, the Decedent's nieces and nephews commonly become the heirs.

If the Decedent has no surviving spouse, issue, parents, siblings, or nieces and nephews, commonly the paternal and maternal grandparents, if they are living, will become the heirs. After this point, the Decedent's cousins may also become heirs of the Decedent's estate.

Finally, without any lineal or legal descendants, the assets of the decedent can "escheat," or go to the state treasury. Once funds escheat, they generally cannot be recovered due to statutes of limitation.

Be sure to follow your state's laws should there be any differences in the way lineal descendants (like half-siblings) or consanguinity considerations (i.e., first, second, and third cousins) are treated. In order to avoid having state law determine how your estate will be distributed, it is important that you update your Will to name new primary or alternate beneficiaries if any beneficiaries named in your Will have predeceased you.

To paraphrase a familiar fuzzy park ranger, only you can prevent estate fires. What follows are details in understanding each section that is important in the construction of your Last Will. Each section can be followed using the sample Last Wills in Chapter 3 as references.

II. Details in Creating a Last Will and Testament

Qualifications of the Testator/Introductory Clause or Recital

The Testator is the creator of the Last Will and the person whose property will be distributed upon death. The first part of the Last Will can be called the "Introduction" or "Recital," where the name and qualifications of the Testator are noted. This paragraph identifies the Testator of the Will and declares the county and state of residence so that the court can confirm that it has jurisdiction over the probate of the estate. In large metropolitan counties where there is more than one courthouse, the Testator's residence can further determine which courthouse within the county the probate should be filed, if procedurally required by the court. Overall, the basic elements supporting the establishment of a valid Will are that the Testator be of legal age, have a sound mind, and be under no undue influence or duress in the preparation and execution of the Will. The typical recital might read like this:

> I, [Name of Testator], a resident of [City, County, and State], am of legal age, of sound and disposing mind and memory, and not acting under any duress, menace, fraud, or undue influence of any person whomsoever regarding the preparation of this instrument, my Last Will and Testament ("Last Will").

Revocation of Former Wills and Codicils

This paragraph revokes all former Wills and Codicils, which means that once this Will is executed, it becomes your valid Last Will. Although most states have codified this language, it is always prudent and safe to make sure it is included in your Last Will.

Identification of Family

First, this section states your marital status. Second, it lists the names and ages of all known biological and adopted children, both minors and adults. Third, if other heirs exist to whom nothing is intended to be given, then it should be written that all others are disinherited, or more specifically, if warranted under the state's statute, it should otherwise contain a statement with the name(s) of the disinherited person(s).

Disposition of the Decedent's Remains

This is an optional section. You can decide to also keep the information more private by instructing the personal representative about funeral arrangements and disposition of remains in a separate letter from the Will. Whether detailed in your Will or in a private letter (left with your Will), your decision about how you wish to have your remains handled after your death should be specified here. Many Testators tend to leave instructions with the personal representative and otherwise make a general statement in the Will that the personal representative shall have the authority to oversee funeral arrangements.

Appointment of the Executor and Other Fiduciaries

An Executor is also referred to as a Personal Representative or Administrator. An Executor is the person who will administer the Will in a fiduciary, or trusted, capacity. Most often, it is a person related to the Testator, such as a spouse or child. Obviously, the Executor named is the Testator's exclusive choice. Professional companies also serve as the "Executor" of an estate (and as a trustee or guardian), should the Testator be unable to find a truly independent and honest fiduciary to fulfill the position. In most all states, statutes are specific as to the qualifications of an Executor, one of which generally includes that the Executor not have any felony convictions or convictions of crimes involving dishonesty.

The Executor is obligated to follow the written terms in the Last Will, as well as conform to the state's laws and the rules of the court in honoring the due process rights on behalf of all the heirs. The person chosen to serve as Executor of an estate is someone who has the Testator's full trust in handling his or her assets, heirs, and creditors. That person holds a position of responsibility and, likewise, a position of trust. The ideal fiduciary is honest, diligent, and independently responsible enough to be able to handle the estate and its assets. It must be someone who will respect and honor the beneficiaries by properly administering and timely distributing assets of the estate.

If you also created a Testamentary Trust within the Last Will, a trustee will also be named in the section or article in the Will where the Testamentary Trust is identified. The same applies to the appointment of a trustee in a Living Trust. Additionally, if you have minor children, you can name a guardian for them in the event of your death.

Shall the Executor be Bonded?

Bonding of an Executor is done generally to ensure that the estate assets are protected in case of embezzlement or other losses of estate property caused by the Executor. In intestate estates, it is not uncommon for the court to issue a bond on the Executor. Often, it will be for the amount of the liquid instruments, such as cash, stock, and bonds owned by the estate, plus an estimated percentage of the value of valuable artwork, jewelry, and other fungible items of value. In most estates, in lieu of bond, heirs would be satisfied to have the Executor provide a regular accounting. Most often, a Testator to the Will chooses not to impose a bond on the Executor. In such cases, the Testator must be certain that they have chosen an Executor he or she trusts without needing a bond to ensure their honesty.

The irony is that the amount of the bond imposed on an Executor can be dependent on that Executor's credit rating. That is, the carrier or surety underwriting the bond wants to be sure that it can recover the funds it pays out as the result of Executor malfeasance. Imagine the situation where the Executor's credit is insufficient to cover the amount of the bond. Then what? The court would need to come to some resolve, such as placing a portion of the liquid assets in trust in an account which requires a court order to get to it. Yes, it can be quite inconvenient for the Executor. But the priority and purpose are to ensure that the assets are there for the creditors and the heirs. Ultimately, the Executor is bound by the fiduciary powers he or she owes to the court and the estate. The sample Last Wills under Chapter 3 all contain clauses that allow the Personal Representative or Executor to serve without bond.

What About the Executor's Powers?

Generally, without more, the default powers in an intestate estate require the Executor to seek court authority to broker the tasks of the estate, from opening bank accounts to selling property, and other tasks to advance the probate proceedings. This is known as court intervention powers that ensures court oversight over the Executor. Most often, especially when the Executor is trusted by the heirs, it is appropriate to allow the Executor to have "non-intervention" powers. This way, the Executor does not have to attend a court hearing to gain approval for every task, but can just accomplish the tasks under the fiduciary veil. Dispensing with the legal bureaucracy and court hearings can save a lot in legal fees, as well as save much time and delay. The sample Last Wills in Chapter 3 all have clauses giving the Executor court non-intervention powers.

What About Naming Co-Executors or Co-Trustees to Serve?

Naming two persons to serve in the same capacity is often done to appease, or to seemingly be fair to, one's children. In reality, more often than not, it causes more friction, frustration, and delays in the proceedings. Decision-making can be grounded in family arguments. Unless there might be a good deal of mistrust among heirs, especially in a very large or complicated estate that demands checks and balances regarding decision-making, it is generally less cumbersome just to have one Executor, or one trustee, or one guardian, appointed where needed. Then, if that person cannot serve in the position, have language appointing an alternate fiduciary to take the primary person's position. A Testator can name as many alternates, in sequential order, as he or she desires. Naming a second or third alternate Executor is not uncommon. This can be a much better planning strategy than two heads making the same decision. The court is always the balance in case of argument about an Executor's action, or inaction. Again, the goal is to choose an honest broker to serve as a fiduciary, either to take charge of an estate as an Executor, take custody over the Decedent's minor child or children as a guardian, or manage a minor child's gifted assets as a trustee. A Testator ideally would want to avoid choosing an Executor who might create unnecessary personality clashes with the heirs. It would be counter-productive to have a biased or confrontational Executor whose individual actions create additional delay and unwanted litigation. Overall, it is every Testator's vision to choose a trusted and considerate individual to handle their assets and take care of any minor or disabled children after they die.

Disposition of the Estate

Identify Property Distribution Clearly for Both Real and Personal Properties

Real Property

Generally, it is easy to divide the more liquid assets, like cash, stocks, and bonds. With real property, often it consists of a single-family residence, which is generally given to the surviving spouse. Other times, the real estate is sold by the Executor of the estate, and the net proceeds distributed equally among the heirs. But if an asset is not sold, such as real estate, and that asset is divided among the children or other heirs, it can become confusing if it is not clearly designated how that real property is to be owned. Many confusing situations can also occur when real estate is layered with different heirs, so be clear in making the right designations. For example, when the Decedent allows one beneficiary to live in or manage real property for the life of that person, then that is a life estate. Further, the other beneficiary who would receive the real property after the life of the first beneficiary is called the remainderman. The remainderman would thereafter inherit the real estate in fee, which means having full title or total ownership in the real estate. Using proper legal terms becomes very important, especially when lawyers on different sides are fighting over any vague interpretations contained in a Will. Any contingencies to a life estate should be spelled out clearly, such as a clause to prevent waste or wasting of the property. For example, if property taxes are left unpaid, the property is not maintained, or left unattended, then the real property can be transferred to the remainderman upon cause showing neglect (i.e., waste).

Good preparation of a Last Will can prevent a lot of heartache and disputes otherwise caused by poor language. A vague Will can cause much debate and adversarial sparring between counsel, which can result in a full course of litigation. An example is shared by this author, who handled a contested and litigious probate case representing the children of the Decedent from a first marriage. The second husband of the Decedent vehemently fought over certain language in the Decedent's Last Will. Although the Decedent had three adult children from her first marriage, she also wanted to care for her second husband. So, her estate lawyer drafted her Last Will with language stating that the second husband can live in the Decedent's house "… during his lifetime, but if it is sold, the proceeds shall go to Decedent's children." The estate lawyer drafting the Will should have more clearly stated that the Decedent intended to give her second husband only a life estate, and that her three children were to receive a remainderman interest in the house, with the net proceeds divided equally among the Decedent's three adult children, or to their issue by right of representation. A life estate allows the designated beneficiary the right to live in the home for his or her lifetime, generally without encumbering it, and while the life estate holder can maintain the household, and not let it go to waste. The Decedent's three children interpreted the language in their mother's Last Will as such. The second husband, however, thought otherwise, doing his best to parse the language to his favor. His interpretation was, "Well, I won't sell it, and as long as I don't sell it, I can keep it." So, he attempted to record it under his name, effectively transferring the real property in its entirety to himself. In his power and position as the estate's Executor, he unilaterally proceeded to quitclaim the real property to himself. Litigation ensued, and the court eventually awarded the Executor only a life estate, after which the house, or sale proceeds, was directed to go to Decedent's three children, or to their heirs, split equally.

The house was eventually given back to the deceased mother's children, but the second husband and his son, as residents, failed to maintain the house; they let it go to waste. All this turmoil lasted 15 years. Preventing such an enduring and expensive incident could have been accomplished simply by using language in the Last Will that could have provided no uncertain interpretation regarding the division of real property of the estate and directing protection of the property from waste, including the responsibility for paying all current property taxes by the life estate holder. Ideally, in a scenario like this, where relationships may be less loving, or otherwise more impersonal, it may be better to direct in the Last Will to liquidate the real estate after death and split the net assets among the beneficiaries chosen by the Testator. That makes it a quick and much cleaner solution. It is not always easy figuring out how to split up one's assets. Also, as seen in this example, finding an honest person to serve in the fiduciary capacity of Executor in one's Will is so vitally important. It is not uncommon that a Testator appoints a bank or professional association to serve as personal representative or Executor of one's estate. Such an appointment also keeps the position neutral and without conflicts of interest between or among individual heirs. A regular accounting by the Executor to all the beneficiaries until the estate is closed may also be a wise move to keep the estate transparent and to compel the Executor to move the case along. Litigation is expensive, time-consuming, and life-disrupting. Try to prevent it by structuring your Will effectively and appropriately.

Personal Property

Personal property items, especially valuables or heirloom property, should be specifically described in a Will when given to certain individuals or entities. This helps to avoid confusion and prevents arguments from arising among family members and various other heirs. These items can be specified and given to particular beneficiaries through a Tangible Personal Property List. This list is incorporated into the Last Will, generally as an attachment. Many estates have lingered on because of infighting among heirs over who should receive particular personal property items.

To help distribute the bulk of most other personal property items smoothly, without family infighting, is to add a fair-minded clause for the heirs to follow. For instance, add language where personal property items are distributed by a sequential selection system. That is, the designated heirs pick out personal property items by taking turns. And if there is a locked contest over the selection of a particular item, such as where two or more heirs want the same item, clauses can be put in the Will where the Executor has the authority to sell and liquidate the property into cash for easier distribution under the Will.

Specific Bequests or Gifts

This is an optional section used for making specific money bequests. This section is also used to list any debts owed to you by someone else that you want to forgive (erase). In our modern day, this section is additionally used to name a caretaker for your pet in the event of your death. In Leona Helmsley's Last Will, she granted $12 million in trust to cover the caretaker's costs to care for her pet dog, Trouble. That amount was later lowered by the court to $2 million, in accordance with a measured accounting of the costs for caring for the pet. The money taken from Trouble's trust was then divided between two grandchildren that Leona had disinherited in her Last Will. This portion of the Will was altered by the court, based in large part on the court's finding that Leona Helmsley was not of sound mind. Typically, changing or tweaking a Last Will by the court is, and should be, a fairly high hurdle to overcome since the court has to look to honoring the wishes of the Decedent.

Disposition of Residue

This section outlines how the remainder of your estate will be distributed to your beneficiaries. In most Wills, it is often stated that if the intended beneficiary predeceases (i.e., dies before) the Testator, then that beneficiary's inheritance shall go to his or her "issue, by right of representation." [See such clauses in: 1) Article 4.5 of the sample simple Will of Jackson Parsons McGee, and; 2) Section VII of the sample blank Will]. Issue means the lineal relationship of descendants and adopted children of that beneficiary. So, if the primary beneficiary (son or daughter) dies before the Testator/ Decedent, then the assets intended for that beneficiary will then go to the next lineal line of that beneficiary, who would receive secondarily, by order. By right of representation means that those who receive an inheritance, as part of the lineal line, like the children of the Decedent, shall each receive the asset, split into equal shares or amounts. Specifically, the children of the primary beneficiary would secondarily inherit, with the primary beneficiary's inheritance split equally among his or her children (Testator's grandchildren) under the law. And if the primary beneficiary's children predecease the Testator/Decedent, then the assets will go to their children (the Testator's great-grandchild or children), and so on. Most often, the named beneficiaries take over the residue of the Will. As to the lineal line of succession, which can vary slightly from state to state, the general line of succession for lineal descendants is examined earlier in this chapter.[32]

32. Take note that if a Will fails to name a secondary (or tertiary) beneficiary, should the named beneficiaries either die before the Testator, disclaim the inherited property from the estate, or cannot be located, then the estate, even with the Will, becomes intestate as to the distribution of assets.

If a family trust is created, and the Last Will is a pour-over Will, then this section can state language that all the residue of the estate can go to the trustee to manage in behalf of the Trust.

Naming a Beneficiary or Beneficiaries

A beneficiary is a person or an organization designated by you to receive money or other property under your Will. The heirs in most Wills tend to be the Decedent's immediate family members. A Last Will allows a Testator to also designate beneficiaries who are friends, non-adopted stepchildren, cousins and other relatives, or charities. In community property states, the Testator can give his or her one-half interest in any community property to the person or entity of choice.[33] Most often, that one-half interest is given to the surviving spouse.

In comparison, without a Last Will, the courts will distribute your assets among your lineal heirs or heirs-at-law under the laws of descent and distribution, which are the default laws and the pre-determined formula set forth under state law. Those heirs-at-law can only include your blood or legal relatives (e.g., adopted children). The primary heirs-at-law are your lineal descendants. They include, in order, the surviving spouse, the Decedent's children, or both, then the children's children, divided equally. If there are no primary heirs, the assets will go to the secondary or tertiary heirs-at-law, which can extend to the Decedent's parents, then grandparents. The details of descent and distribution can vary from state to state.

Providing for Children

In your Will, you should designate someone to act as guardian to care for any of your children who are still minors, as well as designate a trustee to handle and oversee the minor's inherited assets. Generally, a minor child's assets are set aside in a trust, whether created upon death, like a

---

33. There are nine community property states: Arizona, California, Idaho, Louisiana, Nevada, New Mexico, Texas, Washington State, and Wisconsin. Puerto Rico, a U.S. trust territory, is also a community property jurisdiction.

Testamentary Trust built into a Last Will, or in a Living Trust created and funded during one's lifetime. See Chapter 3 for details and samples of Testamentary Trusts and Living Trusts.

Management of Distributions to Minors or to Those Legally Disabled

This section in a Last Will discusses the methods for how property may be distributed to a beneficiary who is under 21 years of age or who is disabled. Most often, a Testamentary Trust is set up within the Will. The Testamentary Trust springs to life after the Decedent's death and can protect money and property over time, with the named Trustee controlling the assets and distributing them in behalf of the beneficiary (a beneficiary is also known as a "grantee" in a trust) in accordance with the trust language that you create.

Miscellaneous Provisions

The Miscellaneous Provisions section does the following:

- Defines terms used throughout the Will;

- Transfers the title of any real property to the Executor of the estate until he/she distributes or sells the property;

- Provides instruction on how to distribute assets if a beneficiary disclaims (does not want) an interest in the Will;

- Identifies your state law as the law your Will is subject to;

- Gives permission to the trustee of any trusts created by the Will to move the administration of the trust without court approval;

- Provides instruction on what to do with property if the Will has no specific instructions on the disposition of that property;

Review Your Document Carefully

Of course, be sure that you carefully review your completed Will. Does the language clearly and accurately reflect your wishes? One of the most important aspects of your Last Will is to make sure that everyone will understand what it says and that it says what you want it to say. You want there to be no vague or ambiguous language that might muddle the proper interpretation of the Will. Make sure that a clause in one part of a Will does not conflict or clash with another clause. Confusing language can result in expensive litigation to resolve for heirs.

Signing Your Last Will

Once you have verified that the Will is accurate, it is critical that you sign the document according to the laws of your state. All states require witnesses view your signing, and attest to the fact that they saw you sign your Will under appropriate conditions. Generally, two witnesses must view and attest to the Testator's signing of his or her Will. Also, the Will must be signed and dated by the Testator before disinterested adult witnesses, who are not beneficiaries under the Will, are otherwise qualified to sign, and who can attest to the Testator's identity and state of mind. Each state has its own requirements about the valid signing of a Will and who can qualify as a witness. Be sure to ask a local estate attorney or conduct research for information about the requirements of your individual state.

What about Notarizing the Will?

Well, this is an interesting situation because most states do not require that the Testator sign his or her Will under a notary. A notary public is an official who applies with the state's secretary of state to serve the public as an impartial witness in performing a variety of official fraud-deterrent acts related to the signing and notarization of documents. But, many courts otherwise require a notarized attestation by way of a self-proving affidavit. Samples of a self-proving affidavit of witnesses attached to the end of sample Wills are included in Chapter 3. So, although state law may not require it, state courts may order it to admit, or accept, a Will to probate. The courts want to have greater assurance, through the confirmation by a notary, that the witnesses saw the Testator sign his or her Will. Often, further attestations are made by the witnesses that they believed the Testator to be of sound mind and appeared to be under no duress when signing his or her Will. A self-proving affidavit helps to settle, in the court's mind, the veracity of the Will's authenticity.

Self-proving affidavits are a contemporary norm so older Wills may not include a self-proving affidavit. If no self-proving affidavit is attached, a court may require the personal representative to seek those witnesses out to submit declarations to the court that each of them witnessed the Testator (now a Decedent) sign the Will. You hope that you can locate those witnesses after all these years and hope that they are still alive! This is one example of a need to update one's Will if it is so aged that is does not contain a self-proving affidavit.

Ensuring Your Will is Legally Valid

Each state follows certain requirements that establish the legality of a valid Last Will and Testament. If every requirement is not met, the court may determine that the Will instrument is not legally enforceable, thus rendering the estate intestate. Be sure to refer to the statutory requirements in the state in which you reside.

III. General Questions and Answers

A Will is also known as a:

- Last Will; or

- Last Will and Testament

What is a Last Will & Testament?

A Last Will and Testament is a legal document that is controlled under state law and generally under a state's Probate and Trust laws. See Chapter 7, which identifies the probate and trust statutes of each of the 50 states and Washington, D.C. The Testator of a valid Last Will dictates control over his or her estate under the protection of the court. In a Last Will, the Testator directs how assets will be distributed, who will receive them, and who will take over as Executor, as Guardian over any minor or disabled children, or as Trustee to handle funds in trust for any minor or disabled children, or for charitable purposes. Wills can, more elaborately, even provide instructions for the set aside of funds in trust for practically any situation, including the care of your pets.

Who Can Prepare a Last Will & Testament?

Any competent person of legal age (usually 18 years of age) can prepare a Last Will, although an exception may be made in your official state of residence if you are married, in the military, or have been legally emancipated. As to being competent, you must be of "sound mind" to make a valid Will, which means:

- You understand that you are making a Will and understand what a Will is;

- You understand your relationship to the people mentioned in your Will;

- You understand what you own, what you are giving away, and how you wish to distribute it; and

- You have an overall intellectual capacity to understand what you are doing with your assets.[34]

In the end, so many people delay making a Will that many die without ever preparing one.[35] For families and friends, it can become an emotional, chaotic, and angry time for them if the Testator failed to create a Will. All

---

34. How to Make a Will Without Spending a Lot of Money. (n.d.). Retrieved November 22, 2016, https://thelawdictionary.org/article/how-to-make-a-will-without-spending-a-lot-of-money/
35. Wills, Trusts and Estates, Ch. 2, §§2.1 to2.1.8"Reasons Most Individuals Die Intestate," Gerry W. Beyer, Aspen Law & Business (1999)

adults should prepare a Last Will to help avoid potential life-long disputes among loved ones. A Last Will is especially important for parents with minor children. Specifically, a Testamentary Trust built within a Will allows the parents, and not the court, to personally appoint a guardian for their children and a trustee for the assets to be held in trust on behalf of their children. The Testamentary Trust further can specify how the assets will be used and distributed, essentially giving the parents a say in how their children will be raised (See Chapter 2 on Testamentary Trusts).

Why is a Last Will Important?

A Last Will essentially allows you to tell the world:

I. who will get your property after you die,

II. who will be your personal representative,

III. who will be the guardian for your minor children, and

IV. who will be the trustee to manage, in trust, the assets you provide for your minor children, disabled individuals, or for other purposes, plus any other testimony like funeral arrangements, and the handling of various other assets.

If you die without a valid Will, your property will otherwise be impersonally handled by a court-appointed Administrator who will distribute the assets to your biological descendants according to the state laws of your residency. Remember that without a Will, you cannot give your property to a stepchild, a friend, or non-relative. And if you have no Will and no relatives, your next-of-kin, so to speak, can be the state of your residency. Yes, your state can wind up getting your assets if they are not otherwise claimed within a specified period established under the state's law. Effectively, your assets can escheat, or go to the state's treasury. Surprisingly, these situations still regularly occur.

What Properties Are Not Given Away in a Will?

You can give away all properties in a Last Will that you own and that you have not implemented any power of transfer upon your death. Typically, the following cannot be given away in a Will because you already have appointed a beneficiary (under a legal transfer known as a power of appointment) for such asset or it is owned as community or jointly-held property:

- 401(k) plan assets

- Annuities

- Bank and brokerage accounts held in joint ownership or in payable-on-death accounts

- Life insurance

- Marital home, held jointly

- Pension plan assets

- Property held in a trust

- Retirement plan assets

Who Should I Name as a Guardian for my Children?

When choosing a guardian, you should consider the following questions:

- Is the guardian of legal age? Your proposed guardian must be a legal adult, and generally, may be required to not possess a certain criminal record, such as felonies, or misdemeanors involving crimes of moral turpitude.[36]

- Is the guardian genuinely concerned for your child's welfare?

---

36. Moral turpitude is a legal concept in the United States and other countries that refers to conduct that is considered contrary to community standards of justice, honesty, or good morals.

- Does the proposed guardian have the time and ability to care for my child?

- Is my child comfortable around the proposed guardian?

- Where does the proposed guardian live? Will my child be able to adapt to the residential area and lifestyle of their guardian?[37]

Can I Dictate how my Pets are to be Cared for?

You can set aside funds in trust for the care of any pet(s), as well as appoint a custodian to care for the pet(s). In a Last Will, this arrangement can be set up within a Testamentary Trust, or the Will can appoint a caretaker and make reference to a separate Trust to distribute any estate funds. A good example can be seen in the Last Will and Testament of Leona Helmsley, a copy of which is provided in Chapter 6. In her Will, Ms. Helmsley appoints her brother, and then her son as alternate, caretaker to care for the life of her beloved white Maltese pet dog named Trouble.[38] Specifics regarding the care of any pet(s) can be discussed or placed in a letter signed by the Testator.

Can I Make a Gift to Charity in my Will?

Yes, you can make a gift(s) to charitable organizations in your Will. In larger estates where estate tax issues may apply, qualified charitable deductions may help to avoid or lessen both federal and state estate taxes.[39]

---

37. (n.d.). How to Appoint a Guardian for Your Children. Retrieved June 18, 2017, from, https://www.lawdepot.com/law-library/estate-articles/how-to-appoint-a-guardian-for-your-children/

38. Helmsley, L. (2005, July 15). Last Will and Testament of Leona Helmsley. Article One Bequests (Item F)

39. Qualified charitable organizations are those entities who are given tax-exempt status by the Internal Revenue Service, such as a 501(c)(3) organization, named after the statute that created it. See 26 U.S. Code Section 501(c)(3). Generally, individuals or businesses who make donations to such tax-exempt entities can receive a corresponding tax deduction on their annual income tax return.

Truly, without a Will, a Trust, or other power of appointment,[40] a charity will not receive any of your properties; your closest lineal heirs will receive everything. This is a significant factor for individuals who want to donate any portion of their estate assets to charity after death. Getting a Will or Trust completed is therefore paramount as the legal pathway to directing estate assets to charity.

Do I Still Need a Will if I Already Have a Power of Attorney?

Yes, you will still need a Will. A Power of Attorney only lets you give another person the authority to deal with your property while you are alive. Since a Power of Attorney officially expires upon death, a Last Will and Testament is required to control how your estate is distributed after death.

What is the Difference Between a Last Will and a Living Will?

A Last Will is used specifically to distribute your property and assets after your death and cannot be used to specify what type of medical treatment you want. In contrast, a Living Will (also known as a Healthcare Directive or an Advance Directive) allows you to specify your preferences for healthcare when you are no longer capable of giving consent yourself.[41] It directs how you want to die. Thus, in a Living Will, when the Principal is in terminal condition and on life-support, the direction is given whether or not life-support should be taken away. Some Living Wills also deal with whether CPR or life-saving drugs should not be administered if one is in a terminal condition. Often, a clause is additionally included to provide that the terminally ill person be kept as comfortable as possible, including receiving pain-relieving medication. Given the constantly changing state of

---

40. Examples of powers of appointment are described above under the heading, "What Properties are not given away in a Will?"
41. "I'm getting older. What documents should I have in place?" (n.d.). Retrieved May 12, 2017, https://www.lawdepot.com/law-library/faq/health-care-directive-faq-united-states/#.XCigvvZFzZg

law, a good lawyer is your best resource when drawing up either a Living Will or a Last Will.

Also see the Durable Power of Attorney for Healthcare under Chapter 3. This instrument can allow the appointed Attorney-in-Fact to make that life and death decision, over that of a Living Will. In simpler terms, would you rather have a trusted friend under a Power of Attorney make a life or death decision for you or pass that right to the last physician or nurse who is medically caring for you?

When Should a Will be Changed or Revised?

If you get married, re-marry, get divorced, have stepchildren with whom you want to share your assets post-mortem, experience the death of a potential beneficiary, or otherwise see a significant change in your life situation, you should review your Will to ensure it continues to not only be valid, but conforms to your every wish.

IV. GLOSSARY: COMMON TERMS AND DEFINITIONS

Ancestor: A person related to a Decedent in an ascending lineal relationship, such as a parent or grandparent. Compare with descendants

Beneficiary: A general term for a person (or entity) who receives either real or personal property under a Will or Trust

Bequest: A gift of personal property in a Will. Contemporary bequests can also include money gifts, which have traditionally been known as legacy gifts (and the person receiving the money gift called a legatee)

Bond: An insurance policy that protects the beneficiaries named in the Will if the Executor wrongfully spends or distributes estate property or embezzles assets of the estate

Charitable Lead Trust: Used by wealthier estates, this is a specialized trust for a term of the years in which a designated charity receives the income stream of the asset placed in the trust. At the end of the term, the property reverts back to the donor/grantor or other designated beneficiaries. The trust still includes the asset within the gross estate so that the grantor's estate can deduct the net present value of the income stream to the charity. Typically, it is set up as a testamentary trust in the donor's Last Will (i.e., funded upon the donor's death). Minimizing estate taxes is the main reason for setting up a testamentary charitable lead trust.

Charitable Remainder Trust: A reverse version of the charitable lead trust, this is a specialized trust[42] in which the donor (i.e., the grantor) will give his/her designated asset or property to a charity after a term of years. The grantor or designated beneficiaries enjoy the property or the income stream from the asset, while the charity receives the property and/or asset at the end of the term. During the term of the trust, the grantor avoids any capital gains taxes and receives an income tax deduction for the fair market value of the remainder interest that the trust has earned. Additionally, the asset is removed from the gross estate, which helps reduce future federal or state estate taxes for that person's estate.

Codicil: A document that is made to amend, replace, revoke, or otherwise modify language in an existing Last Will. Examples in the book are the detailed First and Second Codicils that Thomas Clancy, Jr. attached to his Last Will.

Decedent: A person who has died

Descendants: The issue of an individual, such as children, grandchildren, and their children, followed to the farthest lineal relationship. Descendants are those in a descending line of birth from an individual, rather than an ascending line, such as to the parents or grandparents of the individual. Compare with ancestor.

---

42. 26 U.S. Code § 664.Charitable remainder trusts

Descent: Succession by the heir(s) to real property when the Decedent dies without a Will

Distribution: Succession by the heir(s) to personal property when the Decedent dies without a Will

Emancipation: A court process through which a minor child can become legally recognized as an independent adult

Estate: Everything owned by the Decedent, including but not limited to, personal belongings, real estate, savings, investments, life insurance, business interests, and employee benefits

Executor: The person appointed to handle and distribute property of the Decedent's estate. An Executor is also known as a personal representative if appointed under a Last Will or named an Administrator if appointed by the court without a Last Will.

Fiduciary: A person to whom property or power is entrusted for the benefit of another

Fiduciary Duty: A legal duty to act in the best interests of a person. The Executor and Trustee both possess fiduciary duties to protect, manage, and properly distribute assets of the estate.

Gross estate: The total fair market value of Decedent's estate on the date of death regarding all properties and property interests that include properties real and personal, tangible and intangible, as codified under the Internal Revenue Code, and calculated before subtractions for deductions, qualified debts, administrative expenses, and any casualty losses incurred during administration of the post-mortem estate.

Guardian: A person named in a Will who will assume the physical and legal custody of the Testator's children in the event of the Testator's death

Guardianship: A legal relationship created when a court grants physical and legal custody of a ward to another person or entity; also called a conservatorship

Heir(s) at Law: These are persons who inherit property by law, rather than under a Will, pursuant to the Rules of Descent and Distribution (Intestate Succession)

Inter Vivos: The Latin term for between the living that refers to something done while you are still alive. An inter-vivos trust is a trust created (and funded) while one is alive.

Intestate: This situation occurs when a person with an estate dies without a valid Last Will.

Intestate succession: When the inheritance of a Decedent's estate does not fall under a Will but is succeeded, or obtained, by a lineal relationship, which is codified under the laws of Descent and Distribution of the state jurisdiction where the probate case is filed.

More specifically, intestate succession applies when either:

1) Decedent dies without a Will,

2) Decedent's Will is denied probate due to invalidity, or

3) The Will failed to dispose of all of the estate's properties.[43]

---

43. An example where there is a Will, yet the Will failed to dispose of property, can occur where the Decedent gives all his assets to his wife and his children, but the Decedent, spouse, and children die at the same time. The assets of decedent's now do not have a beneficial direction under the Will. So, the state laws of Descent and Distribution take over. In such a case, the state law may provide the contingency that if there is no spouse, and no children, and no other alternate beneficiaries identified under the Will, then the parents or grandparents, in that order, would inherit the property of the estate. Each state's laws are specific in regard to the order of inheritance by lineal relationship.

Issue: The Decedent's children, grandchildren, great-grandchildren, etc., descending to the most remote degree

Irrevocable: This is a term applied to a document, or to a language clause or term within a document, that is binding and cannot be changed or altered. An example is an irrevocable trust, where the trust terms and funding of such a trust can become binding once signed, and cannot be changed or altered, unless exceptions are specified or unless otherwise determined by a proper court order. See also the term revocable. Irrevocable trusts are created generally to impart favorable tax consequences, where assets of an irrevocable trust can later have estate tax-free status and will not be included in the gross estate of the Grantor for estate tax purposes.

Jurisdiction: The court's power to hear a case

Legitimation: An act that gives the status of legitimacy to a child born to unmarried parents, such as the parents marrying after the birth of a child, a paternity proceeding, or an adoption

Life estate: When someone is designated in a Last Will or Trust who receives a real property asset to keep for the duration of that person's lifetime, or the lifetime of a third-party individual, after which it reverts to the remainderman

Non-intervention power: Language used in a Will that gives the Executor allowance to serve the estate and execute the demands in the Will without having to petition or motion the court each time for authority to undertake the administrative tasks of the estate

Per capita: Each beneficiary takes in equal shares, regardless of whether they are in the same group

Personal representative: See Executor

Per stirpes: Each person in a group or class who takes an equal share

Pretermitted: This occurs when an heir is born after a Will has been drafted but before the death of the Testator.

Pour-over Will: This is a Last Will, which tags to a Living Trust. It essentially states that any properties that by chance are not part of the trust estate will pour over and be part of the trust estate after one's death. The Will ensures that all properties become part of the trust estate.

Probate: This is the method by which the Decedent's estate is administered and processed through the legal system after he or she dies. A state probate court oversees the process.

Remainderman: This is a person who inherits or who is entitled to inherit property upon the happening of a specified event such as the death of a beneficiary. An example is a person who inherits a house after the holder of a life estate on the house dies.

Residue/Residuary Estate/Remainder: The part of a Decedent's estate that remains after all debts, expenses, taxes, and specific bequests (gifts) have been satisfied.

Revocable: A term most often applied to a trust, where the language and funding of a trust generally can be altered or changed at any time during one's life. So, a revocable Living Trust can be amended or terminated by its creator, also known as the Grantor, during that Grantor's lifetime, unless there are intellectual capacity issues of the Grantor. And when the Grantor dies, a revocable Living Trust logically becomes irrevocable. A revocable versus irrevocable trust have considerable tax consequences in an estate plan. All the assets in a revocable trust are still considered assets of the Grantor, personally, so those assets are part of the Grantor's gross estate upon death for tax and estate tax purposes.

Situs: The place where the property is located, which for legal purposes, determines the court of jurisdiction to probate the Last Will

Testamentary Trust: This is a trust that is generally incorporated in a Last Will. Such a trust begins after the Testator's death, is funded post-mortem, and is managed by a trustee appointed under the Will. It expires when the trust funds are expended in behalf of, or distributed to, the designated heirs. This trust is often created to provide funds for the Testator's minor children and assets are distributed to the heirs at a certain adult age designated in the Testamentary Trust. Another reason for creating a Testamentary Trust can be for business succession.

Testator: This is the person who has made a legally binding Last Will and Testament. After the Testator dies, he or she is commonly referred to as the Decedent or the deceased.

Trustee: The person or entity appointed to oversee the day-to-day management of assets owned by a trust

Ward: A minor child or incapacitated adult of whom a guardian has custody

Will: A legal document prepared and signed by the Testator that provides specific instructions about how the Testator's assets should be distributed. The Will names an Executor to handle the administration of the estate, and if needed, can appoint the guardian(s) of any ward(s) of the Testator, can appoint a trustee to oversee the ward's inherited assets, and sets forth all other final wishes of the Testator. It is also referred to as a Last Will or a Last Will and Testament.

Witnesses: This final section of a Will is the statement the witnesses sign, affirming the signature of the Testator to the Will. Additionally, the witnesses also generally sign a self-proving affidavit, which they attest to viewing the Testator sign the Will and that the Testator appeared to be of sound mind and not under any duress.

V. When Should You Consider Constructing a Testamentary Trust or a Living Trust for Your Estate?

> The healthiest response to life is joy.
>
> Deepak Chopra

What kinds of assets are in your estate?

If all you have, for example, are a few bank accounts (in the same state of residence), a life insurance policy, and a 401(k) investment plan, then a Living Trust is likely not necessary — a simple Last Will should satisfy your estate plan. If the estate becomes more complex, as explained below, then move to the next step in considering if a Testamentary Trust or Living Trust is needed to supplement your basic estate plan.[44]

What about real estate ownership?

If you plan simply to transfer ownership of your residential real property[45] to a son or daughter, or to a friend or charitable institution, the transfer can be done in a Last Will. Of course, probating the Last Will makes everything that is filed with the court public information. If the transfer of such property is accomplished through a Living Trust, then the transfer can be done outside of probate, the public eye, and the supervision of the courts.

---

44. You should prepare your basic documents, including your Last Will, Durable Powers of Attorney for Healthcare and Financial management, and possibly a living will.
45. Assumption being that the residential real property, or home, is located in the state where the Last Will is probated.

What if you own properties in more than one state or in other countries?

Theoretically, and practically, you need to probate an estate in the jurisdiction where the asset is located. So, assume that an individual resides in California and dies there. The Last Will is probated in the county where the Decedent claimed residency. But what if the Decedent also owned real property in Florida and Oregon? Then the Decedent's personal representative must also file ancillary (i.e., secondary) probate proceedings in each state where real property is located. So, if you have real properties in two or more states, the best recommendation is to place your assets into a Living Trust, in addition to having a pour-over Will that moves everything you own as a probate asset to pour over to the Living Trust upon your death. In that way, it avoids having to file ancillary probate proceedings in each state where you may own real property. [See Chapter 3 for a sample Living Trust.] And especially if you hold real or personal property assets (e.g., bank or brokerage accounts) in a foreign country, the personal representative will very likely need to set up an ancillary probate proceeding in that foreign country to officially retrieve and transfer the asset(s) to the estate. So, to prevent additional burdens and administrative costs, it is best to hold your assets in a Living Trust if you own real property assets in different states or if you hold real or personal property assets in different countries. The author probated an estate in Washington state for a Decedent who also owned a bank account in the Isle of Man (a self-governing island located between England and Ireland but under the international protection of England). The Decedent only had a Last Will. The Isle of Man required the estate to file an ancillary probate in its jurisdiction for the estate to acquire and transfer the bank account assets to the estate. The additional costs included researching and hiring legal counsel in the Isle of Man to open court probate proceedings and administer the estate in that jurisdiction. Had there existed a Living Trust, the Trustee of the Trust simply would have otherwise been able to handle the administration of the transfer directly with the bank instead of having to hire local legal counsel to file an ancillary probate proceeding in that country.

Do you own a business?

When it comes to a business, having a Living Trust can be more advantageous than simply having a Last Will. In a Living Trust, the smooth transition of your business continues without hiccups or (court) delays. The successor trustee that you appointed in your Living Trust can manage the business immediately after the owner's death. If a business succession must go through the probate process, court decisions can be slow, which can impede business operations.

What if you currently have minor beneficiaries?

Children under 18 years of age, as minors, will need a guardian to make decisions for the child, and a trustee to handle the inherited assets. In such cases, most often, a Testamentary Trust built within a Last Will can handle the financial management of the minor child's inherited assets. Likewise, a separate Living Trust can also serve the same purpose. Language in the trust is crafted according to your wishes as to how the child or children will receive or share in the assets. Deciding upon a Testamentary Trust or a separate Living Trust is a decision that is worthy to receive feedback from a legal professional. A very general rule of thumb is that less complex estates (house, 401(k), a financial account or two) can work well in a Testamentary Trust, while more complex assets (different real estate assets, an ongoing business, and/or various financial accounts, especially in different jurisdictions or countries) would be better in a separate Living Trust. The trust can also specify the use of funds for the health, education and welfare of any designated person. Again, the probate process makes everything public. So, there is a choice to probate the matter through the Testamentary Trust in a Last Will or to construct a Living Trust that essentially spells the same language but stays private, outside of probate, and generally out of the public eye.

What about privacy?

So, once probate proceedings commence, the Last Will becomes a public court document for the whole world to see. Details of the names of heirs, addresses, and how assets are to be handled and distributed all become public, unless otherwise sealed. But a Living Trust is generally handled outside of direct court supervision and public viewing. Just remember that some states may require a Living Trust to be court-filed after your death to allow any interested parties to have a forum to dispute any matters, including how the trustee or guardian is managing the trust estate. Language in a trust can include specifics about what part or parts of the trust can be sealed or not revealed to the public, as long as the beneficiaries can otherwise receive an entire copy, privately, or an overseer is placed to review the accounting and to confirm the trustee's actions regarding the disbursements from the trust.

Other asset designations to consider

Another aspect of estate planning, aside from the consideration of placing assets in a Will or Living Trust, is working directly with the financial institution to designate someone or some entity to receive the assets in a financial account upon one's death. Such funds are not part of your estate, for probate estate purposes, and as such, are designated non-probate assets. Specifically, you can list someone to inherit your funds in a financial institutional account, upon death, which is known as a Payable on death, or POD, account.[46] Ask your financial representative about a POD account. The options offered by banks and other financial institutions can vary.

Be careful when giving another person authority over an account if you only want that added person to help with administering the account funds, but not to legally receive those funds upon your death. This is a common mistake that is made, as this author has often seen. It occurs when an account holder needs help with bookkeeping, writing checks, making deposits, and the like; the individual who owns the financial account most often will add an adult child or friend for helping the owner

---

46. Note: Be careful not to name minor beneficiaries as payable on death beneficiaries, IRA beneficiaries, or 401(k) beneficiaries, since a guardianship for a minor under a court-supervised case will need to be established.

to administer the account only, but not to take the account funds after your death. But, how that added person is listed on the account is crucial. Specifically, an *authorized account holder* can have power to write checks or withdraw funds during the owner's lifetime, but he or she is not allowed to inherit the funds upon the owner's death. That is where you want the added person to only assist with the accounting but not have ownership over the funds when you die. This intended scenario is often seen where one child, among other siblings, helps mom or dad, or both of them. Upon the death of the original account holder(s), the intent thereafter would be to effectively have the net funds distributed in equal amounts among all of the siblings. If a financial institution does not have an authorized account holder designation, one can still have similar access, if not the same as an authorized account holder, by properly using a valid Durable Power of Attorney for financial management to help manage and use the account for the benefit of the account holder. See Chapter 3, which discusses the powers under a Durable Power of Attorney, as well as includes a sample Durable Power of Attorney for healthcare and financial management.

On the other hand, a *joint account holder* will inherit all the funds in a financial account upon your passing. That account is therefore under a designated power of appointment, and it places that account outside of the probate estate assets. Regularly check all your financial accounts to be sure that the designations of any added person(s) to your accounts are in accordance with what you intend to have in place.

So, which direction should you take? It may not be an easy decision to make on your own. As much as this author recommends the importance of consulting with competent legal counsel, you should always ask questions about language you see in your estate planning documents that you do not fully understand.

Other Trust Considerations

Other trust considerations include setting up a separate trust, or trusts, to properly manage assets for a particular use, or for protection for generational beneficiaries. It is often the wealthier clients who seek these more specialized trusts, whether created through a Testamentary or a Living Trust. So, for wealthier estates, trusts become the go-to documents for structuring plans that handle future financial considerations, such as to avoid inclusion in one's gross estate for estate tax reasons, or to set aside funds for charity or for future generations, or both.[47] Charitable lead trusts and charitable remainder trusts are just a couple examples in which wealthier estates may use trusts as tools to avoid or lessen their federal estate taxes, while giving assets away to qualified charities.

In earlier years, trusts were often created to avoid federal estate taxes, which had taxed gross estates valued above the $1 million exemption limit at that time. Today, the exemption limits have drastically increased to the benefit of federal taxpayers.[48] As of January 1, 2018, federal estate taxes are assessed only if the Decedent's gross estate exceeds $11.18 million.[49] That amount doubles to $22.360 million for a married couple. This significantly narrows the number of Americans whose gross estates qualify for the assessment of federal estate taxes. For 2018, a total of only 1,700 Decedents in the United States will be expected to pay federal estate taxes, or only about one-tenth of 1 percent of all Americans who died that year.[50] In contrast, in 2001, a total of 50,500 estates paid federal estate taxes when the tax exemption limit was $1 million.[51]

Ironically, more trusts are now being created to avoid state rather than federal post-mortem taxes. These include state estate taxes as well as

---

47. Examples include a charitable remainder trust or a charitable lead trust. Please refer to the book's glossary included in this Chapter.

48. Tax Cuts and Jobs Act of 2017, Pub. L. 115-97 (Dec. 22, 2017); 26 U.S. Code Section 2010(c)(3)-Unified Credit against tax imposed.

49. Inflation Adjustments Under Recently Enacted Tax Law, IR-2018-94 (April 13, 2018). This is the federal estate tax exemption limit as of January 1, 2018, which is indexed annually for inflation by the Internal Revenue Service.

50. Gleckman, H. (2017, December 6). Only 1,700 Estates Would Owe Estate Tax in 2018. Retrieved December 14, 2018, https://www.taxpolicycenter.org/taxvox/only-1700-estates-would-owe-estate-tax-2018-under-tcja

51. How Many People Pay the Estate Tax? (n.d.). Retrieved October 4, 2018, https://www.taxpolicycenter.org/briefing-book/how-many-people-pay-estate-tax

inheritance taxes. Currently, 17 states and the District of Columbia[52] impose either a state estate tax or inheritance tax. The one exception is the state of Maryland, which imposes both an estate tax and an inheritance tax. In most of the affected states, the reader will see that the various state exemption limits generally range between $1 million and $3 million.[53] These levels are far below today's federal estate tax exemption limits noted above.

Would your gross estate have to pay state estate or inheritance taxes? If so, setting up a specialized trust or trusts would be wise to consider. Review the state estate and inheritance tax chart in Chapter 7 to see if it affects your state of residence. Then view the exemption limits, if any, and whether it is an estate tax or inheritance tax. If you estimate that your gross estate will exceed the exemption limit(s), constructing a specialized trust, such as a credit-shelter trust or a spousal protection trust, might be in order. This book does not provide details of constructing these trusts, which need the attention of specialized tax and trust counsel. But to give the affected reader a general idea of the money that can be saved for creating such a trust, we can view Washington state's estate tax exemption limit of $2.193 million for 2018. If, for example, using stagnant figures, the gross estate of a married couple from Washington state is valued at exactly double the $2.193 million exemption limit ($4.386 million), or about $4.4 million. Thereafter, when the first spouse dies, the surviving spouse would properly elect or otherwise disclaim[54] a marital-deductible amount equal to the current exemption limit allowed, or $2.193 million. That amount is preserved and placed in a credit-shelter or similar type of trust for the first-to-die spouse, which would avoid Washington's estate taxes. This is because the first spouse to die gets to apply the exemption limit if a proper trust is set up for it, coupled with the surviving spouse's timely prepared tax return election and/or written disclaimer. On the other hand, if no credit

---

52. Only two states, Delaware and Hawaii, plus the District of Columbia match the higher federal estate tax exemption limit threshold.

53. *See,* the State Estate Tax and Inheritance Tax Chart for the 50 States and the District of Columbia in Chapter 7

54. Under federal statute, the disclaimer must be made within nine months of the death of the first spouse. *See,* 26 U.S. Code § 2518.Disclaimers, *and* 26 CFR § 25.2518-2

shelter trust was created, and the first-to-die spouse's exemption limit is otherwise waived, then the surviving spouse's estate would be valued at about $4.4 million, and he or she would have to pay state estate taxes above the $2.193 million exemption limit. How much would that amount be? Well, the effective Washington state estate tax rate charged above the exemption limit in this example is 15 percent. Given that the estate has $2.193 million above the exemption limit, the estate would be taxed at 15 percent of $2.193 million, or about $328,950.00 in estate taxes paid to the state of Washington. That amount due would have otherwise been entirely avoided if proper trust planning had been set up. So, as more estates become relatively wealthier over time, it becomes necessary to plan wisely in researching federal as well as state tax issues.

CHAPTER 3

Estate Planning Resources

I do not fear death. I had been dead for billions and billions
of years before I was born, and had not suffered the
slightest inconvenience from it.

MARK TWAIN

Wills and Living Trusts

Following are samples of Last Wills and of a Living Trust. They provide the
reader with examples of what details can be included in such instruments.
Ideally, the consideration in using any of these documents in one's estate
planning is best decided in consultation with a legal advisor.

Uses

Both Living Trusts and Last Wills are used in estate planning; each serves
separate but complementary functions. A Last Will defines a Testator's
instructions, not only for the management and administration of the
estate, but for the care of his or her surviving family, friends and business,
and funeral arrangements. Living Trusts are primarily for managing the
estate's assets, including real property, investments, and business interests.
A Testator who stands to leave behind a spouse and young children needs
a Will to ensure that his or her family is not financially disrupted. A Living
Trust, however, can protect the estate's real and monetary assets, provide

financial support to surviving relatives, and may allow the Testator to take advantage of various tax breaks. A Living Trust can also keep a family's financial estate private. Typically, when and if one prepares a Living Trust, he or she will also prepare a pour-over Will to ensure that an estate includes all other assets that did not or were not placed in the Living Trust.

Advantages

A large majority of citizens generally need only prepare a basic or simple Will to handle their estates. Also, aside from designating asset distributions, the Testator can incorporate language that sets up a Testamentary Trust to care for minor children, appoint a Trustee, provide bequests of money to specific heirs, include a Tangible Personal Property List, and incorporate any other related matters, like funeral arrangements. See the sample Last Wills that follow.

Once you have your Last Will properly drawn up and signed, you will find yourself resting more comfortably. For most of us, it is like reaching the mountaintop — we can relax and breathe easier. Take advantage of a Will to guide your post-mortem estate. Let your Last Will decide how your estate will be managed rather than having state laws decide the fate of your estate without one. The strength of a Last Will, like the one you plan to create, carries the full weight of law that is protected and enforced by the powers of the court. Imagine the court like a personal bodyguard over your estate, enforcing the language under the Will. A Last Will brings a smooth and measured transfer of wealth to the next generation.

Your Last Will has the court's protection in handling the distribution of assets. Further, creditors have a relatively tight bar date, or time limit, in which to file their claims. In Washington state, a creditor has four months from the date of notice[55] to file its claim in a probate proceeding. After the

---

55. Revised Code of Washington §11.40.020(1). Notice to creditors-Manner-Filings-Publication.

bar date, the debt is forever discharged if not properly filed. If no probate is filed, the creditor instead has two years to file an action in court against the estate.[56]

Living Trusts offer the benefit of avoiding probate proceedings, so you can maintain your privacy even after death and save your family potential hassles. Living Trusts are also inherently harder to contest, keeping your assets safer and in the hands of intended beneficiaries. Additionally, a Living Trust offers various tax breaks of which you can take advantage during your lifetime, while your family can continue enjoying the benefits after your passing.

Disadvantages

Administering a Last Will in probate makes it part of a public record — an objectionable point if you want to keep matters more private. Probated Wills are also subject to challenges from outside parties, including disinherited relatives. A minor issue can stall the process for months or years. On the other hand, Living Trusts are limited in function. While you can provide financial support for your children, you cannot appoint a Guardian or define instructions for their care after your death. Living Trusts are explicitly for managing property and assets, forcing the court to administer the remainder of your estate following intestacy guidelines, should you not have a Last Will. As mentioned earlier, having a pour-over Will can allow one to include language about guardianship, while directing the personal representative to give to the Trustee all probated property to administer under the trust.

---

56. Revised Code of Washington §11.40.051(1). Claims against decedent-Time limits.

SIMPLE LAST WILL

The following is a sample of a simple Last Will. It is hypothetically prepared for a person who resides in Washington state. The name of the Testator in the Will is fictional and is purely coincidental to anyone so named. This simple Last Will, unlike a more complex Will that may include a Testamentary Trust, provides a straightforward division of property at death. The last page is known as a self-proving affidavit, where the court can feel satisfied that the Will was witnessed by two other individuals. Before going forward with any estate-planning document, you should not rely solely on any sample document in this book, but you should consult with a lawyer to make sure you are comfortable that every concern of yours is legally resolved and satisfied. Remember that the most important aspect of a Will, or any estate-planning document, is that, foremost, it be clear and understandable. That is, it must not be vague or ambiguous. Second, be sure that the personal representative whom you appoint is someone you trust and is someone who will faithfully carry out your wishes in the Will.

Also, following are other estate planning documents shown here strictly as sample documents for readers to see how they are generally written. They include a Last Will with a built-in Testamentary Trust and a Living Trust. Additional language describes the need to also consider including in one's estate plan Durable Powers of Attorney for Healthcare and Financial Management. Every person knows that his or her estate planning documents are very personal. The author recommends that anyone considering putting together a Last Will and any other related documents seek professional legal advice in customizing his or her estate plan.

LAST WILL AND TESTAMENT OF JACKSON PARSONS MCGEE

I, Jackson Parsons McGee, domiciled in Winthrop, Washington, being of legal age, of sound and disposing mind and memory, and not acting under any duress, menace, fraud, or undue influence of any person whomsoever, do hereby make, publish and declare this to be my Last Will and Testament as follows:

ARTICLE 1. REVOCATION OF FORMER WILLS

I hereby revoke all wills and codicils executed by me prior to the date of this instrument.

ARTICLE 2. FAMILY AND BENEFICIARIES

I am widowed. I have three children. They are *Jackson Parsons McGee, Jr., Melanie Styles, and Markus McGee*. The primary and contingent beneficiaries of my estate are more fully described in Article 4 below.

ARTICLE 3. PERSONAL REPRESENTATIVE

3.1 Designation: I nominate and appoint my son, *Jackson Parsons McGee, Jr.*, residing in Winthrop, Washington, as Personal Representative of my estate. Should Jackson Parsons McGee be unable or unwilling to so act, then I appoint my daughter, *Melanie Styles*, residing in Walla Walla, Washington, as alternate Personal Representative of my estate.

3.2 Bond Waiver; Powers: No bond, surety, or other security shall be required of my Personal Representative in any jurisdiction for any purpose. My Personal Representative shall have non-intervention powers to settle my estate in the manner set forth in this Will. Furthermore, my Personal Representative shall have full power, authority, and discretion to do all that he or she thinks necessary or desirable in administering my estate, including the authority to:

(a) make interim distributions of income and Principal to those beneficiaries who are to receive the income and the Principal of my estate;

(b) sell, lease, exchange, mortgage, pledge, or assign assets of my estate;

(c) invest and reinvest property that is not specifically given, and any form of investment that he or she thinks advisable, including investing in stocks, bonds, certificates of deposit or treasury bills, or money market funds; and

(d) delegate discretionary as well as administrative powers.

3.2.1 Exercise of Powers: Such powers described above may be exercised in the manner and at such times and upon such terms and conditions as in my Personal Representative's judgment is for the best interest of my estate and for such purposes to make, execute and deliver any instruments in writing, which may be necessary or proper.

3.2.2   Ancillary Administration: Should it be necessary for the Personal Representative of my estate to qualify in any jurisdiction outside of the State of Washington, wherein my domiciliary Personal Representative is unable or unwilling to qualify, then I appoint such person or corporation or partnership as may be designated by my domiciliary Personal Representative to serve in such foreign jurisdiction requiring the ancillary probate, to act without bond and without the intervention of any court, to the extent permitted by law.

3.3   Payment of Taxes and Expenses: My Personal Representative shall pay all costs of administration, all properly presented creditor's claims, and all estate, inheritance, succession, legacy and transfer taxes (exclusive of generation-skipping taxes) imposed by and made payable under the laws of the United States and the State of Washington, and any other state or country due to my death, and to charge such payments first against the residue of my probate estate. This direction shall apply to all estate taxes attributable to all property of my estate even though some property does not pass under my Will or is not part of the residue of my estate.

3.4   Adjustment for Tax Deductions: If my Personal Representative elects to claim any expenditures chargeable to Principal as an income tax deduction and such election results in greater estate taxes, my Personal Representative shall make an adjustment in the cash accounting. This adjustment shall be made so that the income account is charged with and the Principal account is credited with an amount equal to the additional estate taxes paid.

ARTICLE 4. DISPOSITION OF ESTATE

4.1   Real Property: I own residential real property in fee absolute, at 2286 W. Main Street, Kennewick, Washington 99352 ("residence"). My residence shall be sold, and the net proceeds divided equally among my three children, or to their issue *per stirpes*, should any child not survive me.

4.2   Certain Tangible Personal Property: I direct my personal Representative to give all my jewelry to my daughter, Melanie Styles. Should Melanie Styles predecease me, then I give all my jewelry to my granddaughter, Kara Styles, or to her issue by right of representation (*per stirpes*). Further, the Personal Representative shall transfer to my son, Jackson Parsons McGee, Jr., all my interests in vehicles that I own. Should Jackson Parsons McGee, Jr. predecease me, then I direct the Personal Representative to transfer or sell my interests in such vehicles in accordance with Article 4.3 below.

4.3   Other Tangible Personal Property: I direct my Personal Representative to give all my other tangible personal property divided equally to my surviving children. Should any son of mine predecease me, then each of their portions shall be re-apportioned equally between my other surviving children. Should my daughter predecease me, then her portion shall be distributed to her issue by right of representation, in as equal shares as possible, since she is my only child with children. My tangible personal property may be liquidated by my Personal Representative to make for a more even distribution or given away to charity provided there is no consensus on the distribution of such property among my children.

4.4   Residue — Definition: The "residue of my estate" means all probate estate property remaining in my estate not otherwise disposed according to this Will, which I own at the time of my death, and after payment of claims, expenses, taxes, and other liabilities of my estate. The residue of my estate shall not include any property over which I may have any power of appointment.

4.5   Residue — Disposition: After payment of funeral and administrative expenses, and payments to creditors, I give the residue of my estate, divided equally, to my children by right of representation (*per stirpes*).

4.6   Expenses: Any expenses incurred in safeguarding or delivering any tangible personal property or residue shall be paid from my estate by my Personal Representative.

ARTICLE 5. CONDITIONS

The current residences of individuals noted in this Will are for reference only and shall not affect the validity of any appointment or any bequest to any individual who has relocated.

ARTICLE 6. SEVERABILITY

If a Court of competent jurisdiction should rule invalid or unenforceable any provision of this Will, the remaining portions of the Will shall remain in full force and effect.

ARTICLE 7. GOVERNING LAW

Any questions of law regarding the execution of this Will or its effect shall be determined in accordance with the laws of the State of Washington.

///

///

IN WITNESS WHEREOF, I have initialed for identification purposes the first three pages of this Will and have hereunto set my hand and official seal in execution of this entire instrument this _____ day of _____, 2017.

_____

Jackson Parsons McGee, Testator

The foregoing instrument was signed, sealed, and declared by Jackson Parsons Mcgee, the above-named Testator, as his Last Will and Testament, in our presence, with all of us being present at the same time, and who has acknowledged signing his name voluntarily and under his own free will for the uses and purposes mentioned in the instrument.

WHEREUPON, at his request and in his presence and in the presence of each other, have hereunto subscribed our names as witnesses.

_____   _____
DATE   *SIGNATURE OF WITNESS*

_____   _____
DATE   *SIGNATURE OF WITNESS*

AFFIDAVIT OF ATTESTING WITNESSES TO THE LAST WILL AND TESTAMENT OF JACKSON PARSONS MCGEE

State of Washington   )
) ss
County of King   )

Each of the undersigned states under penalty of perjury under the laws of the State of Washington that:

1. I am over the age of eighteen years and competent to be a witness to the Last Will and Testament ("Will") of Jackson Parsons Mcgee ("Testator").

2. The Testator, in my presence and in the presence of the other witness whose signature appears below:

   a. declared the attached instrument to be his Will;

   b. requested the other witness and me to act as witnesses to his Will and to make this affidavit; and

   c. signed such instrument.

3. I believe Testator to be of sound mind, and that in so declaring and signing, he appeared to be acting under no duress, menace, fraud, undue influence or misrepresentation.

4. The other witness and I, in the presence of the Testator and of each other, now affix our signatures as witnesses to the Will and make this affidavit.

Signature _____   Signature _____

Name _____   Name _____

Residing at: _____   Residing at: _____

    SUBSCRIBED AND SWORN to before me this _____ day of _____, _____.

                           _____

                           NOTARY PUBLIC in and for the State of Washington

                           Residing at _____.

                           Commission expires _____.

SAMPLE LAST WILL TEMPLATE

Below is a sample blank Will that provides the reader a template and guide to the basic format of a Will. The reader should understand and know what details he or she wants to include in a Will. That is because it is a very personal document, and it needs its own customization. It is wise to have your Will done under the advice and counsel of a competent attorney who can ensure that your wishes are stated very clearly, that no language is left out that is important to the Will, and that it is in conformance with the respective State laws and rules of the court.

The language in this Will, and in the "Parsons McGee" sample Will above, is in the basic optional format that allows the designated Personal Representative to serve without having to obtain and pay for a bond. In an intestate estate (i.e., no Will), the court can order that the bond on the Executor be set at an amount equivalent to the value of the estate's more liquid assets (i.e., stocks, cash, bonds, auctionable property items), or a percentage of the entire value of the estate. Whatever the amount, it will be at the discretion of the court. But to otherwise allow the Personal Representative in a Will to serve without a bond does allow him or her to dispense with the time and cost of obtaining the bond itself. The Testator has the incentive to appoint someone he or she trusts to handle the estate without a bond.

The added challenge of a bond on the Executor is that it can be based on the Executor's own credit report and rating. Should the Executor happen to have a low or challenged credit rating, it could make the bond premium relatively costly. Even worse, he or she could fail to qualify for the requisite amount of the bond under the rules of the bonding carrier or surety.

Additionally, the sample blank Will and the "Parsons McGee" sample Will contain language that allows the Executor to hold non-intervention powers. That power allows the Executor to complete fiduciary tasks to advance the probate without first needing to notice parties for hearings to seek court authority to accomplish each fiduciary task.

Section VI in the sample blank Will contains a list where the Testator can identify certain personal property items (known as a tangible personal property list) or cash allotments (known as a bequest list) that can be designated to certain heirs. The Testator will describe or identify those items, and specify which heir shall receive each item.

So, to serve without bond and to have non-intervention powers are signs of faith of the Testator that he or she fully trusts the Executor or Personal Representative to execute the language specified in the Will and to distribute assets to the designated heirs as promptly as is practicable under the Will.

Another aspect of this Will is the self-proving affidavit at the end of the document. It is generally not a statutory requirement that it is included, but it can be required by the Court Commissioner, the Judge, or under the Rules of the Court. A self-proving affidavit provides greater assurance of authenticity of the Will to the Court. In Washington state, as is the requirement for Wills in all other states, at least two witnesses must view the Testator when he or she signs the Will and must attest to that fact with their signatures on the Will.[57] Also in the self-proving affidavit, the witnesses must additionally affirm that the Testator appeared to be of sound mind and not under any noticeable duress when he or she signed the Will. The self-proving affidavit is notarized, as is shown in the example below.

The attorney who prepares a Last Will for the client must also, under the Rules of Professional Conduct,[58] ethically adjudge the client to have the intellectual capacity to understand that he or she is signing a Will and giving assets away to particular heirs. The same assessment applies to other situations in the context of estates where the client is giving up his or her rights to someone else, such as through a Durable Power of Attorney, or a Living Will. [See Chapter 3, which details language about Durable Powers of Attorney and discusses aspects about a Living Will]. If the Testator is not able to clearly comprehend what he or she is doing, then the Testator may be intellectually challenged enough to have a diminished capacity[59]

---

57. Most all States require two witnesses to the Testator's signing of a Last Will. Be sure to check your state's laws regarding the minimum requirements in preparing a Last Will. For a summary resource, see the chart of the probate and trust laws listed in Chapter 7. One interesting matter worthy of inclusion in this footnote is a story where the author's wealthy client directed him to include three witnesses to the signing of client's Will since she feared individual family members who might try to "knock the legs off the Will," i.e., find a way to invalidate the Will, such as by finding a witness' signature to be invalid.

58. The Rules of Professional Conduct of Washington State ("RPC") are the ethical rules that all licensed Washington attorneys must follow. These rules are generally promulgated and set into practice by the State Supreme (or highest) Court of each state. The ethical rules may be titled differently in each state, but all steer toward what conduct is condoned or not allowed for an attorney.

59. RPC 1.14 *Client with Diminished Capacity.* The Washington State Supreme Court provides a comment describing indications of diminished capacity that an attorney use in assessing a client under RPC 1.14:

In determining the extent of the client's diminished capacity, the lawyer should consider and balance such factors as: the client's ability to articulate reasoning leading to a decision, variability of state of mind and ability to appreciate consequences of a decision; the substantive fairness of a decision; and the consistency of a decision with the known long-term commitments and values of the client. In appropriate circumstances, the lawyer may seek guidance from an appropriate diagnostician.

that could interfere with or prevent getting a Will and other estate-planning documents completed. In such an instance, the Testator may be advised to seek a second legal opinion, or else a medical examination by a physician. Capacity in Washington state is ultimately a legal decision and not a medical one regarding completing Wills and other estate-planning instruments.[60] No attorney should prepare a Will or other estate-planning document if the client does not understand what he or she is signing due to intellectual incapacity. A significant number of court challenges have included intellectual capacity issues of the Testator. For example, the New York Surrogate court in Leona Helmsley's estate determined that she did not have or possess the full capacity or competency to have drafted a valid Will. This action allowed the court to lower the trust fund for the care of her pet dog from $12 million to $2 million and to redirect a good portion of those proceeds to the two other grandchildren who were originally disinherited in the Will. Leona Helmsley's estate was valued between $4 and $5 billion at the time of her death.

---

60. Revised Code of Washington §11.88.010(1)(c): "A determination of incapacity is a legal not a medical decision, based upon a demonstration of management insufficiencies over time in the area of person or estate…"

The author thanks the Internet Legal Research Group (www.ilrg.com) for providing the sample fill-in Will below. The self-proving affidavit attached to the back of the sample Will was prepared and provided by the author:

LAST WILL AND TESTAMENT OF

_____
[Name of Testator]

I, _____ [Name of Testator], a resident of _____, Washington, being of sound and disposing mind and memory and over the age of eighteen (18) years or lawfully married or having been lawfully married or a member of the armed forces of the United States or a member of an auxiliary of the armed forces of the United States or a member of the maritime service of the United States, and not being actuated by any duress, menace, fraud, mistake, or undue influence, do make, publish, and declare this to be my Last Will, hereby expressly revoking all Wills and Codicils previously made by me.

I. MARRIAGE AND CHILDREN

I am married to _____, and all references in this Will to my _____ [husband or wife] are references to _____ [him or her]. I have the following children:

Name:_____Date of Birth:_____

Name:_____Date of Birth:_____

Name:_____Date of Birth:_____

Name:_____Date of Birth:_____

II. EXECUTOR: I appoint _____ as Executor of this my Last Will and Testament and provide if this Executor is unable or unwilling to serve then I appoint _____ as alternate Executor. My Executor shall be authorized to carry out all provisions of this Will and pay my just debts, obligations and funeral expenses.

III. GUARDIAN: In the event I shall die as the sole parent of minor children, then I appoint _____ as Guardian of said minor children. If this named Guardian is unable or unwilling to serve, then I appoint ___ _____ as alternate Guardian.

IV. SIMULTANEOUS DEATH OF SPOUSE: In the event that my _____ [wife or husband] shall die simultaneously with me or there is no direct evidence to establish that my _____ [wife or husband] and I died other than simultaneously, I direct that I shall be deemed to have survived my _____ [wife or husband], notwithstanding any provision of law to the contrary, and that the provisions of my Will shall be construed on such presumption.

V. SIMULTANEOUS DEATH OF BENEFICIARY: If any beneficiary of this Will, including any beneficiary of any trust established by this Will, other than my _____ [wife or husband], shall die within 30 days of my death or prior to the distribution of my estate, I hereby declare that I shall be deemed to have survived such person.

VI. BEQUESTS:

I will, give, and bequeath unto the persons named below, if he or she survives me, the Property described below:

Name: _____

Address: _____

Relationship: _____

Property: _____

_____

_____

Name: _____

Address: _____

Relationship: _____

Property: _____

_____

_____

Name: _____

Address: _____

Relationship: _____

Property: _____

_____

_____

Name: _____

Address: _____

Relationship: _____

Property: _____

_____

_____

If a named beneficiary to this Will predeceases me, the bequest to such person shall lapse, and the property shall pass under the other provisions of this Will. If I do not possess or own any property listed above on the date of my death, the bequest of that property shall lapse.

VII. ALL REMAINING PROPERTY; RESIDUARY CLAUSE: I give, devise, and bequeath all the rest, residue, and remainder of my estate, of whatever kind and character, and wherever located, to my _____ [wife or husband], provided that my _____ [wife or husband] survives me. I make no provision for my children, knowing that, as their parent, my _____ [wife or husband] will continue to be mindful of their needs and requirements. If my _____ [wife or husband] does not survive me, then I give, devise, and bequeath all of the rest, residue, and remainder of my estate, of whatever kind and character, and wherever located, to my children per share, but if any child predeceases me, then his or her share will pass, per share, to his or her lineal descendants, natural or adopted, if any, who survive me; but if there are none, then his or her share will lapse and pass equally as part of the shares of my other named children; but if none of my named children survives me or leaves a lineal descendant who survives me, then according to the order of intestate succession in the State of Washington.

VIII. ADDITIONAL POWERS OF THE EXECUTOR: My Executor shall have the following additional powers with respect to my estate, to be exercised from time to time at my Executor's discretion without further license or order of any court.

_____

_____

_____

_____

IX. WAIVER OF BOND, INVENTORY, ACCOUNTING, REPORTING AND AP-PROVAL: My Executor and alternate Executor shall serve without any bond, and I hereby waive the necessity of preparing or filing any inventory, accounting, appraisal, reporting, approvals or final appraisement of my estate. I direct that no expert appraisal be made of my estate unless required by law.

X. OPTIONAL PROVISIONS: I have placed my initials next to the provisions below that I adopt as part of this Will. Any unmarked provision is not adopted by me and is not a part of this Will.

_____ If any beneficiary to this Will is indebted to me at the time of my death, and the beneficiary evidences this debt by a valid Promissory Note payable to me, then such person's portion of my estate shall be diminished by the amount of such debt.

_____ All debts of my estate shall first be paid from my residuary estate. Any debts on any real property bequeathed in this Will shall be assumed by the person to receive such real property and not paid by my Executor.

_____ I direct that my remains be cremated and that the ashes be disposed of according to the wishes of my Executor.

_____ I direct that my remains be cremated and that the ashes be disposed of in the following manner:

_____

_____

_____

_____ I desire to be buried in the _____ cemetery in _____ County, Washington.

XI. CONSTRUCTION: The term "Testator" as used in this Will is deemed to include me as Testator or Testatrix. The pronouns used in this Will shall include, where appropriate, either gender or both, singular and plural.

XII. SEVERABILITY AND SURVIVAL: If any part of this Will is declared invalid, illegal, or inoperative for any reason, it is my intent that the remaining parts shall be effective and fully operative, and that any Court so interpreting this Will and any provision in it construe in favor of survival.

IN WITNESS WHEREOF, I, _____
__ [Name of Testator], hereby set my hand to this Last Will, on each page of which I have placed my initials, on this _____ day of _____,
20_____ at _____
_____, State of Washington.

_____ [Signature]

_____ [Printed or typed name of Testator]

_____ [Address of Testator, Line 1]

_____ [Address of Testator, Line 2]

WITNESSES

The foregoing instrument, consisting of _____ pages, including this page, was signed in our presence by _____
__ [name of Testator] and declared by _____ [him or her] to be _____ [his or her] Last Will. We, at the request and in the presence of _____ [him or her] and in the presence of each other, have subscribed our names below as witnesses. We declare that we are of sound mind and of the proper age to witness a will, that to the best of our knowledge the Testator is of the age of majority, or is otherwise legally competent to make a will, and appears of sound mind and under no undue influence or constraint. Under penalty of perjury, we declare these statements are true and correct on this _____ day of _____, 20_____ at _____
_____, State of Washington.

_____ [Signature of Witness #1]

_____ [Printed or typed name of Witness #1]

_____ [Address of Witness #1, Line 1]

_____ [Address of Witness #1, Line 2]

_____ [Signature of Witness #2]

_____ [Printed or typed name of Witness #2]

_____ [Address of Witness #2, Line 1]

_____ [Address of Witness #2, Line 2]

AFFIDAVIT OF ATTESTING WITNESSES TO THE LAST WILL AND TESTAMENT OF _____

State of Washington   )

) ss

County of King   )

Each of the undersigned states under penalty of perjury under the laws of the State of Washington that:

1. I am over the age of eighteen years and competent to be a witness to the Last Will and Testament ("Will") of _____ ("Testator").

2. The Testator, in my presence and in the presence of the other witness whose signature appears below:

    a. declared the attached instrument to be her Will;

    b. requested the other witness and me to act as witnesses to her Will and to make this affidavit; and

    c. signed such instrument.

3. I believe Testator to be of sound mind, and that in so declaring and signing, she appeared to be acting under no duress, menace, fraud, undue influence or misrepresentation.

4. The other witness and I, in the presence of the Testator and of each other, now affix our signatures as witnesses to the Will and make this affidavit.

_____   _____
Signature   Signature

_____   _____
Name   Name

Residing at: _____   Residing at: _____

SUBSCRIBED AND SWORN to before me this ____ day of _____, _____.

                          _____
                          NOTARY PUBLIC in and for the State of
                          Washington

                          Residing at _____.

                          Commission expires _____.

LAST WILL WITH TESTAMENTARY TRUST

Note: Below is a sample Last Will with a Testamentary Trust included. The name and address of the Testator, and the names of all the fiduciary Appointees and the Beneficiaries, except for the non-profit entity The Columbus Foundation[61], are fictional and purely coincidental to anyone so named.

---

61. The author inserted the correct address of this tax-exempt non-profit organization as just one example of giving to non-profit organizations through estate plans. Helping our community through philanthropy is a vital resource to non-profits that helps promote the general welfare of our communities. Other than gifting while alive, there is no other way. If no Last Will is made, then non-profits receive nothing. Only lineal heirs receive assets in an intestate estate-a precious reason to complete a Last Will and to give assets to those entities who survive on the goodwill and love of able donors. The Columbus Foundation has as its mission statement the opportunity "…[t]o assist donors and others in strengthening and improving our community for the benefit of all its residents." See https://columbusfoundation.org/about-us/overview/

LAST WILL AND TESTAMENT OF
ROGER JOHN GALETKA

I, Roger John Galetka, am a resident of Mahoning County, Youngstown, Ohio, residing at 5264 W. Elmendorf Street, Youngstown, Ohio 44512. I am of legal age, of sound and disposing mind and memory, and not acting under any duress, menace, fraud, or undue influence of any person whomsoever in regard to the preparation of this instrument, my Last Will and Testament ("Will" or "Last Will").

ARTICLE 1: REVOCATION OF PRIOR WILLS

I revoke all other Wills and Codicils made by me prior to the date of this Will.

ARTICLE 2: FAMILY; BENEFICIARIES

I am a single, widowed individual. My immediate family consists of my son, Harrison Galetka ("Mr. Galetka"). As of the writing of this instrument, my son is 14 years old. Any references to "my son" in this instrument shall refer to Harrison Galetka. The beneficiaries of my estate are specifically identified in Article 4 below.

ARTICLE 3: PERSONAL REPRESENTATIVE

3.1 Designation: I nominate and appoint *Ms. Elizabeth Sealy* as the Personal Representative of my estate. If Elizabeth Sealy is unable or unwilling to serve, then I appoint *Ms. Margaret Boardman* as Alternate Personal Representative.

3.2 Bond Waiver; Powers: No bond, surety, or other security shall be required of my Personal Representative in any jurisdiction for any purpose. My Personal Representative shall have non-intervention powers to settle my estate in the manner set forth in this Will. Furthermore, my Personal Representative shall have full power, authority, and discretion to do all that he or she thinks necessary or desirable in administering my estate, including the authority to:

(a) make interim distributions of income and principal to those beneficiaries who are to receive the income and the principal of my estate. The beneficiaries may include, in lieu of my Trustee, the beneficiaries of any trust under this instrument. If distributions are made to trust beneficiaries, my Personal Representative shall have and exercise the same power, authority, and discretion given my Trustee; (b)   sell, lease, exchange, mortgage, pledge, or assign assets of my estate;

(c) invest and reinvest property that is not specifically given, and any form of investment that he or she thinks advisable; and

(d) delegate discretionary as well as administrative powers.

3.2.1 Exercise of Powers: Such powers described above may be exercised in the manner and at such times and upon such terms and conditions as in my Personal Representative's judgment is for the best interest of my estate and for such purposes to make, execute, and deliver any instruments in writing, which may be necessary or proper.

3.2.2 Ancillary Administration: Should it be necessary for a representative of my estate to qualify in any jurisdiction outside the State of Ohio, wherein my domiciliary Personal Representative is unable or unwilling to qualify, then I appoint such person or corporation or partnership as may be designated by my domiciliary Personal Representative to serve in such foreign jurisdiction requiring the ancillary probate, to act without bond and without the intervention of any court, to the extent permitted by law.

3.3 Distribution of Trust Property: If any property would be distributable to a trust beneficiary immediately upon receipt by my Trustee, my Personal Representative may distribute such property directly to the beneficiary.

3.4 Payment of Taxes and Expenses: My Personal Representative shall pay all costs of administration, all properly presented creditor's claims, and all estate, inheritance, succession, legacy, and transfer taxes (exclusive of generation-skipping taxes) imposed by and made payable under the laws of the United States and the State of Ohio, and any other state or country by reason of my death, and to charge such payments first against the residue of my probate estate. This direction shall apply to all estate taxes attributable to all property of my estate even though some property does not pass under my Will or is not part of the residue of my estate.

3.5 Adjustment for Tax Deductions: If my Personal Representative elects to claim any expenditures chargeable to principal as an income tax deduction and such election results in greater estate taxes, my Personal Representative shall make an adjustment in the cash accounting. This adjustment shall be made so that the income account is charged with and the principal account is credited with an amount equal to the additional estate taxes paid.

ARTICLE 4. DISPOSITION OF ESTATE

4.1 Real Property: I give all my interests in real property which I own to the *Trustee* to be administered as part of the Family Trust that is described in Article 6 below, which includes my vacation residence located at 41 Sandpiper Strand, Coronado Cays, California 92118.

4.2 Tangible Personal Property: I give and dispose all my interest in tangible personal property to my son. Such property shall include, but not be limited to, motor vehicles, boats, furniture, furnishings, books, objects of art, sporting equipment, jewelry, clothing, and other property of a household or personal kind. My Personal Representative may liquidate any such personal property to cash to be used for expenses as is necessary.

4.3 Expenses: Any expenses incurred in safeguarding or delivering any tangible personal property shall be paid from my estate as an administrative expense.

4.4   Residue — Definition: The "residue of my estate" means all other probate estate property which I own at the time of my death, and after payment of claims, expenses, taxes, and other liabilities of my estate. The residue of my estate shall not include any property over which I may have any power of appointment.

4.5   Residue — Disposition: I distribute the residue of my estate to the *Trustee* to be administered as part of the Family Trust described in Article 7 herein below.

ARTICLE 5. FUNERAL ARRANGEMENTS AND REMAINS

My Personal Representative shall have sole responsibility for my funeral arrangements, except that any writing I may provide to the Personal Representative concerning my funeral arrangements shall be followed.

ARTICLE 6. FAMILY TRUST

Hereafter, I will refer to myself as "Trustor," and to my Trustee as "Trustee."

6.1   Trustee: I nominate and appoint *Harold Warren Brown* as Trustee. Should Harold Warren Brown at any time be unable or unwilling to serve as Trustee, then I appoint *Mr. Henry Girard* to serve as Successor Trustee of the Family Trust.

6.2   The Trust Estate: The Trust estate shall consist of the following property received by the Trustee for administration under this Article, and the proceeds, investments, and reinvestments of that property:

(a) property received from Trustor's Personal Representative, including real property located at 41 Sandpiper Strand, Coronado Cays, California 98112;

(b) insurance proceeds payable to Trustee on behalf of any beneficiaries by reason of Trustor's death;

(c) payments to Trustee from any pension or profit-sharing plan, employee savings plan, deferred compensation agreement, or other employee benefit plan; and

(d) other property transferred to, and accepted by, Trustee.

6.3   Beneficiaries; Purposes: The beneficiaries of the Trust estate shall be those individuals specified below in Articles 6.10 and 6.11. The trust purposes shall be to provide for any future bequests to each beneficiary, as well as to provide for the health, education, support, and maintenance of any certain beneficiary as more specified below.

6.4   Duties of Trustee.

6.4.1   Annual Accountings: After the end of each income tax year for each trust, Trustee shall prepare a statement showing how the property of the trust is invested and all transactions relating to the trust for the preceding tax year. Within 60 days after the end of the tax year, Trustee shall furnish a copy of the statement to each adult income beneficiary or to the Guardian of a minor beneficiary of the Trust estate.

6.4.2 Investments: In acquiring, investing, reinvesting, exchanging, selling, and managing the property of the Trust, Trustee shall exercise the judgment and care, under the circumstances then prevailing, which persons of prudence, discretion, and intelligence exercise in the management of their own affairs, not in regard to speculation but in regard to the permanent disposition of their funds. In determining the prudence of a particular investment, Trustee shall consider the proposed investment or investment course of action in relation to all properties of the Trust estate.

6.4.3 Income: If all of the income of a trust is not distributed during an income tax year, the undistributed portion shall be added to principal.

6.5 Powers of Trustee: Trustor grants to Trustee the continuing, absolute, discretionary power to deal with any property, real or personal, held in the Trust estate or in any trust, as freely as Trustor might in the handling of Trustor's own affairs, except as specifically directed herein. In addition, Trustee shall have all of the power, authority, and discretion given a trustee under the laws of the State of Ohio on this date. Such powers may be exercised independently and without the prior approval of any court or judicial authority, and no person dealing with Trustee shall be required to inquire into the propriety of any of Trustee's actions.

6.6 Agents and Attorneys: Trustee may employ agents and attorneys as Trustee thinks necessary or desirable for the proper administration of the trust or for any litigation, controversy, or uncertainty that may arise in connection with the trust. Trustee may pay reasonable compensation to agents and attorneys for their services and be fully protected in relying on advice of legal counsel.

6.7 Resignation of Trustee; Appointment of Successor Trustee: Trustee shall have the right to resign as trustee without court proceedings by giving written notice to that effect to the successor trustee. Notice shall also be provided to any adult income beneficiaries of the Trust estate. If the successor Trustee fails or is unable to serve as trustee, then such successor trustee has the power to choose a successor trustee who holds fiduciary controls, such as an attorney, professional service corporation or partnership, or bank.

6.8 Reasonable Compensation: The trustee shall be compensated for services reasonably expended in the operation and maintenance of the trust, based on reasonable fees at the then prevailing rate.

6.9 Spendthrift Clause; Transfer of Beneficial Interest: The interest of any beneficiary in income or principal shall not be subject to claims of creditors or others, or to legal process, and shall not be assigned, alienated or encumbered. This provision shall not prevent a beneficiary from exercising a power of appointment or disclaiming an interest. Additionally, the Trustee shall make no distribution of either income or principal to Harrison Galetka if the Trustee determines that there is a reasonable possibility that any such distributions will primarily benefit Harrison's creditors or others than Harrison himself.

6.10 Maintenance and Liquidation of Trust Property: The Trustee shall have the right to sell or lease the real property of the trust. The property shall be sold and liquidated no later than my son's 18th birthday. Until then, the house shall serve as the family retreat.

6.11 Distributions and Allocation of Family Trust Assets: After the real property is liquidated to cash, the Trustee of the Family Trust shall have the right to distribute funds to Mr. Harrison Galetka as follows:

a) Of the net total proceeds, 50% of the proceeds shall continue to be held *in trust* for Harrison Galetka, through any of his minor years and until his 30th birthday and distributed as follows: The Trustee of the Family Trust shall have the right to distribute funds to Harrison Galetka during and up to his 30th birthday for his health, education, support, and maintenance. Such amounts are to be determined by the Trustee, in his sole discretion, as to those funds reasonably calculated for living expenses; and distributions shall be made out of net income to the extent available and the balance shall be made out of principal. On Harrison Galetka's 30th birthday, the remaining net funds from this 50% pool, after payments for expenses, shall be distributed in full to him.

b) The Trustee shall distribute the other one-half interest of trust proceeds being held *in trust* for Harrison Galetka, as follows: 1.) 25% of the one-half net interest given on his 18th birthday; 2.) 50% of the remaining one-half interest given him on his 25th birthday, and; 3.) the remaining net amount of this one-half interest given to him on his 30th birthday.

6.12 Trustee's Good Faith Actions Binding: Every action taken in good faith by Trustee shall be conclusive and binding upon all persons interested in the property of the trust.

6.13 Merger of Similar Trusts: If Trustee manages two or more trusts, under this or any other instrument, which are to fulfill similar purposes for the same beneficiary or beneficiaries, Trustee may merge any two or more of such trusts.

6.14 Alternate Trust Beneficiaries: Should my son die prior to receiving any portions of funds from the Family Trust under this Article, then those funds shall continue to be distributed in accordance with Article 6.11 above, except that distributions shall inure to my son's children by right of representation as alternate trust beneficiaries. And my son's children shall receive the continued portions of trust fund distributions until each alternate trust beneficiary reaches 30 years of age. If my son dies before his 30th birthday and has no children, then the Family Trust, and all related trusts, shall terminate. The Trustee shall thereafter distribute all remaining trust property as soon as practicable to the The Columbus Foundation, 1234 East Broad Street, Columbus, Ohio 43205-1453.

6.15   Expenses of Trust: The Trustee shall pay all administrative expenses of the trust from trust assets, after which net proceeds can be distributed from the liquidation of real property as described in Article 6.11 above.

ARTICLE 7. APPOINTMENT OF GUARDIAN FOR MINOR CHILD

At the time of my death, should my son still be a minor child, then I appoint *Mr. Andrew Taylor* as Guardian of my son, Harrison Galetka. Should Mr. Andrew Taylor be unable or unwilling to serve as Guardian, then I appoint *Ms. Randi Edwards* as Alternate Guardian of my son.

ARTICLE 8. SEVERABILITY

If a court of competent jurisdiction rules invalid or unenforceable any of the provisions of this Will, the remaining portions of this Will shall remain in full force and effect.

ARTICLE 9. GOVERNING LAW

Any questions of law regarding the execution of this Will or its effect shall be determined in accordance with the laws of the State of Ohio.

///

///

///

IN WITNESS WHEREOF, I have initialed for identification purposes each of the previous pages herein of my Last Will and Testament and have hereunto set my hand and official seal in execution of this entire instrument.

DATED this _____ day of _____, 2018.

_____
Signature of Testator

The foregoing instrument was signed, sealed, and declared by Roger John Galetka, the above-named Testator, as his Last Will and Testament, in our presence, with all of us being present at the same time.

WHEREUPON, at his request and in his presence and in the presence of each other, have hereunto subscribed our names as witnesses.

DATE:_____ WITNESS: _____

(Print Name) : _____

DATE:_____ WITNESS: _____

(Print Name) : _____

AFFIDAVIT OF ATTESTING WITNESSES TO THE LAST WILL AND TESTAMENT OF ROGER JOHN GALETKA

STATE OF OHIO   )

) ss

COUNTY OF MAHONING   )

Each of the undersigned states under penalty of perjury and under the laws of the State of Ohio that:

1. I am over the age of eighteen years and competent to be a witness to the Last Will and Testament ("Will") of Roger John Galetka ("Testator").

2. The Testator, in my presence and in the presence of the other witness whose signature appears below:

    a. declared the attached instrument to be his Will;

    b. requested the other witness and me to act as witnesses to his Will and to make this affidavit; and

    c. signed such instrument.

3. I believe Testator to be of sound mind, and that in so declaring and signing, he appeared to be acting under no duress, menace, fraud, undue influence or misrepresentation.

4. The other witness and I, in the presence of the Testator and of each other, now affix our signatures as witnesses to the Will and make this affidavit.

_____   _____

Signature   Signature

_____   _____

Printed name   Printed name

Residing at: _____   Residing at: _____
        (City, State)   (City, State)

SUBSCRIBED AND SWORN to before me this ____ day of _____, 2018.

NOTARY SEAL:

                              _____

                              NOTARY PUBLIC in and for the State of Ohio

                              Residing at _____.

                              Commission expires _____.

LIVING TRUST

A Living Trust, also popularly known by its Latin term as an inter vivos trust, is created while one is alive. A Living Trust is funded once assets are placed into it, such as naming a bank account under the trust and placing funds into the account or transferring real or personal property to the trust. Generally, it must be funded for the instrument to be valid and effective. A Living Trust can be revocable, which allows the person a chance to freely change his or her mind about the trust. Changing a revocable trust is possible if the one who created the trust (called the Grantor) is alive and is intellectually competent to understanding what he or she is doing with the assets and beneficiaries. Alterations include changing the language in the trust, eliminating or adding beneficiaries and the amounts of any gifts or bequests, or to terminate it. The sample Living Trust below is a revocable Living Trust. An irrevocable trust cannot generally be changed once it is created and funded; such trusts are created to generally handle tax matters, while setting aside funds for heirs, or for charitable purposes.

[NAME OF PERSON] INTER VIVOS TRUST

THIS TRUST AGREEMENT is entered into and executed on this _____ day of _____, (Year), by and between the Trustor, Mr./Ms. _____, of the County of King, State of Washington, herein called "Trustor," and Trustee, _____, herein called "Trustee."

RECITAL

The Trustee hereby declares that Trustor has transferred and delivered to the Trustee, without consideration, real property described in *Schedule A*, which is attached to this instrument.

The Trustee shall hold, manage, and distribute the Trust Estate exclusively for the uses, purposes and objectives set forth in this TRUST AGREEMENT, and upon and subject to the terms, provisions, conditions, powers and limitations herein set forth below.

ARTICLE 1. FAMILY; BENEFICIARIES

1.1 Trustor's Family Members: The Trustor is currently a single unmarried individual with no children surviving.

1.2 Trust Beneficiaries: The benefactors under this Trust instrument shall apply to the Trustor, the Trustor's children, the Trustor's community interest, and/

or to the Trustor's designation of charities, all more specifically defined in Article 4. The distribution of trust assets is more specifically described in Article 5.

ARTICLE 2. RIGHTS RESERVED BY TRUSTOR

2.1 While Trustor is Living: The Trustor reserves the right to:

(a) Direct the distribution of all income and Principal of the Trust;

(b) Amend or revoke this Trust, in whole or in part, by an instrument in writing delivered to the Trustee;

(c) Accept transfers into the Trust, from the Trustor or any other person, by will or otherwise, and may designate the Trust to which the property shall be added; and

(d) To withdraw from the operation of the Trust any part of the property of the Trust estate.

2.2 Powers and Duties of Trustee: The powers and duties of the Trustee shall not be changed without the Trustor's written consent, or otherwise by court order.

2.3 Disposition of Property of Trust: Any revocation, withdrawal of property or properties, or modification exercisable by the Trustor shall be valid and fully effective whenever the Trustee receives from the Trustor written notice thereof. In the case of revocation or withdrawal of property, the Trustee shall have a reasonable time to transfer or deliver any properties out of the Trust.

2.4. Rights Reserved to Trustor: The rights reserved to the Trustor are personal to Trustor and shall not be exercised by any other person, including an attorney-in-fact or a guardian of Trustor's estate, except upon court order.

ARTICLE 3. ADMINISTRATION

3.1 Trustor to Direct During His Lifetime: While the Trustor is alive, the Trustee shall pay to the Trustor or to his assigns so much of the net income and Principal of the Trust as the Trustor shall direct. Any payments made by Trustor from the Trust to any beneficiaries shall be deemed to have passed first through the Trustor individually.

3.2 Trust Administration During Trustor's Lifetime While Not Incapacitated or Disabled: During the lifetime of the Trustor, and as Trustee, the Trustor shall have all rights and powers designated in this Trust Agreement. Specifically, the Trustor shall have all the rights and powers designated in the Trust instrument.

3.3 Successor Trustee Designated for Trust Administration After Life of Trustor or While Incapacitated or Disabled: After the life of the Trustor, or during periods of incapacity or inability of the surviving Trustor to act as Trustee, ****, shall act as Trustee of the Trust estate and all other trusts created herein, with all rights and powers designated in this Trust Agreement.

3.4   Investments: In acquiring, investing, reinvesting, exchanging, selling, and managing the property of the Trust, as is authorized in this Trust instrument, the Trustee shall exercise the judgment and care, under circumstances then prevailing, which persons of prudence, discretion, and intelligence exercise in the management of their own affairs. In determining the prudence of a particular investment, the Trustee shall consider the proposed investment or investment course of action in relation to all property of the Trust.

3.5   Trustee's Bond: Neither the original Trustee named herein, nor any successor Trustee shall be required to give any bond of any kind or character for the performance of such Trustee's duties pursuant to this Trust Agreement.

3.6   Power of Attorney: The powers and authorities conferred upon the Trustee or any successor Trustee shall constitute and be construed to be "powers of attorney" sufficient to permit the Trustee to convey title to or for any beneficial interest in all personal or real property which are part of the Trust estate of any trust created and established herein.

3.7   Trustee's Powers: Additionally, the Trustee shall have all rights, powers and duties given by law on the date hereof, including those set forth in the Washington Trust Act and other relevant law in force as of the date of execution of this instrument. Such powers may be exercised independently and without the prior approval of any court or judicial authority, and no person dealing with the Trustee shall be required to inquire into the propriety of any of Trustee's actions.

3.8   Trustee's Additional Powers: The Trustee shall have authority:

(a) To determine what is Principal or income, which authority shall specifically include the right to make any adjustments between Principal and income for premiums, discounts, taxes, depreciation or depletion;

(b) To reasonably compensate and employ agents and attorneys as the Trustee thinks necessary or desirable for the proper administration of the Trust, or for any litigation, controversy, or uncertainty, which may arise in connection with the Trust. The Trustee shall employ such agents or attorneys without liability for their omissions or errors;

(c) To borrow money on behalf of the Trustor, or on behalf of any other trust beneficiary when needed under exigent circumstances, with or without security, and to repay any such borrowings;

(d) To invest and reinvest the Trust assets as the Trustee shall determine to be prudent under circumstances then prevailing. Such includes opening accounts to trade securities for stocks, bonds, and other securities, options, and other negotiable instruments.

3.9   Directions to Trustee: In addition to written directions, the Trustee is entitled to rely upon directions given to Trustee in person, by telephone, facsimile, telex, cable or otherwise. A person giving any direction to the Trustee shall give written confirmation of any such direction when requested by the Trustee.

3.10 Restraint on Alienation: No right, title, interest or equity in any of the Trust estate or the income or increase thereof shall vest in any beneficiary until actual payment to him or her by the Trustee, and no part hereof, either Principal, interest, or increase, shall be liable for the debts, present or future, of any beneficiary, and shall not be subject to the right on the part of any creditor of any beneficiary to seize or reach the same under any writ or by any proceeding at law or in equity. No beneficiary shall have any power to give, grant, sell, convey, mortgage, pledge, or otherwise dispose of, encumber, or anticipate the Principal, income or increase of the Trust estate, or any portion thereof, of any installment thereof.

3.11 Trustee Removal and Appointment of Successor Trustee(s): Trustor shall have, at any time during his lifetime while not incapacitated or disabled, the absolute right to resign as Trustee, to remove any existing Trustee, or to appoint a successor Trustee to any of the trust-related assets. Such removal or appointment shall be made in writing.

3.12 Successor Trustee Powers and Duties:

(a) A Successor Trustee may accept a predecessor's accounting without independent review or audit and shall not be liable for any loss sustained during or attributable to the period in which a predecessor served as Trustee.

(b) A Successor Trustee shall have full power and authority, without procuring any order, consent or confirmation of any court, to manage the trust assets during the existence of this Trust.

3.13 Profits and Losses: Any taxes owed on trust income transferred during the taxable year to any of the income beneficiaries shall be chargeable to the respective beneficiaries receiving such income.

3.14 Resignation of Trustee; Appointment of Successor Trustee: Trustee shall have the right to resign as Trustee without court proceedings by giving written notice to that effect to Trustor if Trustor is then living, or otherwise to each adult income beneficiary of the Trust and each guardian of any minor children of the Trust if Trustor is not living. Trustor, or a majority of the adult income beneficiaries and guardians of any minor children of the Trust shall then have the right, without court proceedings, to appoint a successor Trustee.

ARTICLE 4. BENEFICIARIES OF THE ESTATE

4.1 Beneficiaries; Purposes: The Trustor shall be the primary beneficiary of the Trust estate while living. The primary trust purposes shall be to provide for the health, support, and maintenance of the Trustor's accustomed manner of living. Secondary trust purposes shall be to permit Trustor to provide funds for the reasonable health, support, maintenance, and education of the Trustor's children, or to any community interest, or to any charities, as specifically described herein below.

4.2   Distributions While Trustor Is Living:

4.2.1   As Directed by Trustor: As long as the Trustor is living, the Trustee shall make such distributions of income and Principal to Trustor, or to others, as Trustor shall direct. Notwithstanding any restrictions on the Trustee as designated in this Trust instrument, the Trustor shall have full power and authority over the trust assets pursuant to Article 2 herein. If the Trustor is disabled or incapacitated, the Trustee may either continue or discontinue any distributions previously directed by Trustor based on what would be in the best interest of the Trustor.

4.2.2   Upon Disability of Trustor: In the event of incapacity or disability of the Trustor, the Trustee may make to, or for the benefit of, the Trustor such distributions from the Trust estate as the Trustee thinks necessary to accomplish the Trust purposes.

ARTICLE 5. DIVISION AND ALLOCATION UPON TRUSTOR NOT LIVING

5.1   Upon Trustor Not Living: The Trustee may distribute the assets in the Trust no earlier than ninety (90) days after the life of the Trustor to the beneficiary or beneficiaries of the trust.

5.2   Beneficiaries: Purposes: The Trustor's children surviving, if any, shall be the primary beneficiaries, in equal shares, to receive all properties of the trust, after payments for all administrative costs and other expenses. Distribution shall be made in trust to any child who is a minor, benefiting primarily for their health, education, maintenance and welfare. Should the Trustor have no children, then the net assets of the trust shall be divided equally, that is one-half going to the Trustor's community interest or estate, and the other half going to a proper non-profit charity or charities (as defined by the Internal Revenue Code), which actively protect old-growth forests, either regionally or worldwide. Should Trustor have neither any issue or community interest or estate, then such remaining non-claimed portion shall also go to a charity or charities as defined above, which actively protect wildlife and the environment, either regionally or worldwide.

ARTICLE 6. PROPERTY OF THE TRUST ESTATE

Any real property transferred to the Trust described in *Schedule A* shall retain all tax benefits that have inured to Trustor. Trustor shall have all rights during his lifetime to sell, mortgage, lease or otherwise dispose of any property held by the Trust estate. Should any real property be sold or leased, the Principal and any income gained shall remain part of the Trust estate unless otherwise directed to be distributed by the Trustor. The properties of the Trust, together with such other property as may be added to this Trust, shall be held, managed, and distributed by the Trustee as herein provided.

ARTICLE 7. CONDITIONS

7.1   Incapacity: If the surviving Trustor shall become incapacitated, all distributions of his income and Principal shall be discretionary with the Trustee for the duration of such incapacity. These include providing funds for the complete care of Trustor up to the limits of the assets available in the Trust estate.

7.2   Costs and Expenses: After the life of the Trustor, the Trustee may pay, based upon availability of liquid assets in the Trust, the Trustor's debts, funeral expenses, administration expenses, and expenses of last illness, and all estate, transfer, succession, inheritance or other death taxes (except generation-skipping taxes), together with interest and penalties thereon, assessed due to such Trustor's death, whether attributable to property passing under this Trust or outside it. This would include having to liquidate, if necessary, any properties in the trust.

7.3   No Contest Clause: If any beneficiary under this Trust Agreement, or under the Trustor's estate, in any legal manner, contests or attacks any provisions in the Trusts or Will, including any property or any interest in the Trustor's estate going to the contesting beneficiary, or any distributions of the assets of the trust or estate, then that beneficiary's trust or estate interest shall be revoked in its entirety and shall be disposed of as if that contesting beneficiary had predeceased Trustor without issue.

7.4   Address Locations: The current addresses of any individual as may be noted in reference to this Trust Agreement are for reference only and shall not affect the validity of any appointment or bequest to any individual who has relocated.

7.5   Validity of Copy of Trust Agreement: Third parties shall be entitled to rely upon a copy of the signed original hereof, as opposed to a certified copy of the same.

ARTICLE 8. IRREVOCABILITY

The Trustor reserves the right to alter, amend, revoke, cancel or terminate this instrument, or to withdraw or receive property of the Trust estate. The Trustor, or other person or estate, reserves the right to transfer to the Trustee, at any time during the term thereof, additional property acceptable to the Trustee to be administered as a part of the Trust estate. This Trust, however, becomes irrevocable after the life of the Trustor. Successor Trustee shall have no right to revoke or terminate this instrument.

ARTICLE 9. TERMS AND DEFINITIONS

9.1   Incapacity: As used in this instrument, "incapacity" with respect to a Trustee's duties and responsibilities shall mean that the Trustee is either unwilling or unavailable to manage the Trust's affairs, whether due to illness, physical abduction, or for any other reason. A written letter, either from the then-existing Trustor, the Trustee, or his or her physician, stating that the Trustor or Trustee is unavailable or unwilling to direct or manage the Trust's affairs, is sufficient, unless otherwise superseded by court order or a current Durable Power of Attorney to the contrary.

9.2   Net Income: Net income shall include all interest income and dividends earned by the Trust estate, less any amounts charged for all expenses, costs, taxes and fees, and amounts transferred to Principal.

9.3   Trustee's Good Faith Actions Binding: Actions taken in good faith by Trustee shall be conclusive and binding upon all persons interested in property of the trust.

9.4   Trustor Not Living: The wording, "upon Trustor not living" or "after the life of Trustor" or "Trustor's passing," means the date of death of Trustor.

9.5   Merger of Similar Trusts: If the Trustee is trustee of two or more trusts, under this or any other instrument, the purposes of which serves the same beneficiary or beneficiaries, the Trustee may merge any two or more of such trusts into one combined trust for administrative sufficiency.

9.6   Successor Trustee: All referrals to "Trustee" or "Trustee" shall also refer to the role and responsibility of the Successor Trustee, and his or her successors or Co-Trustee.

9.7   Governing Law and Savings Clause: This instrument shall be governed by the laws of the State of Washington. Any provision prohibited by law or unenforceable shall not affect the remaining provisions of this instrument.

IN WITNESS WHEREOF, Trustor has initialed for identification purposes the preceding pages of this Trust Agreement, and the Trustor and the Trustee hereunto set their hand and official seal in execution of this entire instrument as of the date subscribed on page one (1) of this Trust Agreement:

TRUSTOR:

_____

[Print Name]

TRUSTEE:

_____

[Print Name]

STATE OF WASHINGTON   )
) ss
COUNTY OF KING   )

On this _____ day of _____, _____, before me, a Notary Public, State of Washington, duly commissioned and sworn, personally appeared Mr. [ ], known to me to be the person whose name is subscribed to the Trust instrument known as the [ ] Inter Vivos Trust, and acknowledged to me that he executed the same.

WITNESS my hand and official seal.

_____

NOTARY PUBLIC

Residing at_____

Commission expires _____

[Name of Person] INTER VIVOS TRUST

SCHEDULE A

This SCHEDULE *A* includes the following assets placed IN TRUST immediately following the creation of this Trust Agreement:

1.   REAL PROPERTY located at 1211 Main Street, Seattle, Washington 98105 (see attached quitclaim deed);

2.   BANK ACCOUNTS at NASA Federal Credit Union, Bremerton, Washington 98312;

3.   Other assets as itemized herein:

      1932 Chicago Bears Championship Football Program (Chicago Bears v. Portsmouth Lions)

      1955 Chevrolet Convertible

      1955 Mickey Mantle Rookie Card-Graded PSA 8

///

///

///

AFFIDAVIT OF ATTESTING WITNESSES
TO [Name of Person] INTER VIVOS TRUST

State of Washington   )

) ss

County of King   )

Each of the undersigned states under penalty of perjury under the laws of the State of Washington that:

1. I am over the age of eighteen years and competent to be a witness to the Last Will and Testament ("Will") of *** ("Testator").

2. The Testator, in my presence and in the presence of the other witness whose signature appears below:

   a. declared the attached instrument to be his Will;

   b. requested the other witness and me to act as witnesses to his Will and to make this affidavit; and

   c. signed such instrument.

3. I believe Testator to be of sound mind, and that in so declaring and signing, he appeared to be acting under no duress, menace, fraud, undue influence or misrepresentation.

4. The other witness and I, in the presence of the Testator and of each other, now affix our signatures as witnesses to the Will and make this affidavit.

_____   _____
Signature   Signature

_____   _____
Name   Name

Residing at: _____   Residing at: _____

SUBSCRIBED AND SWORN to before me this ____ day of _____, _____.

                                   _____

                                   NOTARY PUBLIC in and for the State of Washington

                                   Residing at _____.

                                   Commission expires _____.

OTHER ESTATE PLANNING DOCUMENTS TO CONSIDER

Durable Powers of Attorney For Healthcare and Financial Management

Other documents should be considered to ensure full coverage of your person and your estate. While your Last Will provides instructions to be followed after death, a healthcare Power of Attorney and a financial management Power of Attorney provide instructions in case you become incapacitated and are unable to make decisions for yourself during your lifetime.

While one is alive, there are always situations that can and will arise where one is unavailable, either intellectually or physically or both. During these periods of incapacity, it is wise to have a document available that allows another person to act on your behalf and to handle pressing matters regarding your health or financial situation.

The person creating the Power of Attorney is the Principal. The individual or entity appointed by the Principal to act as the Principal's agent is known as the Attorney-in-fact. Although the word attorney is used, that does not mean a lawyer. Any individual who has the capacity to act can serve as the Attorney-in-fact. The Principal can also appoint an alternate Attorney-in-fact, should the primary Attorney-in-fact be unable or unwilling to serve. In earlier years, a Power of Attorney primarily served to appoint someone to serve as your agent. But the Power of Attorney is terminated if the Principal became incapacitated since the Principal could not, thereafter, competently monitor the Attorney-in-fact. In the 1950s, states began enacting their own statutes, allowing the Power of Attorney more durability to extend into and serve the rights of the Principal even during periods of the Principal's incapacity. Thus, the term durable was applied to the Power of Attorney. Today, all 50 states have Durable Power of Attorney instruments.

There are two primary Durable Power of Attorney agreements that everyone should create. One of them is a Durable Power of Attorney for Financial

Management, where the Attorney-in-fact serves as the Principal's agent to manage accounts, pay bills, write checks, and handle financial matters on behalf of the Principal, including during any period where the Principal may be incapacitated mentally or unavailable physically.

The other agency agreement is a Durable Power of Attorney for Healthcare. It allows another person to act in your behalf to make healthcare decisions for you. Another important aspect of this document is the ability to determine whether you should live with or without life-sustaining equipment. Having a real person whom you trust to determine your healthcare and medical needs is a wiser decision versus preparing a Living Will (explained below).

Often, the Principal will name the same individual as the Attorney-in-fact for both healthcare and financial management. Below is a sample document of a combined Durable Power of Attorney for Financial Management and Healthcare. It contains very thorough authorities over healthcare and financial management, including authority over digital information and healthcare authority to seek all information protected under the Health Insurance Portability and Accountability Act of 1996 (HIPAA),[62] as amended. Remember that any Durable Power of Attorney should be customized according to the intent and desires of the individual creating it (known as the Principal).

The Attorney-in-fact is a fiduciary, who is fully responsible to act in strict accordance with the language in the Durable Power of Attorney. That person *must* be a trusted individual because he or she can, and will, be making healthcare decisions for you or handling assets of your estate and managing your financial accounts. When all of us get older, and especially if we become incapacitated, we are going to need trusted help. The Durable Power of Attorney will get you there. It can be a very vital and important document that can save you much work and frustration by having a trusted Attorney-in-fact accomplish your day-to-day activities when needed. If the author can emphasize the most important aspect about making this instrument work well, it is to study thoroughly and find the best and most

---

62. Health Insurance Portability and Accountability Act. Pub. L. No. 104-191 (1996).

trusted individuals (or entities) to serve as Attorney-in-fact, or as alternates. Embezzlement and other thefts of assets from vulnerable adults continue to remain a problem. A recent study found that vulnerable adults lose $37 billion annually to corrupt telephone marketers, online scammers, and yes, family members.[63] A well-trusted Attorney-in-fact can help fight against others illegally trying to gain your assets.

Living Will

You can also allow a healthcare professional to determine your fate through a Living Will. It is also known as a healthcare directive. This is your choice. A Living Will is a document that informs doctors and other healthcare professionals about the kind of life-sustaining medical treatment you want or do not want if you become unable to communicate your wishes verbally should you ever be diagnosed to be in terminal condition and on life support. A Living Will is limited to choices involving artificial life support, feeding tubes, and hydration. Most people who choose to have a Living Will also have a healthcare Power of Attorney, as explained above. The designated Attorney-in-fact in a healthcare Power of Attorney will often have powers to make decisions about sustaining the life of the Principal. Do you want the healthcare Attorney-in-fact to make the decision to take you off life support (through a healthcare Durable Power of Attorney), or would you prefer to have the healthcare professional at the hospital (like a physician, nurse, or physician's assistant) decide? This author definitely prefers a close relative or friend to have the power to decide because it is a decision of the soul and eliminates from the equation the emotionless, objective (and *any* economically-driven) diagnosis by a healthcare professional.

Sample Durable Power of Attorney For Healthcare and Financial Management

The following Durable Power of Attorney for Healthcare and Financial Management (DPOA) is presented as a framework or guide to create your

---

63. Leiber, N. (2018, May 3). How Criminals Steal $37 Billion a Year from America's Elderly. Bloomberg News.

own instrument. Any person who creates their own DPOA must craft it according to their preferences. Most importantly, remember that the Attorney-in-fact, and any alternates you select, need to be individuals whom you fully trust and who will handle your financial or healthcare decisions, or both, and make decisions as you would for yourself. The Attorney-in-fact can also be an entity. This DPOA shows the following selected options:

1) It does not become effective immediately but becomes effective *upon* the written determination by a medical professional or other qualified person regarding the disability or incapacity of the Principal [Paragraph 2]. Note: The *other* option is to allow the Attorney-in-fact to act in your behalf, effective immediately, without any further authority, and without the Principal being declared incapacitated. In such case, the DPOA becomes effective for the Attorney-in-fact as soon as it is validly prepared.

2) It allows the healthcare Attorney-in-fact to have general powers over your person, with authority to make decisions as you would give yourself. Examples include deciding to take you off life support [Paragraph 3-Powers-Section (C), Item (i)], or having full access into healthcare records that include all records protected by the Health Insurance Portability and Accountability Act of 1996 (HIPAA), as amended [Paragraph 3-Powers-Section (C), Item (ii)].

3) It allows various financial powers and access, including safe-deposit box entry, and authority to discover digital information [Paragraph 3-Powers-Section (B), Items (xii) and (xiii)]. You may choose to be more selective.

4) That you give the Attorney-in-fact powers to be your guardian, if necessary [Paragraph 5].

5) The wording is done in the female gender [See the Notary certification].

DURABLE POWER OF ATTORNEY
FOR [NAME OF PRINCIPAL]

1. Designation: The undersigned individual, [*NAME OF PRINCIPAL*] ("Principal"), currently domiciled and residing in [*City, County, State*], designates [*NAME #1, address, email, phone number*], as Attorney-In-Fact for the Principal. Should [*NAME #1*] be unable or unwilling to act, then Principal designates [*NAME #2, address, email, phone number*], as alternate Attorney-In-Fact for the Principal.

2. Effectiveness and Duration: This Power of Attorney shall become effective upon the disability or incapacity of the Principal. Disability shall include the inability of the Principal to manage her property and affairs effectively for reasons such as mental illness, mental deficiency, physical illness or disability. Disability may be evidenced by a written statement of a qualified physician attending the Principal and relating to Principal's health, or by other qualified persons with knowledge of Principal's appearance due to confinement, detention or disappearance. This Power of Attorney shall remain in effect until revoked or terminated as defined herein, notwithstanding any uncertainty as to whether the Principal is dead or alive.

3. Powers:

(A) General Powers: The Attorney-in-Fact, as fiduciary, shall have all powers of an absolute owner over the assets and liabilities of the Principal, whether located within or without the State of _____. Without limiting the powers herein, the Attorney-in-Fact shall have full power, right, and authority to sell, lease, rent, exchange, mortgage and otherwise deal in and with all property, real or personal, belonging to the Principal the same as if he or she were the absolute owner thereof.

(B) Specific Powers: In addition, the Attorney-in-Fact shall have specific powers including, but not limited to, the following:

    (i) Personal Property: The Attorney-in-Fact shall have authority to purchase, receive, take possession of, lease, sell, assign, endorse, exchange, release, mortgage and pledge personal property or any interest in personal property.

    (ii) Real Property: The Attorney-in-Fact shall have authority to purchase, take possession of, lease, sell, convey, exchange, release and encumber real property or any interest in real property.

    (iii) Claims Against Principal: The Attorney-in-Fact shall have authority to pay, settle, compromise or otherwise discharge all claims of liability or indebtedness against the Principal and, in so doing, use any of the assets of the Attorney-in-Fact and obtain reimbursement out of the Principal's funds or other assets.

    (iv) Financial Accounts: The Attorney-in-Fact shall have authority to deal with accounts maintained by or on behalf of the Principal with institutions (including, without limitation, banks, savings and loan associations, credit unions and securities dealers). This shall include the authority to manage, maintain and close existing accounts, to open, maintain and close other accounts, and to make deposits and withdrawals with respect to all such accounts.

(v) Moneys Due: The Attorney-in-Fact shall have authority to request, demand, recover, collect, endorse and receive all moneys, debts, accounts, gifts, bequests, dividends, annuities, rents and payments due the Principal.

(vi) Beneficiary Designations: The Attorney-in-Fact shall have authority to make, amend, alter or revoke any of the Principal's life insurance beneficiary designations and retirement plan beneficiary designations so long as, in sole discretion of the Attorney-in-Fact, such action would be in the best interests of the Principal and those interested in the Principal's estate.

(vii) Transfers to Trust: The Attorney-in-Fact shall have authority to make transfers of the Principal's property, both real and personal, to any trust created by the Principal of which the Principal is the primary beneficiary during the Principal's lifetime.

(viii) Legal proceedings: The Attorney-in-Fact shall have authority to participate in any legal action in the name of the Principal or otherwise. This shall include:

(a) actions for attachment, execution, eviction, foreclosure, indemnity and any other proceeding for equitable or injunctive relief; and (b) legal proceedings in connection with the authority granted herein.

(ix) Written Instruments: The Attorney-in-Fact shall have the power and authority to sign, seal, execute, deliver and acknowledge all written instruments and perform each and every act and thing whatsoever which may be necessary or proper in the exercise of the powers and authority granted to the Attorney-in-Fact as fully as the Principal could do if personally present.

(x) Disclaimer: The Attorney-in-Fact shall have authority to disclaim any interest in any property to which the Principal would otherwise succeed, by Will, community property agreement or otherwise, and to decline to act or resign, if appointed or serving as an officer, director, Executor, trustee or other fiduciary.

(xi) Gifting Power: The Attorney-in-Fact shall have certain powers to make gifts, whether outright or in trust, during the Principal's lifetime which are consistent with Principal's interest. Specifically, such gifting powers, as authorized by law, shall be for purposes of Medicaid or Medicare or other local, state and federal funding requirements for nursing or managed care of the Principal, or for estate planning and tax purposes on behalf of the Principal.

(xii) Safe Deposit Box: The Attorney-in-Fact shall have the authority to enter any safe deposit box in which the Principal has a right of access.

(xiii) Digital Information: The Attorney-in-Fact shall have complete and unfettered authority to access any digital or internet accounts and devices on behalf of the Principal. This includes without limitation financial institution accounts, credit card accounts, debit card accounts, internet stores, email accounts, social-network accounts, domain names, computers (including smart phones, tablet computers, e-readers and all other devices), web pages, blogs and anything else "in the cloud" belonging to the Principal. The Attorney-in-Fact may, in the Attorney-in-Fact's sole discretion, make or change logins, user names, passwords and security settings as well as create, merge, terminate and liquidate accounts and services, and take any other action with respect to such accounts and devices.

(xiv) Other Powers: The Attorney-in-Fact shall have all other powers and authority necessary to reasonably manage the Principal's estate.

(C) Healthcare Decisions:

(i) General Statement of Authority Granted: The Attorney-in-Fact shall have full power and authority to make healthcare decisions for the Principal to the same extent that the Principal could make such decisions if the Principal had the capacity to do so. In exercising this authority, the Attorney-in-Fact shall make healthcare decisions that are consistent with the Principal's desires as stated in this document or otherwise made known to the Attorney-in-Fact, including, but not limited to, the Principal's desires concerning obtaining or refusing or withdrawing life-prolonging care, treatment, services, and procedures. "Healthcare decisions" shall include consent, refusal of consent, or withdrawal of consent to any care, treatment, service, or procedure to maintain, diagnose, or treat the Principal's physical condition.

(ii) Inspection and Disclosure of Information Relating to the Principal's Physical or Mental Health: The Attorney-in-Fact shall have the following powers and authority:

(a) In furtherance of the foregoing, and in contemplation of the protections afforded by the *Health Insurance Portability and Accountability Act of 1996* (HIPAA), as amended, any and all physicians and related healthcare facilities are hereby authorized to release to the Attorney-in-Fact or to the successor Attorney-in-Fact designated herein, any and all of Principal's medical and health records, and individually identifiable health information including, but not limited to, mental health records;

(b) Execute, on the Principal's behalf, any releases or other documents that may be required to obtain the above information;

(c) Consent to the disclosure of the above information; and

(d) Consent to donation of Principal's organs for medical purposes.

(iii) Signing Documents, Waiver, and Releases: Where necessary to implement the healthcare decisions that the Attorney-in-Fact is authorized by this document to make, the Attorney-in-Fact has the power and authority to exercise and execute, on the Principal's behalf, all of the following:

(a) Documents titled or purporting to be a "Refusal to Permit Treatment" and "Leaving Hospital Against Medical Advice;" and

(b) Any necessary waiver or release from liability required by a hospital or physician.

4. Prior Designations Revoked: *This Durable Power of Attorney revokes any prior Durable Power of Attorney of the Principal for healthcare and/or financial management, and any prior guardianship Power of Attorney.*

5. Intent to Obviate Need for Guardianship: It is the Principal's intent that the power given to the Attorney-in-Fact designated herein be interpreted to be so broad as to obviate the need for the appointment of a guardian for the person or estate of the Principal. If the appointment of a guardian or limited guardian of the person or estate of the Principal is sought, however, the Principal nominates the Attorney-in-Fact designated above as the Principal's guardian or limited guardian for the person and estate of the Principal.

6. Revocation: This Durable Power of Attorney may be revoked, suspended or terminated in writing by the Principal with written notice to the designated Attorney-in-Fact, and if the same has been recorded, then by recording the written instrument of revocation with the Auditor of the county where the Durable Power of Attorney is recorded.

7. Termination:

(A) By Appointment of Guardian: The appointment of a guardian of the estate of the Principal vests in the guardian the power to revoke, suspend or terminate this Durable Power of Attorney, upon court approval, as to the powers enumerated in subsections (A) and (B) of Section 3 herein. The appointment of a guardian of the Principal empowers the guardian to revoke, suspend or terminate, upon court approval, those powers concerning healthcare decisions as enumerated in subsection (C) of Section 3 herein.

(B) <u>By Death of Principal</u>: The death of the Principal shall be deemed to revoke this Durable Power of Attorney upon actual knowledge or actual notice being received by the Attorney-in-Fact.

8. Accounting: Upon request of the Principal, or the Guardian of the estate of the Principal, or the personal representative of the Principal's estate, the Attorney-in-Fact shall account for all actions taken by the Attorney-in-Fact for or on behalf of the Principal.

9. Reliance: Any person acting without negligence and in good faith in reasonable reliance on this Power of Attorney shall not incur any liability thereby. The designated and acting Attorney-in-Fact and all persons dealing with the Attorney-in-Fact shall be entitled to rely upon this Durable Power of Attorney so long as neither the Attorney-in-Fact nor any person with whom he or she was dealing at the time of any act taken pursuant to this Durable Power of Attorney had received actual knowledge or actual notice of any revocation, suspension or termination of the Durable Power of Attorney by death or otherwise. Any action so taken, unless otherwise invalid or unenforceable, shall be binding on the heirs, devisees, legatees or personal representatives of the Principal. In addition, third parties shall be entitled to rely upon a photocopy of the signed original hereof, as opposed to a certified copy of the same.

10. Indemnity: The estate of the Principal shall hold harmless and indemnify the Attorney-in-Fact from all liability for acts done in good faith and not in fraud of the Principal.

11. Release: The Attorney-in-Fact shall not be obligated to incur any financial liability on his or her part and may withdraw as Attorney-in-Fact without incurring liability so long as the Attorney-in-Fact acts in good faith pursuant to Paragraph 10 herein.

12. Applicable Law: The laws of the State of California shall govern this Durable Power of Attorney.

///

///

///

IN WITNESS WHEREOF, I have hereunto set my hand and official seal as Principal in execution of this entire instrument dated this _____ day of _____, _____.

_____

(Print Name): _____

STATE OF _____   )

) ss

COUNTY OF _____   )

    I certify that I know or have satisfactory evidence that [NAME OF PRINCIPAL] is the person who appeared before me, and the person who acknowledged that she signed this Durable Power of Attorney and acknowledged it to be her free and voluntary act for the uses and purposes mentioned in the instrument.

SUBSCRIBED AND SWORN before me on this _____ day of _____, _____.

                    _____

                    Notary Public in and for the State of

                    _____

                    Residing at _____.

                    My commission expires _____.

CHAPTER 4

SELECTED LAST WILLS

When you were born, you cried and the world rejoiced.
Live your life in a manner so that when you die the
world cries and you rejoice.

NATIVE AMERICAN PROVERB

WARREN E. BURGER
September 17, 1907 — June 25, 1995
Chief Justice, U.S. Supreme Court 1969-1986

Here is the Last Will of Warren E. Burger, the 15th Chief Justice of the United States Supreme Court. Chief Justice Burger wrote out his own Last Will, probably out of concern for his personal privacy. It is very short, which left a ton of direction and interpretation to be desired. His self-written Will failed to give any authority to his Executors and did not include any estate tax provisions. The oversights limited what could be done with the estate. The brevity of description unfortunately created vague and ambiguous language in Chief Justice Burger's Last Will. The resulting confusion in its interpretation led to infighting among his heirs and needlessly cost the estate hundreds of thousands of dollars to litigate and resolve the eventual distribution of assets. Much of the liquid assets were consumed by litigation costs.

LAST WILL AND TESTAMENT OF WARREN E. BURGER

I hereby make and declare the following to be my Last Will and testament.

1. My Executors will first pay all claims against my estate;

2. The remainder of my estate will be distributed as follows: one-third to my daughter, Margaret Elizabeth Burger Rose and two-thirds to my son, Wade A. Burger;

3. I designate and appoint as Executors of this will, Wade A. Burger and J. Michael Luttig.

IN WITNESS WHEREOF, I have hereunto set my hand to this my Last Will and Testament this 9th day of June, 1994.

/s/Warren E. Burger

We hereby certify that in our presence on the date written above WARREN E. BURGER signed the foregoing instrument and declared it to be his Last Will and Testament and that at this request in his presence and in the presence of each other we have signed our names below as witnesses.

/s/Nathaniel E. Brady residing at 120 F St., NW, Washington, DC

/s/Alice M. Khu residing at 3041 Meeting St., Falls Church, VA

DIANA, PRINCESS OF WALES
July 1, 1961 — August 31, 1997

Diana, Princess of Wales, in the Yellow Oval Room of the White House, Nov. 9, 1985.

Although Princess Diana had a proper and valid Last Will, she also wrote a "letter of wishes" to her Executors to leave some personal possessions worth well over 100,000 British pounds (about $130,000 U.S. dollars at the time), to each of her sons and godchildren. Of course, her children, Prince William and Prince Harry, received her fortune in her Will, but unfortunately, the godchildren did not receive any possessions of value noted in the letter from Princess Diana. The letter was invalid in the transfer of estate property because it was not a part of her Last Will.

The lesson here is that unless otherwise and properly described in a Will, make sure your wishes are included in a properly drafted Will (or trust) rather than a separate hand-written letter if you want any bequests carried out. Instead of the letter of wishes, a Tangible Personal Property List in the Last Will would have accomplished the legal transfer of the personal property items to the godchildren.[64]

LAST WILL AND TESTAMENT OF PRINCESS DIANA

I DIANA PRINCESS OF WALES of Kensington Palace London W8 HEREBY RE-VOKE all former Wills and testamentary dispositions made by me AND DECLARE this to be my Last Will which I make this First day Of June One thousand nine hundred and ninety three.

    1 I APPOINT my mother THE HONOURABLE MRS FRANCES RUTH SHAND KYDD of Callinesh Isle of Seil Oban Scotland and COMMANDER PATRICK DESMOND CHRISTIAN JERMY JEPHSON of St James's Palace London SW1 to be the Executors and Trustees of this my Will;

    2 I WISH to be buried;

    3 SHOULD any child of mine be under age at the date of the death of the survivor of myself and my husband I APPOINT my mother and my brother EARL SPENCER to be the guardians of that child and I express the wish that should I predecease my husband he will consult with my mother with regard to the upbringing education and welfare of our children;

    4 (a) I GIVE free of inheritance tax all my chattels to my Executors jointly (or if only one of them shall prove my Will to her or him);

        (b) I DESIRE them (or if only one shall prove her or him);

            (i) To give effect as soon as possible but not later than two years following my death to any written memorandum or notes of wishes of mine with regard to any of my chattels;

            (ii) Subject to any such wishes to hold my chattels (or the balance thereof) in accordance with Clause 5 of this my Will;

---

64. See Chapter 2, §2 regarding Disposition of the Estate under Personal Property, which explains the incorporation of a Tangible Personal Property List or money bequests in a Last Will.

(c) FOR the purposes of this Clause "chattels" shall have the same meaning as is assigned to the expression "personal chattels" in the Administration of Estates Act 1925 (including any car or cars that I may own at the time of my death);

(d) I DECLARE that all expenses for the safe custody of and insurance incurred prior to giving effect to my wishes and for packing transporting and insurance for the purposes of the delivery to the respective recipients of their particular chattels shall be borne by my residuary estate;

5 SUBJECT to the payment or discharge of my funeral testamentary and administration expenses and debts and other liabilities I GIVE all my property and assets of every kind and wherever situate to my Executors and Trustees Upon trust either to retain (if they think fit without being liable for loss) all or any part in the same state as they are at the time of my death or to sell whatever and wherever they decide with power when they consider it proper to invest trust monies and to vary investments in accordance with the powers contained in the Schedule to this my Will and to hold the same UPON TRUST for such of them my children **PRINCE WILLIAM** and **PRINCE HENRY** as are living three months after my death and attain the age of twenty five years if more than one in equal shares PROVIDED THAT if either child of mine dies before me or within three months after my death and issue of that child are living three months after my death and attain the age of twenty one years such issue shall take by substitution if more than one in equal shares per stirpes the share that the deceased child of mine would have taken had he been living three months after my death but so that no issue shall take whose parent is then living and so capable of taking;

6 MY EXECUTORS AND TRUSTEES shall have the following powers in addition to all other powers over any share of the Trust Fund;

(a) POWER under the Trustee Act 1925 Section 31 to apply income for maintenance and to accumulate surplus income during a minority but as if the words "my Trustees think fit" were substituted in sub-section (1)(i) thereof for the words "may in all the circumstances be reasonable" and as if the proviso at the end of sub-section (1) thereof was omitted;

(b) POWER under the Trustee Act 1925 Section 32 to pay or apply capital for advancement or benefit but as if proviso (a) to sub-section (1) thereof stated that "no payment or application shall be made to or for any person which exceeds altogether in amount the whole of the presumptive or vested share or interest of that person in the trust property or other than for the personal benefit of that person or in such manner as to prevent limit or postpone his or her interest in possession in that share or interest";

7 THE statutory and equitable rules of apportionment shall not apply to my Will and all dividends and other payments in the nature of income received by the Trustees shall be treated as income at the date of receipt irrespective of the period for which the dividend or other income is payable;

8 IT is my wish (but without placing them under any binding obligation) that my Executors employ the firm of Mishcon de Reya of 21 Southampton Row London WC1B 5HS in obtaining a Grant of Probate to and administering my estate;

9 ANY person who does not survive me by at least three months shall be deemed to have predeceased me for the purpose of ascertaining the devolution of my estate and the income thereof;

10 IF at any time an Executor or Trustee is a professional or business person charges can be made in the ordinary way for all work done by that person or his firm or company or any partner or employee;

THE SCHEDULE

MY Executors and Trustees (hereinafter referred to as "my Trustees") in addition to all other powers conferred on them by law or as the result of the terms of this my Will shall have the following powers:

1 (a) FOR the purposes of any distribution under Clause 5 to appropriate all or any part of my said property and assets in or toward satisfaction of any share in my residuary estate without needing the consent of anyone;

(b) FOR the purposes of placing a value on any of my personal chattels (as defined by the Administration of Estates Act 1925) so appropriated to use if they so decide such value as may have been placed on the same by any Valuers they instruct for inheritance tax purposes on my death or such other value as they may in their absolute discretion consider fair and my Trustees in respect of any of my personal chattels which being articles of national scientific historic or artistic interest are treated on such death as the subject of a conditionally exempt transfer for the purposes of the Inheritance Tax Act 1984 Section 30 (or any statutory modification or re-enactment thereof) shall in respect of any such appropriation place such lesser value as they in their absolute discretion consider fair after taking into account such facts and surrounding circumstances as they consider appropriate including the fact that inheritance tax for which conditional exemption was obtained might be payable by the beneficiary on there being a subsequent chargeable event;

(c) TO insure under comprehensive or any other cover against any risks and for any amounts (including allowing as they deem appropriate for any possible future effects of inflation and increasing building costs and expenses) any asset held at any time by my Executors and Trustees And the premiums in respect of any such insurance may be discharged by my Executors and Trustees either out of income or out of capital (or partly out of one and partly out of the other) as my Executors and Trustees shall in their absolute discretion determine and any monies received by my Executors and Trustees as the result of any insurance insofar as not used in rebuilding reinstating replacing or repairing the asset lost or damaged shall be treated as if they were the proceeds of sale of the asset insured PROVIDED ALWAYS that my Executors and Trustees shall not be under any responsibility to insure or be liable for any loss that may result from any failure so to do;

2   (a) POWER to invest trust monies in both income producing and non-income producing assets of every kind and wherever situated and to vary investments in the same full and unrestricted manner in all respects as if they were absolutely entitled thereto beneficially;

  (b) POWER to retain or purchase as an authorised investment any freehold or leasehold property or any interest or share therein of whatever nature proportion or amount (which shall be held upon trust to retain or sell the same) as a residence for one or more beneficiaries under this my Will and in the event of any such retention or purchase my Trustees shall have power to apply trust monies in the erection alteration improvement or repair of any building on such freehold or leasehold property including one where there is any such interest or share And my Trustees shall have power to decide (according to the circumstances generally) the terms and conditions in every respect upon which any such person or persons may occupy and reside at any such property (or have the benefit of the said interest or share therein);

  (c) POWER to delegate the exercise of their power to invest trust monies (including for the purpose of holding or placing them on deposit pending investment) and to vary investments to any company or other persons or person whether or not being or including one or more of my Trustees and to allow any investment or other asset to be held in the names or name of such person or persons as nominees or nominee of my Trustees and to decide the terms and conditions in every respect including the period thereof and the commission fees or other remuneration payable therefor which commission fees or other remuneration shall be paid out of the capital and income of that part of the Trust Fund in respect of which they are incurred or of any property held on the same trusts AND I DECLARE that my Trustees shall not be liable for any loss arising from any act or omission by any person in whose favour they shall have exercised either or both their powers under this Clause;

(d) POWER to retain and purchase chattels of every description under whatever terms they hold the same by virtue of the provisions of this my Will And in respect thereof they shall have the following powers;

    (i) To retain the chattels in question under their joint control and custody or the control and custody of any of them or to store the same (whether in a depository or warehouse or elsewhere); (ii) To lend all or any of the chattels to any person or persons or body or bodies (including a museum or gallery) upon such terms and conditions as my Trustees shall determine; (iii) To cause inventories to be made; (iv) Generally to make such arrangements for their safe custody repair and use as having regard to the circumstances my Trustees may from time to time think expedient (v) To sell the chattels or any of them and (vi) To treat any money received as the result of any insurance in so far as not used in reinstating replacing or repairing any chattel lost or damaged as if it were the proceeds of sale of the chattel insured;

(e) POWER in the case of any of the chattels of which a person of full age and capacity is entitled to the use but when such person's interest is less than an absolute one;

    (i) To cause an inventory of such chattels to be made in duplicate with a view to one part being signed by the beneficiary for retention by my Trustees and the other part to be kept by the beneficiary and to cause any such inventory to be revised as occasion shall require and the parts thereof altered accordingly (ii) To require the beneficiary to arrange at his or her expense for the safe custody repair and insurance of such chattels in such manner as my Trustees think expedient and (where it is not practicable so to require the beneficiary) to make such arrangements as are referred to under paragraph (iv) of sub-clause (d) of this Clause;

PROVIDED THAT my Trustees shall also have power to meet any expenses which they may incur in the exercise of any of their powers in respect of chattels out of the capital and income of my estate or such one or more of any different parts and the income thereof as they shall in their absolute discretion determine AND I FURTHER DECLARE that my Trustees shall not be obliged to make or cause to be made any inventories of any such chattels that may be held and shall not be liable for any loss injury or damage that may happen to any such chattels from any cause whatsoever or any failure on the part of anyone to effect or maintain any insurance;

IN WITNESS whereof I have hereunto set my hand the day and year first above written.

SIGNED by HER ROYAL HIGHNESS) in our joint presence and) then by us in her presence)

LEONA HELMSLEY
July 4, 1920 — August 20, 2007

Ms. Leona Helmsley (Federal photo taken in 1988 when Ms. Helmsley was arrested and indicted by the U.S. Attorney's Office in the Southern District of New York for tax evasion)

Leona Helmsley, the widow of billionaire real estate tycoon Harry Helmsley, set off a legal battle by leaving $12 million in trust for her dog when she died in 2007 while effectively disinheriting certain family members. Specifically, the hotel tycoon cut two of her grandkids out of her $5 billion estate and left $12 million for her dog. The disinherited grandchildren sued the estate, claiming that she wasn't mentally fit to create her Last Will and Trust.

Helmsley left the bulk of her estate — one that was estimated to be between $4 and $5 billion — to the Leona M. and Harry B. Helmsley Charitable Trust. In addition to providing for her own dog in her Last Will, she left separate instructions that the trust, which grew in value upwards to $8 billion, was to be used to benefit dogs. The courts ruled that the trust was not legally bound to wishes separate from the trust documents.

The Will left her Maltese dog, Trouble, a $12 million trust fund. Trouble lived in Florida with Carl Lekic, the general manager of the Helmsley Sandcastle Hotel. Lekic, Trouble's caretaker, stated that $2 million would pay for the dog's maintenance for more than 10 years — the annual $100,000 for full-time security, $8,000 for grooming and $1,200 for food. Lekic was paid a $60,000 annual guardianship fee.[65] Trouble died at age 12 in December 2010, with the remainder of the funds reverted to the Leona M. and Harry B. Helmsley Charitable Trust. Although Helmsley's wishes were to have Trouble interred next to her in the mausoleum, New York

---

65. Affidavit of Carl Lekic filed in the Estate of Leona Helmsley.

state law excluded interment of pets in human cemeteries, so Trouble was subsequently cremated.

Helmsley had four grandchildren. Two of them each received $5 million in trust and $5 million in cash under the condition that they visit their father's gravesite once each calendar year.[66] Their signing a registration book would prove that they had visited the grave. Her other two grandchildren, Craig and Meegan Panzirer, received nothing under her Last Will.[67]

In a judgment published on June 16, 2008, Manhattan Surrogate Court Judge Renee Roth ruled that Helmsley was mentally unfit when she executed her Last Will. The Court, through discussion with the estate, reduced the $12 million trust fund for the pet to $2 million. Of the $10 million originally bequeathed to Trouble, $4 million was instead awarded to the Charitable Trust, and $6 million was awarded to Craig and Meegan Panzirer, who had been disinherited in Leona's Last Will. The ruling requires the Panzirers to keep silent about their dispute with their grandmother and deliver to the court any documents they have about her. It has been alleged that they were omitted from the Will because they failed to name any of their children after Helmsley's late husband.[68] She left $15 million for her brother, Alvin Rosenthal. Helmsley also left $100,000 to her chauffeur, Nicholas Celea.[69] Ms. Helmsley's Last Will appeared to be clear in stating that she disinherited two of her grandchildren and would leave $12 million to care for her dog, Trouble. If the Surrogate Court found the Decedent Helmsley mentally unfit, why did it only "tweak" a relatively tiny portion of the estate, and order beneficiary distributions to the two grandchildren that the Testator did not intend to inherit? Such a ruling on Helmsley's mental competence could have possibly been ripe for reversal in the appel-

---

66. Article 4(D): Trusts, *Last Will and Testament of Leona Helmsley,* dated July 15, 2005.
67. Article 1(G): Bequests, *Last Will and Testament of Leona Helmsley,* dated July 15, 2005.
68. "Helmsley, Leona, Queen of Mean," InmateAid, https://www.inmateaid.com/famous-inmates/helmsley-leona-queen-of-mean
69. NY judge trims dog's $12 million inheritance. (2008, June 16). Retrieved April/May, 2017, from https://uk.reuters.com/article/oukoe-uk-helmsley-dog-idUKN1634773920080617

late court. She may have been quite eccentric, but her Last Will did not look to be vague and ambiguous. But with the disinherited grandchildren getting something, and the dog's caretaker being resolved with the settlement, the ruling stood. The lesson here is that if you are planning on doing something unusual, like bequeathing a relatively good amount of money to care for your pet and leaving unhappy family members behind, it might be prudent to have a lawyer conduct an evaluation attesting to your mental competence.[70]

LAST WILL AND TESTAMENT OF LEONA M. HELMSLEY

I, LEONA M. HELMSLEY, a resident of the State, City and County of New York, declare this to be my Last Will and Testament. I revoke all of my prior Wills and Codicils. I acknowledge in this Will, as I often did during my life, my love, affection and admiration for my late husband, HARRY B. HELMSLEY. I direct that I be interred wearing my gold wedding band (which is never to be removed from my finger) and that my remains be interred next to my beloved husband. HARRY B. HELMSLEY, and next to my beloved son, JAY PANZIRER, at the Helmsley Mausoleum at Woodlawn Cemetery, Bronx, New York. If the remains of my husband HARRY B. HELMSLEY and my son JAY PANZIRER are relocated to another mausoleum in another cemetery, then I direct that my remains be interred next to them, in any such other mausoleum in such other cemetery. I further direct that permission be granted as the need arises for the interment in the Helmsley Mausoleum of the remains of my brother, ALVIN ROSENTHAL, if he wishes, and my brother's wife, SUSAN ROSENTHAL, if she wishes, but for no other person. I also direct that anything bearing the Helmsley name must be maintained in "mint" condition and in the manner that it has been accustomed to, maintaining the outstanding Helmsley reputation.

ARTICLE ONE BEQUESTS

A. I direct my Executors to sell all my personal residences that I may own at my death and to add the net proceeds of sale to my residuary estate to be disposed of in accordance with the provisions of Article THREE hereof.

---

70. Mental competency is a legal decision and not a medical one since it is the court that interprets whether the medical facts underlying one's mental state is determinative of being competent or not.

B. I direct my Executors to sell all my furniture, furnishings, books, paintings and other objects of art, wearing apparel, jewelry, automobiles, and all other tangible personal property and to add the net sales proceeds to my residuary estate, to be disposed of in accordance with the provisions of Article THREE hereof.

C. I give the sum of Three Million Dollars ($3,000,000) to a separate trust to be known as "THE HELMSLEY PERPETURAL CARE TRUST" (referred to within this paragraph as the "Trust"), upon the terms set forth in this paragraph C.

(1) The Trust shall provide for the perpetual care and maintenance of (i) the Helmsley Mausoleum at Woodlawn Cemetery, Bronx, New York, containing the remains of my husband, Harry B. Helmsley and my son, Jay Panzirer, and my remains, or such other final resting place as may be designated as indicated above, (ii) the Brakmann Mausoleum at Woodlawn Cemetery, Bronx, New York, and (iii) the Rosenthal/Roman burial plots located at the Mt. Hebron Cemetery, Flushing, New York, containing the remains of my mother, Ida Rosenthal my father, Morris Rosenthal, my sister, Sylvia Roman, and my brother-in-law, Irving Roman (collectively (i), (ii) and (iii) shall be referred to as the "Final Resting Places").

(2) My Trustees shall distribute any part of the trust income and principal, at any time or times, as my Trustees shall determine in their sole discretion is advisable (i) for the care, cleaning, maintenance, repair and preservation of the interior and exterior of the Final Resting Places, and (ii) for the care, planting and cultivation of the lawn, trees, shrubs, flowers, plant or hedges located on the cemetery plots on which the Final Resting Places are located. I direct that my Trustees arrange for the Mausoleums to be acid washed or steam cleaned at least once a year. Any undistributed net income shall be added to principal at intervals determined by my Trustees. I direct my Trustees to maintain the Final Resting Places in excellent condition, and to arrange for inspection of the Final Resting Places as often as may be necessary (but not less often than quarterly) to ensure their proper care and maintenance.

(3) The duration of this trust shall be perpetual, it being my intention to create a trust for cemetery purposes pursuant to Section 8-1.5 of the New York Estates, Powers and Trusts Law ("EPTL"), and I direct that all of the provisions of this Article shall be construed accordingly. If any of the Final Resting Places are in cemeteries which are razed or otherwise cease to function as cemeteries, I direct that such Final Resting Places be moved to another cemetery and the provisions of this paragraph C continue to apply to said new Final Resting Place or Places.

(4) Any funds which a court determines are no longer needed to carry out the purposes of this trust for cemetery purposes shall be paid over to The Leona M. and Harry B. Helmsley Charitable Trust created by a Trust Agreement dated April 23, 1999, of which I am the Settlor and initially

the sole Trustee, as such Trust Agreement may be amended and re-stated form time to time in accordance with its provisions ("THE LEONA M. AND HARRY B. HELMSLEY CHARITABLE TRUST") and I direct the trustees of THE LEONA M. AND HARRY B. HELMSLEY CHARITABLE TRUST to add the same to the principal of THE LEONA M. AND HARRY B. HELMSLEY CHARITABLE TRUST and dispose of the same for chari-table purposes in accordance with the provisions thereof.

D. I direct that the following bequests be made in trust for each of the following persons. It is my intention that each of them will receive a flow of "income" as defined in the trust and (except as expressly provided) after each person dies, the trust assets will pass to THE LEONA M. AND HARRY B. HELMSLEY CHARITABLE TRUST. The detailed trust provisions are in Paragraphs A and B of Article FOUR, and with respect to sub-paragraphs 1-2, paragraph D of Article FOUR.

(1) If my grandson DAVID PANZIRER survives me, I leave the sum of Five Million Dollars ($5,000,000) to the trust established for his benefit under paragraph A of Article FOUR.

(2) If my grandson WALTER PANZIRER survives me, I leave the sum of Five Million Dollars ($5,000,000) to the trust established for his benefit under paragraph A of Article FOUR.

(3) If my brother ALVIN ROSENTHAL survives me, I leave the sum of Ten Million Dollars ($10,000,000) to the trust established for his benefit un-der paragraph B of Article FOUR.

E. I direct that the following bequests be made for each of the following per-sons, outright and not in trust.

(1) If my brother ALVIN ROSENTHAL survives me, I leave the sum of Five Million Dollars ($5,000,000) to him.

(2) If my grandson DAVID PANZIRER survives me, I leave the sum of Five Million Dollars ($5,000,000) to him.

(3) If my grandson WALTER PANZIRER survives me, I leave the sum of Five Million Dollars ($5,000,000) to him.

(4) If my chauffeur NICHOLAS CELEA survives me and at the time of my death is employed by me or any Helmsley entity, I leave the sum of One Hundred Thousand Dollars ($100,000) to him.

F. I leave the sum of Twelve Million Dollars ($12,000,000) to the Trustees of the LEONA HELMSLEY JULY 2005 TRUST, established under an instrument dated on or about the date of this Will, to be disposed of in accordance with the provisions of that Trust agreement. I leave my dog Trouble, if she survives me, to my brother ALVIN ROSENTHAL, if he survives me, or if he does not survive me, to my grandson DAVID PANZIRER. I direct that when my dog, Trouble, dies, her remains shall be buried next to my remains in the

Helmsley Mausoleum at Woodlawn Cemetery, Bronx, New York, or in such other mausoleum as I may be interred pursuant to this will.

G. I have not made any provisions in this Will for my grandson CRAIG PAN-ZIRER or my granddaughter MEEGAN PANZIRER for reasons which are known to them.

ARTICLE TWO TAXES AND EXPENSES

All of my funeral expenses, last illness expenses, and estate administration expenses shall be paid from my residuary estate. All estate and inheritance taxes (including interest and penalties thereon but not including any generation-skipping transfer taxes imposed under Chapter 13 of the Internal Revenue Code of 1986, as amended (the "Code")) on all assets passing under this Will shall be charged against my residuary estate.

ARTICLE THREE RESIDUARY ESTATE

A. The term "my residuary estate" includes all the residue of my assets of every kind, wherever located, including all assets which I have not otherwise effectively disposed of in this Will.

B. I leave my residuary estate to THE LEONA M. AND HARRY B. HELMSLEY CHARITABLE TRUST, to be disposed of for charitable purposes in accordance with the provisions of that Trust Agreement. If THE LEONA M. AND HARRY B. HELMSLEY CHARITABLE TRUST is not then an organization which can receive contributions eligible for income tax and estate tax charitable deductions, my Executors shall distribute my residuary estate to charitable organizations having purposes similar to those provided in such Trust Agreement, contributions to which are eligible for income tax and estate tax charitable deductions, as my Executors shall select in their sole discretion.

ARTICLE FOUR TRUSTS

A. Any amount or amounts distributed to trusts for my grandchildren to be held pursuant to this paragraph A of Article FOUR shall be held in separate trusts, in accordance with the following provisions:

In each taxable year of the trust, the beneficiary (hereinafter in this paragraph A of Article FOUR referred to as "the Recipient") shall receive, during the Recipient's life, an amount equal to five percent (5%) of the net fair market value of the assets of the trust valued as of the first day of each taxable year of the trust. Provisions for distribution of the "income" of the trust are intended to mean this percentage distribution, in accordance with my understanding that certain tax benefits are available for the trust only if the distribution is determined in this way. The distribution shall be paid in quarterly installments out of income and, to the extent income is not sufficient, out of principal. Any income of the trust which is not required to be distributed shall be added to principal at the end of each taxable year and at the termination of the trust. The amount to be distributed shall be prorated on a daily basis for a short taxable year and for the taxable year ending with the Recipient's death. In the taxable year ending with the Recipient's death, any amount which is due to the Recipient shall be paid to the Recipient's estate.

Upon the death of the Recipient, all of the then principal and income of the trust (other than any amount due the Recipient or his or her estate under the provisions above) shall be distributed to THE LEONA M. AND HARRY B. HELMSLEY CHARITABLE TRUST and disposed of for charitable purposes in accordance with the provisions of that Trust Agreement. If THE LEONA M. AND HARRY B. HELMSLEY CHARITABLE TRUST is not an organization described in sections 170(c) and 2055(a) of the Code at the time when any principal or income of the trust is to be distributed to it, then such principal or income shall be distributed to such one or more organizations, having purposes similar to those described in that Trust Agreement, and which are described in Sections 170(c) and 2055(a), as my Trustees shall select in their sole discretion.

I intend that the trust under this paragraph A shall qualify as a charitable remainder unitrust within the meaning of Section 6 of Rev. Proc. 90-30 and Section 664(d)(2) of the Code. Accordingly, the provisions of such trust under this paragraph A shall be construed and such trust created under this paragraph A shall be administered solely in accordance with said intention and in a manner consistent with Section 664(d)(2) of the Code and the regulations thereunder and with any successor section or regulations and any revenue rulings, revenue procedures, notices or other administrative pronouncements that may be issued thereunder by the Internal Revenue Service. Should the provisions of such trust under this paragraph A be inconsistent or be in conflict with any such section, regulation, or administrative pronouncement, as issued from time to time, then such section, regulation or administrative pronouncement shall be deemed to override and supersede the provisions which are set forth herein. If any such section, regulation or administrative pronouncement at any time requires a charitable remainder unitrust to contain provisions that are not expressly set forth herein, such provisions shall be incorporated into this Will by reference and shall be deemed to be a part of this Will to the same extent as though they had been expressly set forth herein. However, anything to the contrary notwithstanding, I direct that even if the value of the charitable remainder trust is less than the minimum amount which is required for a trust to qualify as a charitable remainder trust (such minimum is currently ten percent), I nevertheless direct that the unitrust amount of five percent not be changed, even if it means the trust would therefore not qualify as a charitable remainder trust.

B. Any amount distributed to a trust for my brother ALVIN ROSENTHAL to be held pursuant to this paragraph B of Article FOUR shall be held in a separate trust, in accordance with the following provisions.

If my brother, ALVIN ROSENTHAL ("ALVIN"), survives me, in each taxable year of the trust, ALVIN shall receive, during his life, an amount equal to five percent (5%) of the net fair market value of the assets of the trust valued as of the first day of each taxable year of the trust (the "valuation date"). The distribution amount shall be paid in quarterly installments out of income and, to the extent income is not sufficient, out of principal. Any income of the trust which is not required to be distributed shall be added to principal at the end of each taxable year and at the termination of the trust. The distribution amount shall be prorated on a daily basis for a short taxable year and for the taxable year ending with ALVIN'S death. In the taxable year ending with ALVIN'S death, any amount which is due to him shall be paid to his estate.

Upon the death of ALVIN, my Trustees shall distribute all of the then principal and income of the trust (other than any amount due ALVIN or his estate under the provisions above to THE LEONA M. AND HARRY B. HELMSLEY CHARITA-BLE TRUST, to be disposed of for charitable purposes in accordance with the provisions of that Trust Agreement. If THE LEONA M. AND HARRY B. HELMS-LEY CHARITABLE TRUST is not an organization described in Sections 170(c) and 2055(a) of the Code at the time when any principal or income of the trust is to be distributed to it, then such principal or income shall be distributed to such one or more organizations, having purposes similar to those described in that Trust Agreement, and which are described in Section 170(c) and 2055(a), as my Trustees shall select in their sole discretion.

I intend that the trust under this paragraph B shall qualify as a charitable remainder unitrust within the meaning of Section 6 of Rev. Proc. 90-30 and Section 664(d)(2) of the Code. Accordingly, the provisions of the trust under this paragraph B shall be construed and the trust created under this paragraph B shall be administered solely in accordance with said intention and in a manner consistent with Section 664(d)(2) of the Code and the regulations thereunder and with any successor section or regulations and any revenue rulings, revenue procedures, notices or other administrative pronouncements that may be issued thereunder by the Internal Revenue Service. Should the provisions of the trust under this paragraph B be inconsistent or in conflict with any such section, regulation, or administrative pronouncement, as issued from time to time, then such section, regulation, or administrative pronouncement, as issued from time to time, then such section, regulation, or administrative pronouncement shall be deemed to override and supersede the provisions which are set forth herein. If any such section, regulation or administrative pronouncement at any time requires a charitable remainder unitrust to contain provisions that are not expressly set forth herein, such provisions shall be incorporated into this Will by reference and shall be deemed to be a part of this Will to the same extent as though they had been expressly set forth herein. However, anything to the contrary notwithstanding, I direct that even if the value of the charitable remainder interest is less than the minimum amount which is required for a trust to qualify as a charitable remainder trust (such minimum is currently ten percent), I nevertheless direct that the unitrust amount of five percent not be changed, even if it means the trust would therefore not qualify as a charitable remainder trust.

C. The following provisions shall be applicable to the trusts created under paragraphs A and B, above:

If for any year the net fair market value of the trust assets is incorrectly determined, then within a reasonable period after the value is finally determined for federal tax purposes, the Recipient shall receive from the trust (in the case of an undervaluation) or pay back to the trust (in the case of an overvaluation) an amount equal to the difference between the unitrust amount properly payable and the unitrust amount actually paid.

The obligation to pay the unitrust amount shall commence with the date my death but payrnea4 of the unitrust amount may be deferred from such date until the end of the taxable year of the trust in which occurs the complete funding of the trust. Within a reasonable time after he end of the taxable year in which the complete funding of the trust occurs, my Trustees must pay to the Recipient (in the case of an underpayment) or receive from the Recipient (in the case of an overpayment) the difference between (1) any unitrust amounts actually paid, plus interest, compounded annually, computed for any period at the rate of interest that the federal income tax regulations under Section 664 of the code prescribe for the trust for such computation for such period, and (2) the unitrust amounts payable, plus interest, compounded annually, computed for any period at the rate of interest that the federal income tax regulations under Section 664 prescribe for the trust for such computation for such period.

No additional contributions shall be made to the Trust after the initial contribution The initial contribution, however, shall consist of all property passing to the trust as a result of my death.

My Trustees shall make distributions at such time and in such manner as not to subject the trust to tax under Section 4942 of the Code. Except for the payment of the unitrust amount to the Recipient, my Trustees shall not engage in any act of self-dealing, as defined in Section 4941(d) of the Code, and shall not make any taxable expenditures, as defined in Section 4945(d) of the Code. My Trustees shall not make any investments that jeopardize the charitable purposes of the trust within the meaning of Section 4944 of the Code and the regulations thereunder, and shall not retain any excess business holdings, within the meaning of Section 4943(c).

The taxable year of the trust shall be the calendar year.

The operation of the trust shall be governed by the laws of the State in which this Will is first admitted to probate. The trustees, however, are prohibited from exercising any power of discretion granted under said laws that would be inconsistent with the qualification of the Trust under section 664(d)(2) of the Code and the corresponding regulations.

I intend to create charitable remainder trusts as described in section 664(d)(2) of the Internal Revenue Code, and this Will shall be interpreted in accordance with this intent. My trustees may, by an instrument filed in the court in which this Will is probated, amend the trust for the sole purpose of effecting this intent, except that the five percent annual payments may not be changed.

Nothing in this Trust instrument shall be construed to restrict the trustees from investing the Trust assets in a manner that could result in the annual realization of a reasonable amount of income or gain from the sale or disposition of Trust assets.

D. Notwithstanding any provision of this Will to the contrary, my grandchildren DAVID PANZIRER and WALTER PANZIRER shall not be entitled to any distributions from any trust established for such beneficiary's benefit under this Will unless such beneficiary visits the grave of my late son JAY PANZIRER, at least once each calendar year, preferably on the anniversary of my said son's death (March 31, 1982) (except that this provision shall not apply during any period that the beneficiary is unable to comply therewith by reason of physical or mental disability as determined by my Trustees in their sole and absolute discretion). If DAVID or WALTER fails to visit the grave during any calendar year, her or his interest in the separate trust established for her or his benefit shall be terminated at the end of such calendar year and the principal of such trust, together with all accrued and undistributed net income, shall be disposed of as if such beneficiary had then died.

My Trustees shall have placed in the Helmsley Mausoleum a register to be signed by each visitor and shall rely on it in determining whether the provisions of this paragraph have been complied with, and my Trustees shall have no duty to make, and shall be prohibited from making, any further inquiries after determining whether or not such beneficiary signed such register. At the end of any calendar year, my Trustees shall have the right to presume that the beneficiary did not visit the grave during that calendar year if his or her signature does not appear on the register for such calendar year.

E. To the extent permitted by law, and except for a disclaimer or renunciation, no interest of any beneficiary in the income or principal of any trust shall be subject to pledge, encumbrance, assignment (except to a trust for the beneficiary's benefit) sale or transfer in any manner, nor shall the interest of any beneficiary be liable while in the possession of my Trustees for the debts, contracts, liabilities, engagements or torts of the beneficiary.

ARTICLE FIVE ULTIMATE DISPOSITIONS

If upon my death or upon the termination of any trust created under my Will there shall be no beneficiary then entitled to receive the residue of my estate or the remaining assets of such trust, then in such event I direct that the residue of my estate or the remaining assets of such trust, as then constituted, shall be distributed to THE LEONA M. AND HARRY B. HELMSLEY CHARITABLE TRUST, to be disposed of for charitable purposes in accordance with the provisions thereof.

ARTICLE SIX FIDUCIARIES

A. I appoint my brother ALVIN ROSETHAL, my grandson DAVID PANZIRER, my grandson WALTER PANZIRER, my attorney SANDOR FRAMKEL, and my friend JOHN CODEY (herein called the "individual fiduciaries"), or such of them who qualify as Executors of my Will and as Trustees of all of the trusts established under this Will.

B   (I) At such time as there are fewer than three individual fiduciaries acting as such fiduciaries, then such individual fiduciaries as are then acting shall promptly designate a corporate fiduciary to serve as an Executor hereof and/or a Trustee of the trusts hereunder when there are fewer than two individual fiduciaries acting in such capacity.

    (i) In selecting such corporate fiduciary, and fixing the terms of compensation, the individual fiduciaries shall first approach CITIBANK, N.A., New York, New York; and if an agreement satisfactory to the individual fiduciaries is not reached, the individual fiduciaries shall then approach such other corporate fiduciary as I shall have designated by an acknowledged written instrument or, in the absence of such designation, then such other corporate fiduciary as the individual fiduciaries shall select.

    (ii) In all events, it is my wish and expectation that a corporate fiduciary selected in the manner provided above (or any entity that succeeds such institution by merger or acquisition), and which shall have agreed to terms of compensation and other matters satisfactory to the individual fiduciaries, shall be selected as a successor Executor and/or Trustee to commence serving at such time as there is only one individual Executor and/or Trustee acting hereunder.

    (iii) In reaching a determination, the individual Executor(s) and Trustee(s) shall act in a manner consistent with their fiduciary duties.

  (2) Any action by my Executors or Trustees pursuant to this paragraph B shall be absolute and binding on all persons interested in my estate or any trust hereunder.

C. If any Executor or Trustee becomes disabled, that determination of disability shall also constitute that individual's immediate resignation as an Executor or Trustee, without any further act. For the purposes of this paragraph, a person shall be considered disabled if either (i) a committee, guardian, conservator or similar fiduciary shall have been appointed for such person or (ii) a court shall have determined, or two physicians shall have certified, that the person is incompetent or otherwise unable to act prudently and effectively in financial affairs.

D. Each successor Executor and successor Trustee shall have all rights and discretions which are granted to the Executor and Trustee who preceded that successor, except those which may be specifically denied in this Will.

E. No bond or other security shall be required in any jurisdiction of any Executor herein or Trustee hereunder named or appointed as herein provided.

F. To the extent not prohibited by law, my fiduciaries shall have the right to maintain physical possession of any tangible or intangible property in my estate or any trust hereunder in any jurisdiction, notwithstanding that my Will may have been probated in another jurisdiction or that my Executor may have qualified pursuant to the laws of such other jurisdiction.

G. No fiduciary shall have any power whatsoever to make or participate in making decisions affecting in any way the disposition of the income or the principal of such trust to or for the benefit of such person or in discharge of a legal obligation of support which such person has.

H. All decisions regarding my estate or any trust shall be made by a majority of my Executors or Trustees not disqualified to act thereon, or by both if only two are then serving. My fiduciaries may from time to time authorize one of their number, or each of them acting singly, to execute instruments of any kind on their behalf (including, but not by way of limitation, any check, order demand, assignment, transfer, contract, authorization, proxy, consent, notice or waiver). As to third parties dealing with my fiduciaries, instruments executed and acts performed by one fiduciary shall be fully binding as if executed or performed by all of them. All authorization shall be valid until those acting in reliance on it receive actual notice of its revocation.

I. No fiduciary shall be liable or responsible in any way or manner for any action or inaction unless such fiduciary shall have acted in bad faith or shall have failed to exercise reasonable care, diligence and prudence. In no event shall any fiduciary be liable on account of any default of any other fiduciary unless liability may be imposed upon such fiduciary for such fiduciary's own misconduct.

J. No one dealing with any Executor or Trustee shall be required to investigate such fiduciary's authority for entering into any transaction or to see to the application of the proceeds of any transaction.

K. If ancillary or separate administration of my property in any jurisdiction becomes necessary or desirable, I authorize my Executors to be, or to designate an individual or a bank or trust company to be, ancillary executor or to occupy such other fiduciary positions as may be appropriate to accomplish such ancillary or separate administration.

L. No individual Executor or individual Trustee shall be entitled to statutory commissions for serving as such.

M. Any one or more executors or trustees may render services to the Estate or any Trust hereunder as an officer, manager or employee of the Estate or any Trust hereunder, or in any other capacity, notwithstanding the fact that they may appoint themselves to serve in such capacities, and they shall be entitled to receive reasonable compensation for such services No such person shall be required to furnish any bond in connection with any such employment.

ARTICLE SEVEN FIDUCIARIES' POWERS

In addition to all powers conferred upon them by law, I hereby give to my fiduciaries the following powers, authority and discretion, to be exercised by them without regard to present or future statutory limitations thereon and with respect to all property, real or personal, which I own or in which I have any interest or which may at any time under any of the provisions of this Will be subject to administration by my fiduciaries:

1. To retain and hold (including the retention of any such property owned, beneficially or of record, by me at the time of my death) securities of HELMSLEY ENTERPRISES, INC., or of any successor corporation or other business entity, irrespective of the proportion of the total assets of my estate or of any trust which such investment may represent and irrespective of the fact that one or more of my fiduciaries may be a director or an officer of or otherwise connected with any act of such corporations; and my fiduciaries shall not be liable or responsible for any loss, either of income or of capital value, incurred by reason of their retention of securities of such corporations or to seek other information regarding any of such corporations; and I designate my Executors, or an individual designated by my Executors, as successor to me as a member of any partnership in which I have an interest at my death; subject, however, to my overriding intention as provided in Paragraph D of this Article;

2. Subject to the provisions of Paragraph D and E or this Article, to manage, operate, repair, improve, mortgage and lease for any term any real estate; and to determine whether or not to establish any reasonable reserves to be charged against income for depreciation of any buildings or capital improvements thereon;

3. To borrow such amounts, from such persons other than my individual fiduciaries (or any beneficiary of my estate or any trust hereunder) upon such terms and conditions and for such purposes as they may deem advisable and to pledge any assets of my estate or any trust hereunder to secure the repayment of any amounts so borrowed, provided that all loans shall be made at a reasonable rate of interest;

4. To divide any trust estate held hereunder (or any bequest directed to be held in trust hereunder) into separate identical trusts, and to allocate to each such separate trust such assets from the original trust (or bequest) as they shall deem advisable, and to combine or merge any two or more separate trusts held hereunder for the benefit of the same individual, and having identical or substantially identical provisions, into one trust, all as they shall determine in their discretion and without application to any court;

5. Except to the extent prohibited by law, to delegate in whole or in part, to any agent or agent (who may be one or more of my fiduciaries), any of the powers granted to my fiduciaries, including but not limited to the authority and power to (a) sign checks, drafts or orders for the payment or withdrawal of funds from any bank account in which funds of my estate or any trust shall be deposited, (b) endorse for sale, transfer or delivery, or sell transfer or deliver, or purchase or otherwise acquire, any and all stocks, bonds or other securities whatsoever, and (c) gain access to any safe deposit box or boxes in which assets of my estate or any trust may be located or which may be in the names of my fiduciaries and remove part or all of the contents of any such safe deposit box or boxes and release and surrender the same;

6. To commingle in one of more funds and to hold and administer in solido the income from and principal of any two or more trusts held hereunder;

7. To employ such attorneys, accountants, custodians, investment advisors, real estate consultants and other persons (including any firm with which any of my fiduciaries may be affiliated) as they may deem advisable in the administration of my estate or any trust hereunder, and to pay them such compensation as they may deem proper;

8. In general, to exercise all powers in the management of my estate and any trust hereunder which any individual could exercise in the management of similar property owned in his own right, upon such terms and conditions as to them may seem best, and to execute and deliver all instruments and to do all acts which they deem necessary or advisable to carry out the purposes of my Will, and my fiduciaries shall have no liability by reason of any action, inaction, determination or exercise of discretion taken or made in good faith nor by reason of any loss sustained as a result of the purchase, retention, sale, exchange or other disposition of any property made in good faith.

B. Notwithstanding the foregoing, subject to the provisions of the Internal Revenue Code and state law relating to charitable split interest trusts, my fiduciaries shall be limited in the investment and reinvestment of funds held by my estate or by any trust under this Will to U.S. Treasury obligations and state and municipal obligations, such investments to be purchased based on the highest investment standards in the opinion of brokerage firms and/or investment advisors. These investments shall be held by a financial institution, preferably one which does not charge for such service. This restriction shall not affect the power of my fiduciaries to retain and deal with any assets which I may own at my death or which my fiduciaries may receive by reason of my death.

C. No power or discretion granted to my Executors and Trustees by this Will or by law, including, without limitation any investment power, shall apply to any disposition of property hereunder to any charitable organization (including THE LEONA M. AND HARRY B. HELMSLEY CHARITABLE TRUST) if the authority to exercise such power or discretion would affect the availability to my estate of a Federal estate tax charitable deduction for such dispositions. All powers or discretion conferred on my Executors and Trustees may be exercised only in such manner as is consistent with the allowance of such deduction. This paragraph C shall be construed as a precedent (and not as a subsequent) limitation or condition.

D. As to each and any corporation, partnership or other business entity, public or private, in which my Executors in that capacity hold any equity interest exceeding one percent (1%) of the net value of such corporation, partnership or other business entity (each such corporation, partnership or other business entity being hereafter referred to as the "Entity"). My Executors are directed to dispose of such interests in excess of one percent (1%) as promptly as they shall determine to be reasonably practical without adversely affecting the value realizable on the sale of such interests.

In furtherance of my intent as expressed above, I authorize and empower my Executors, to the extent permitted by law, to exercise their rights and powers as holders of such shares or interests, to sell or otherwise dispose of the assets or business or, in their sole discretion, to sell, exchange, offer for redemption or otherwise dispose of the shares of or interests in the Entity owned by my estate, or to effect the liquidation or dissolution of the Entity, at such time or times and upon such terms and conditions as shall, in the opinion of my Executors, be in the best interests of my estate.

During the period of administration required before the disposition of the interests described above, any one or more of my Executors may act as officer, partner, director manager or employee of the Entity, and the Executors are specifically authorized to exercise their rights of ownership as Executors for the election or appointment of any person or persons, including themselves, as directors, officers, managers or the like, and I direct that no such person shall be required to furnish any bond in connection with such employment.

I am aware that conflicts of interest may arise by reason of service on the part of my Executor as such and as officer, partner, director, manager or employee of the Entity and by reason of my Executors owning an interest in the Entity in their own right. I intend that my Executors shall, in all respects, be free to exercise the powers and discretion herein conferred as fully and unrestrictedly as if there were no such conflicting interests. With this thought in mind, I expressly exempt my Executors from the adverse operation of any rule of law which might otherwise apply to them in the performance of their fiduciary duties by reason of conflict of interest. Without limiting the generality of the foregoing, I specifically direct that my Executors shall not have any greater burden of justification in respect of their acts as Executors by reason of conflict of interest than they would have in the absence of any such conflict.

E. Anything herein to the contrary notwithstanding, I direct that during any period of administration required before the disposition of such property as described above, the management of any property which at my death was owned or controlled (directly or indirectly) by me shall be performed by an entity which is also owned, operated or controlled (directly or indirectly) by my Executors or Trustees, as the case may be, except that this provision shall not preclude a corporate fiduciary from serving as an Executor or a Trustee.

ARTICLE EIGHT FURTHER CONDITION

If any beneficiary under this Will shall directly or indirectly, file or cause to be filed objections to this Will, or shall in any other manner contest this Will, in part or in whole, or attempt to prevent the probate thereof, or shall, directly or indirectly, institute or prosecute any action or proceeding to invalidate or set aside this Will or any of its provisions, or shall assert any claim against me or my estate, then any bequest under this Will to for the benefit of such beneficiary (whether outright or in trust) and his or her issue shall not be paid to them or for their benefit and such beneficiary and his or her issue shall be deemed to have predeceased me for all purposes of this Will. The determination of my Executors concerning the application of this Article shall be conclusive on all interested parties.

ARTICLE NINE CONSTRUCTION

Whenever the masculine or feminine or neutral gender is used in this Will, it shall be deemed, when appropriate to the context, to include any other gender as well. Whenever appropriate, the singular shall include the plural and the plural shall include the singular, as the context may require. The headings in this Will have been inserted solely for convenient reference, and shall be ignored in its construction.

IN WITNESS WHEREOF, I have hereunto set my hand to this my Last Will and Testament this 15th day of July 2005.

The foregoing instrument was signed, published and declared by the said Testatrix, THE LEONA M. HELMSLEY, as and for her Last Will and Testament, in our presence, and we at her request and in her presence, and in the presence of each other, have hereunto subscribed our names as witnesses on the day and year last above written.

STATE OF NEW YORK)) ss: COUNTY OF NEW YORK)

Each of the undersigned, individually and severally being duly sworn, deposes and says:

The within Will was subscribed in our presence and sight at the end thereof by THE LEONA M. HELMSLEY, the within named Testatrix, on the 15th day of July 2005 at 36 Central Park South, New York, New York.

Said Testatrix was, at the time of so executing said Will, over the age of 18 years and, in the respective opinions of the undersigned, of sound mind, memory and understanding and not under any restraint or in any respect incompetent to make a will.

The Testatrix, in the respective opinions of the undersigned, could read, write and converse in the English language and was suffering from no defect of sight, hearing or speech, or from any other physical or mental impairment which would affect her capacity to make a valid Will. The Will was executed as a single, original instrument and was not executed in counterparts.

Each of the undersigned was acquainted with said Testatrix at such time and makes this affidavit at her request. The within Will was shown to the undersigned at the time this affidavit was made, and was examined by each of them as to the signature of said Testatrix and of the undersigned.

The foregoing instrument was executed by the Testatrix and witnessed by each of the undersigned affiants under the supervision of Sandor Frankel, attorney-at-law.

Severally sworn to before me this 15th day of July 2005

/s/ Sandor Frankel Notary Public State of New York No. 31-8382085 Qualified in New York County Commission Expires 10/25/06

THOMAS L. CLANCY, JR.
April 12, 1947 — October 1, 2013

Battle over Tom Clancy's Estate

It is ironic that one of the best-selling authors of all time, a masterful and prolific writer, had a Last Will that was vague and ambiguous. Specifically, conflicting language arose concerning which trust or trusts had to pay the Estate's estate taxes. The unclear language grew out of added language contained in Clancy's Second Codicil to his Last Will.

The Last Will was signed in 2007. It divided Clancy's assets into three trusts: one-third for his wife, another third for his wife to use while she was alive, and then those assets would pass to their daughter, and the last third to be split among his four adult children from a prior marriage.

Clancy signed his second codicil weeks before he passed away.[71] It included this key sentence:

> No asset or proceeds of any assets shall be included in the Marital Share of the Non-Exempt Family Residuary Trust as to which a marital deduction would not be allowed if included.[72]

What did the sentence mean? Even the seven justices of Maryland's highest court struggled with it. The vote came down to a closely divided 4 to 3 decision on the interpretation of this language, which gives clear indication that the language was highly-conflicted and poorly written. The four justices who ruled for the court and in favor of Clancy's widow believed the clause to mean that all estate taxes from Tom Clancy's Estate would have to be paid by the children's trust, not the two trusts controlled by the widow, because that was the only way to fully protect the marital deduction under federal estate tax laws.

The other three justices dissented and sided with Clancy's four children from a prior marriage. The dissenting justices had no argument that the clause protected the marital estate tax deduction, but they also agreed that it did not trump or alter another provision contained in Clancy's Will, which said that the estate taxes were to be paid equally from two of the three trusts, but not from the children's trust alone. As such, the dissent felt that the children should only pay one-half the tax bill, not all of it, and that the clause did not alter the estate tax outcome. Essentially, the dissenting justices felt that Tom Clancy wanted to protect the marital deduction, but not solely at the expense of his children's trust assets.

---

71. Mayoras, A., & Mayoras, D. (2016, August 30). Tom Clancy estate battle ends but valuable lesson remains. Retrieved November 10, 2017, from http://www.probatelawyerblog.com/2016/08/tom-clancy-estate-battle-ends-but-valuable-lesson-remains.html

72. *See below, Second Codicil to the Last Will of Thomas J. Clancy, Jr.,* dated September 18, 2007.

What was interesting in this case was that the very lawyer who drafted the second codicil that contained the challenging language had sided with the children. Now, that was very telling, knowing that he had the ear of Tom Clancy when drafting the second codicil and thus had the best feedback to what Tom Clancy really wanted. Who better to know the interpretation than the attorney who worked with Clancy to write the language of his Last Will? That lawyer also had initially acted as Executor of Tom Clancy's estate. He did not last long in the Executor's position, understanding the potential conflict of interest by siding with the children while representing Clancy's widow. Logically, it would seem that the lawyer's thoughts strongly attest to the interpretation of the language that the children's trust was to pay for only half of the estate taxes. Unfortunately, the law in Maryland does not turn on what was originally intended but on what the documents actually say. This is true in all other states where your thoughts and wishes must be expressed clearly in writing in a Last Will.

What does all this mean for Tom Clancy's heirs? The four children had to pay the entire estate tax bill to the IRS of almost $12 million. If they had won, the total tax bill, readjusted to account for a lesser marital deduction and a revised tax accounting under the separate trusts, would have been closer to $16 million, but that amount would have been split equally ($8 million each) between the children and Clancy's widow.[73]

An additional $4 million for federal estate taxes ($12 million vs. $8 million) is a lot of money that Clancy's four children from his first marriage had to pay over one vague sentence. On top of that, the legal fees were likely quite significant, given that the legal challenges were appealed to Maryland's highest state court.

---

73. Mayoras, D., & Mayoras, A. (2014, September 26). TOM CLANCY ESTATE IN FAMILY FIGHT DUE TO POOR ESTATE PLANNING. Retrieved August 28, 2017, https://danielleandandy.com/tom-clancy-estate-in-family-fight-due-to-poor-estate-planning/

061107

LAST WILL
OF
THOMAS L. CLANCY, JR

I, THOMAS L. CLANCY, JR. of Calvert County, Maryland, declare this to be my Last Will, hereby revoking all other Wills and Codicils heretofore made by me.

ITEM FIRST

A.   ALEXANDRA M. CLANCY is my Wife, and, for brevity, she is referred to in this Will simply as my "Wife." I have one daughter by my Wife: ALEXIS JACQUELINE CLANCY.

B.   I have four children by my prior marriage: MICHELLE CLANCY BANDY, CHRISTINE CLANCY BLOCKSIDGE, THOMAS L. CLANCY, III, and KATHLEEN W. CLANCY. For brevity, they are referred to collectively as "my older children" and individually as an "older child."

ITEM SECOND

I direct my personal representative or personal representatives, hereinafter named and, for convenience, sometimes referred to in the singular neuter, to expend such sums for my funeral and burial and for the erection of a suitable stone or marker at my grave as it, in its discretion, may deem proper, without the necessity of obtaining an order of court approving the payment.

ITEM THIRD

A.   All estate, inheritance, legacy, succession and transfer taxes (including any interest and any penalties thereon) lawfully payable with respect to all property includible in my gross estate or taxable in consequence of my death by any State or Territory of the United States, or under the laws of the United States, or by any other taxing authority, whether or not such property passes under this my Will, and whether such taxes are payable by my estate, or, in the absence of this provision, by any recipient of any such property (including, but only in the discretion of my personal representative, any inheritance taxes that may, but need not, be prepaid), shall be paid by my personal representative out of my residuary estate, subject, however, to the provisions hereinafter contained in Item SIXTH hereof with respect to the Marital Share therein created; and my personal representative shall not be entitled to any reimbursement for any such taxes from any person or entity.

B.   This provision to pay all such taxes out of my residuary estate shall not apply, however, to any death taxes occasioned by my death attributable to the assets of any Irrevocable Trust of which I am a Settlor.

ITEM FOURTH

A.   I give and bequeath to my Wife, if she survives me for thirty days, all of my tangible personal property of domestic or personal use.

B.   If my Wife does not so survive me, I give and bequeath all of my tangible personal property of domestic or personal use to my then surviving children in substantially equal shares. If my children are unable to agree on the division, my personal representative shall make the division.

ITEM FIFTH

A.   I give and devise to my Wife, if she survives me for thirty days, all of my right, title, and interest in and to my real property in Calvert County, Maryland, known as Peregrine Cliff, which includes my residence and all contiguous parcels of land, whether improved or unimproved, and has a post office address of 5000 Camp Kaufmann Road, Huntingtown, MD 20639.

B.   I give and devise to my Wife, if she survives me for thirty days, all of my right, title, and interest in and to my real property on Martha's Vineyard, Dukes County, Massachusetts, that has a post office address of 12 Naushon Avenue, Oak Bluffs, MA 02557.

ITEM SIXTH

I give, bequeath, and devise all of the rest and residue of my estate, real and personal, and wheresoever situate (hereinafter referred to as my "residuary estate"), including all property over which I may have any power of appointment, as follows:

A.   If my Wife survives me, there shall be first set apart and promptly transferred as set out below a separate fund (hereinafter sometimes referred to as the Marital Share) equal to one-third of my net estate, as calculated pursuant to Section 3-203(c) of the Estates and Trusts Article of the Annotated Code of Maryland.

(1)   My personal representative shall select and designate the cash, securities and other property, including real estate and interests therein, that shall be allocated to the Marital Share, regardless of cost basis, and the determinations so made by my personal representative shall be final and binding.

-2-

(2)   No asset or proceeds of any asset shall be included in the Marital Share as to which a marital deduction would not be allowable if included.

(3)   The Marital Share shall not be charged with or reduced by any estate, inheritance, succession or other tax of any kind or nature assessed by any State or under the laws of the United States or by any other taxing authority whatsoever.

(4)   My personal representative shall have full power to treat expenses as either estate tax or income tax deductions, to select tax valuation methods and dates, and to exercise any other allowable tax election, regardless of the effect thereof on the Marital Share. No adjustment to this fund shall be required by reason of any such election, and the determinations so made by my personal representative shall be final and binding.

(5)   The amount of the Marital Share shall be based upon values as finally determined for federal estate tax purposes. Assets may be allocated in cash or in kind to this fund. All assets allocated to the Marital Share shall have an aggregate fair market value fairly representative of the appreciation or depreciation in the value, to the date of each distribution, of all property then available for distribution.

(6)   This fund shall abate to the extent that it cannot be satisfied in the manner hereinabove provided.

(7)   I direct that the amount of the Marital Share created for my Wife pursuant to Paragraph A hereof shall be reduced by the value of all property passing to her pursuant to Items FOURTH and FIFTH of this Will.

(8)   The Marital Share shall be paid over and transferred to and held by my trustee or trustees, hereinafter named and sometimes, for convenience, referred to in the singular neuter, as a separate trust, called the "Marital Trust," which shall be administered as set out below in Item SEVENTH.

B.   I direct that one-half of the remainder of my residuary estate shall be paid over and distributed to my trustee as a separate trust, called the "Non-Exempt Family Residuary Trust," which shall be administered as set out below in Item EIGHTH.

- 3 -

C.   I direct that the other one-half of the remainder of my residuary estate shall be administered as follows:

(1)   I direct that an amount equal to the applicable credit amount allowed to my Estate pursuant to Section 2010 of the Internal Revenue Code of 1986, as amended ("IRC"), shall be paid over and distributed to my trustee as a separate trust, called the "Exempt Residuary Trust," which shall be administered as set out below in Item NINTH.

(2)   I direct that the balance of my residuary estate, after funding the Exempt Residuary Trust, shall be paid over and distributed to my trustee as a separate trust, called the "Non-Exempt Older Children's Residuary Trust," which shall be administered as set out below in Item TENTH.

ITEM SEVENTH

THE MARITAL TRUST

A.   My trustee shall pay over the entire net income from the Marital Trust to my Wife, at least quarter-annually, during her lifetime.

B.   My trustee shall have full power, in its discretion, to pay to my Wife or to apply for her benefit such sums out of the principal of the Marital Trust from time to time as it, in its discretion, deems advisable or proper for her continued maintenance, support, and health.

C.   In addition, my Wife shall have the right from time to time, by a simple request in writing delivered to my trustee, to withdraw any part or all of the principal of the Marital Trust.

D.   Upon the death of my Wife, the remainder of the Marital Trust, if any, both principal and undistributed income, shall be paid over and distributed by my trustee to or among such one or more persons and legal entities, including her estate, her creditors and the creditors of her estate, in such amounts and proportions and upon such terms and conditions, in further trust or otherwise, as my Wife may validly appoint by her Last Will and Testament, by specific reference to, and express exercise of, the general testamentary power of appointment herein granted to her, which shall be exercisable by her alone and in all events.

E.   The remainder of the Marital Trust, if any, both principal and undistributed income, not so validly appointed by her Will, shall be by my trustee added to and merged with the principal of the Non-Exempt Family Residuary Trust, to be held, administered and disposed of as a part thereof.

- 4 -

ITEM EIGHTH

THE NON-EXEMPT FAMILY RESIDUARY TRUST

A.   My trustee shall pay over the entire net income from the Non-Exempt Family Residuary Trust to my Wife, at least quarter-annually, during her lifetime.

B.   Upon the exhaustion of the Marital Trust, my trustee shall have full power, in its discretion, to pay to or apply for the benefit of my Wife or my child or children by my Wife who are living from time to time, out of the principal of the Non-Exempt Family Residuary Trust, such amounts and in such proportions as my trustee, in its absolute discretion, from time to time may deem advisable and proper to provide for her or their continued maintenance, support, health, and education (including secondary, college, postgraduate, professional or other education).

C.   In determining whether, when, and for whom any such payments pursuant to Paragraph B hereof shall be made, and the amounts thereof, if any, my trustee is hereby requested to take into consideration the respective needs and best interests of the beneficiaries without any duty or obligation with respect to my children to pay over equal amounts to or for all of them. Nevertheless, the decisions of my trustee shall be final and binding on all parties.

D.   Upon the death of my Wife, or upon her remarriage, whichever event shall first occur, my trustee shall divide the then remainder of the Non-Exempt Family Residuary Trust, if any, together with all additions from the Marital Trust, both principal and undistributed net income, into a sufficient number of equal shares, if more than one, so that there shall be set apart one share for each of my children by my Wife who are then living and one such share for the descendants (as a group) of each of my children by my Wife who are not then living, but of whom there shall be one or more then living descendants.

E.   (1)   Each share so set apart in Paragraph D for a then living child of mine by my Wife shall be held by my trustee as a separate trust.

(a)   Until such child shall attain the age of twenty-one years, my trustee shall have power, in its discretion, to pay to or apply for the benefit of such child, from the net income of her or his respective trust, as much thereof as the trustee, in its sole judgment and discretion, shall deem to be advisable or proper to provide for the child's maintenance, support, health, and education (including secondary, college, postgraduate, professional, or other education). All net income not so distributed pursuant to this sub-paragraph (a) hereof shall be

- 5 -

accumulated and periodically added to the principal of the child's separate trust estate.

(b)   Upon and after attaining the age of twenty-one years, each child shall be entitled to receive the entire net income from her or his respective trust during her or his lifetime, in installments not less frequent than quarter-annually.

(2)   If, in the opinion and sole discretion of my trustee, the payments herein provided for any such child of mine shall be insufficient to provide for her or his continued maintenance, support, health, and education (including secondary, college, postgraduate, professional or other education) and generally for her or his best interests, my trustee shall have full power, in its discretion, to pay to or apply for the benefit of such child, from the principal of her or his respective trust, as much thereof as it, in its sole judgment and discretion, shall deem to be advisable and proper under the circumstances.

(3)   Each child shall have the right, upon attaining the age of thirty years, or at any time and from time to time thereafter, to withdraw free of trust, from the principal of her or his respective trust, upon her or his written request, such sum or sums as the child may see fit, not exceeding in the aggregate, however, before she or he attains the age of thirty-five years, one-third of the value of the principal of the trust as valued by my trustee at the time of the first withdrawal; and upon attaining the age of thirty-five years, or at any time and from time to time thereafter until attaining the age of forty years, the child shall have the right to withdraw free of trust such sum or sums as she or he may see fit, not exceeding in the aggregate, however, two-thirds of the value of the principal of the trust, likewise so valued and including, for the purpose of computing the two-thirds, all withdrawals, if any, by the child prior to having attained the age of thirty-five years; and upon attaining the age of forty years, or at any time and from time to time thereafter, each child shall have the right so to withdraw any part or all of the balance of the trust, free and clear of any further trust.

(4)   Upon the death of each child, whatever then remains, if any, of her or his trust, both principal and undistributed income, shall be paid over and delivered by my trustee to or among such one or more persons and legal entities, including the child's estate, her or his creditors, and the creditors of her or his estate, in such amounts and proportions and upon such terms and conditions, in further trust or otherwise, as my child may, by her or his Last Will and Testament, validly appoint by specific reference to and express exercise of the general testamentary power herein granted to the child, which shall be exercisable by him or her alone

- 6 -

and in all events. If no notice of the existence of a Last Will and Testament exercising this power shall have been received by my trustee within sixty days after the death of the child, my trustee may assume that she or he did not exercise the power, either in whole or in part.

(5)   Upon the death of each child, whatever then remains, if any, of her or his trust, not so validly appointed, shall be divided for the benefit of the child's then living descendants, if any, per stirpes and shall be held in further trust in accordance with the provisions of Paragraph G hereof, but if none, then one equal share to each of my children by my Wife then living and one equal share to the then living descendants (as a group) of each of my children by my Wife then deceased, per stirpes as to the descendants, and shall be held in further trust in accordance with the provisions of Paragraph G, and provided, further, that if any of my children who would be entitled, under the foregoing provisions of this sub-paragraph (5) of this Paragraph E, to receive all or any part of such trust, shall be the beneficiary of an existing trust created pursuant to the provisions of this Item EIGHTH, then that trust or part thereof shall not be paid over absolutely to the child, but shall be added to and merged with and shall become a part of the principal of the existing trust.

F.   Each share set apart as hereinbefore in Paragraph D provided for the descendants of a deceased child shall be divided among the descendants, per stirpes, and shall be administered in trust in accordance with the terms of Paragraph G hereof.

G.   (1)   (a)   Each share set apart for a then living descendant of a deceased child as provided in sub-paragraph (5) of Paragraph E hereof or as provided in Paragraph F hereof shall be held by the trustee as a separate trust.

(b)   Each descendant, upon and after attaining the age of twenty-one years, shall be entitled to receive the entire net income of her or his respective trust estate during her or his lifetime, payable in installments not less frequent than quarter-annually.

(c)   In the event that the descendant shall not have attained the age of twenty-one years at the time of the creation of her or his separate trust, my trustee shall have full power, in its discretion, to pay to or apply for the benefit of such descendant, from the income of her or his respective trust, as much thereof as my trustee, in its sole discretion, shall deem to be advisable or proper to provide for such descendant's continued maintenance, support, health, and education (including secondary, college, postgraduate, professional or other education). My trustee shall accumulate and add periodically to the principal of the descendant's separate trust all

-7-

income not required for the purposes set forth in this sub-paragraph (1)(c).

(2)   Each descendant shall have the right, upon attaining the age of thirty years, or at any time and from time to time thereafter, to withdraw free of trust, from the principal of her or his respective trust, upon her or his written request, such sum or sums as such descendant may see fit, not exceeding in the aggregate, however, before she or he attains the age of thirty-five years, one-third of the value of the principal of the trust as valued by my trustee at the time of the first withdrawal; and upon attaining the age of thirty-five years, or at any time and from time to time thereafter until attaining the age of forty years, the descendant shall have the right to withdraw free of trust such sum or sums as she or he may see fit, not exceeding in the aggregate, however, two-thirds of the value of the principal of such trust, likewise so valued and including, for the purpose of computing the two-thirds, all withdrawals, if any, by the descendant prior to having attained the age of thirty-five years; and upon attaining the age of forty years, or at any time and from time to time thereafter, each descendant shall have the right so to withdraw any part or all of the balance of her or his trust, free and clear of any further trust.

(3)   If, in the opinion and sole discretion of my trustee, the payments herein provided for a descendant shall be insufficient to provide for her or his continued maintenance, support, health, and education (including secondary, college, post-graduate, professional or other education) and generally for her or his best interests, my trustee shall have full power, in its discretion, to pay to or apply for the benefit of such descendant, from the principal of her or his respective trust, as much thereof as it, in its sole judgment and discretion, shall deem to be advisable and proper under the circumstances.

(4)   Upon the death of each descendant, the remainder, if any, of her or his trust estate shall be paid over and delivered to the personal representative of the descendant's estate.

H.   Any assets that are not finally distributable free of trust pursuant to the provisions of the Non-Exempt Family Residuary Trust shall be paid over and delivered by my trustee or personal representative as the case may be to my older children and their descendants, per stirpes.

ITEM NINTH

THE EXEMPT RESIDUARY TRUST

A.   My trustee shall divide the Exempt Residuary Trust into a sufficient number of

- 8 -

equal shares, if more than one, so that there shall be set apart one such share for the then living descendants (as a group) of each of my older children. If there is more than one descendant of an older child, the share shall be divided, per stirpes into separate trusts for the descendants.

B.   Each share so set apart in Paragraph A shall be held by my trustee as a separate trust.

(1)   Until the descendant shall attain the age of twenty-one years, my trustee shall have power, in its discretion, to pay to or apply for the benefit of the descendant, from the net income of her or his respective trust, as much thereof as the trustee, in its sole judgment and discretion, shall deem to be advisable or proper to provide for the descendant's maintenance, support, health, and education (including secondary, college, postgraduate, professional, or other education). All net income not so distributed pursuant to this sub-paragraph (a) shall be accumulated and periodically added to the principal of the child's separate trust estate.

(2)   Upon and after attaining the age of twenty-one years, each descendant shall be entitled to receive the entire net income from her or his respective trust during her or his lifetime, in installments not less frequent than quarter-annually.

(3)   If, in the opinion and sole discretion of my trustee, the payments herein provided for a descendant shall be insufficient to provide for her or his continued maintenance, support, health, and education (including secondary, college, postgraduate, professional or other education) and generally for her or his best interests, my trustee shall have full power, in its discretion, to pay to or apply for the benefit of such child, from the principal of her or his respective trust, as much thereof as it, in its sole judgment and discretion, shall deem to be advisable and proper under the circumstances.

(4)   Each descendant shall have the right, upon attaining the age of thirty years, or at any time and from time to time thereafter, to withdraw free of trust, from the principal of her or his respective trust, upon her or his written request, such sum or sums as the descendant may see fit, not exceeding in the aggregate, however, before she or he attains the age of thirty-five years, one-third of the value of the principal of the trust as valued by my trustee at the time of the first withdrawal; and upon attaining the age of thirty-five years, or at any time and from time to time thereafter until attaining the age of forty years, the descendant shall have the right to withdraw free of trust such sum or sums as she or he may see fit, not exceeding in the aggregate, however, two-thirds of the value of the principal of the trust, likewise so valued and

- 9 -

including, for the purpose of computing the two-thirds, all withdrawals, if any, by such child prior to having attained the age of thirty-five years; and upon attaining the age of forty years, or at any time and from time to time thereafter, each descendant shall have the right so to withdraw any part or all of the balance of such trust, free and clear of any further trust.

(5)   Upon the death of each such descendant, whatever then remains, if any, of her or his trust estate shall be paid over and delivered to the personal representative of the descendant's Estate.

ITEM TENTH
THE NON-EXEMPT OLDER CHILDREN'S RESIDUARY TRUST

A.   My trustee shall divide the Non-Exempt Older Children's Residuary Trust into a sufficient number of equal shares, if more than one, so that there shall be set apart one such share for each of my older children then living and one such share for the descendants (as a group) of my older children who shall not be then living, but of whom there shall be one or more then living descendants.

B.   (1)   Each share so set apart in Paragraph A for a then living older child shall be held by my trustee as a separate trust.

(a)   Until the child shall attain the age of twenty-one years, my trustee shall have power, in its discretion, to pay to or apply for the benefit of such child, from the net income of her or his respective trust, as much thereof as the trustee, in its sole judgment and discretion, shall deem to be advisable or proper to provide for the child's maintenance, support, health, and education (including secondary, college, postgraduate, professional, or other education). All net income not so distributed pursuant to this sub-paragraph (a) shall be accumulated and periodically added to the principal of the child's separate trust estate.

(b)   Upon and after attaining the age of twenty-one years, each child shall be entitled to receive the entire net income from her or his respective trust during her or his lifetime, in installments not less frequent than quarter-annually.

(2)   If, in the opinion and sole discretion of my trustee, the payments herein provided for a child shall be insufficient to provide for her or his continued maintenance, support, health, and education (including secondary, college, postgraduate, professional or other education) and generally for her or his best interests, my trustee shall have full power, in its discretion, to pay to or apply for the benefit of such child, from the principal of her or his

- 10 -

respective trust, as much thereof as it, in its sole judgment and discretion, shall deem to be advisable and proper under the circumstances.

(3)   Each child shall have the right, upon attaining the age of thirty years, or at any time and from time to time thereafter, to withdraw free of trust, from the principal of her or his respective trust, upon her or his written request, such sum or sums as the child may see fit, not exceeding in the aggregate, however, before she or he attains the age of thirty-five years, one-third of the value of the principal of the trust as valued by my trustee at the time of the first withdrawal; and upon attaining the age of thirty-five years, or at any time and from time to time thereafter until attaining the age of forty years, such child shall have the right to withdraw free of trust such sum or sums as she or he may see fit, not exceeding in the aggregate, however, two-thirds of the value of the principal of the trust, likewise so valued and including, for the purpose of computing the two-thirds, all withdrawals, if any, by such child prior to having attained the age of thirty-five years; and upon attaining the age of forty years, or at any time and from time to time thereafter; each such child shall have the right so to withdraw any part or all of the balance of such trust, free and clear of any further trust.

(4)   Upon the death of a child, whatever then remains, if any, of her or his trust shall be divided for the benefit of the child's then living descendants, if any, per stirpes and shall be held in further trust in accordance with the provisions of Paragraph G hereof, but if none, then one equal share to each of my older children then living, and one equal share to the then living descendants (as a group) of each then deceased older child, per stirpes as to such descendants, and shall be held in further trust in accordance with the provisions of Paragraph D, and provided, further, that if any child who would be entitled under the foregoing provisions of this sub-paragraph (4) to receive all or any part of the trust shall be the beneficiary of an existing trust created pursuant to the provisions of this Item NINTH, then the trust or part thereof shall not be paid over absolutely to that child, but shall be added to and merged with and shall become a part of the principal of the existing trust for that child.

C.   Each share set apart pursuant to Paragraph B for the descendants of a deceased child shall be divided among the child's descendants, per stirpes, and shall be administered in trust in accordance with the terms of Paragraph G hereof

D.   (1)   (a)   Each share so set apart for a then living descendant of a deceased child of mine, as provided in sub-paragraph (4) of Paragraph E hereof, or as provided in

- 11 -

Paragraph F hereof, shall be held by the trustee as a separate trust.

(b)   Each descendant, upon and after attaining the age of twenty-one years, shall be entitled to receive the entire net income of her or his respective trust estate during her or his lifetime, payable in installments not less frequent than quarter-annually.

(c)   In the event that the descendant shall not have attained the age of twenty-one years at the time of the creation of her or his separate trust, my trustee shall have full power, in its discretion, to pay to or apply for the benefit of such descendant, from the income of her or his respective trust, as much thereof as my trustee, in its sole discretion, shall deem to be advisable or proper to provide for such descendant's continued maintenance, support, health, and education (including secondary, college, postgraduate, professional or other education). My trustee shall accumulate and add periodically to the principal of the descendant's separate trust all income not required for the purposes set forth in this sub-paragraph (1)(c).

(2)   Each descendant shall have the right, upon attaining the age of thirty years, or at any time and from time to time thereafter, to withdraw free of trust from the principal of her or his respective trust upon her or his written request, such sum or sums as the descendant may see fit, not exceeding in the aggregate, however, before she or he attains the age of thirty-five years, one-third of the value of the principal of the trust as valued by my trustee at the time of the first withdrawal; and upon attaining the age of thirty-five years, or at any time and from time to time thereafter until attaining the age of forty years, the descendant shall have the right to withdraw free of trust such sum or sums as she or he may see fit, not exceeding in the aggregate, however, two-thirds of the value of the principal of such trust, likewise so valued and including, for the purpose of computing the two-thirds, all withdrawals, if any, by such descendant prior to having attained the age of thirty-five years; and upon attaining the age of forty years, or at any time and from time to time thereafter, each such descendant shall have the right so to withdraw any part or all of the balance of her or his trust, free and clear of any further trust.

(3)   If, in the opinion and sole discretion of my trustee, the payments herein provided for any descendant shall be insufficient to provide for her or his continued maintenance, support, health, and education (including secondary, college, post-graduate, professional or other education) and generally for her or his best interests, my trustee shall have full power, in its discretion to pay to or apply for the benefit of the descendant, from the principal of her or his respective trust, as much thereof as it, in its sole judgment and discretion, shall

- 12 -

deem to be advisable and proper under the circumstances.

(4)   Upon the death of each such descendant, whatever then remains, if any, of her or his trust estate shall be paid over and delivered to the personal representative of such descendant's estate.

ITEM ELEVENTH

A.   Any provision in this Will to the contrary notwithstanding, if at any time after the death of the last to die of my Wife and me, my trustee, in its discretion, shall determine that the size of any trust arising hereunder does not warrant the cost of continuing the trust or if its administration would be otherwise impractical, my trustee, in full discharge of its duty and without formal court accounting, may pay the remaining principal and income of the trust to the person then entitled or permitted to receive the income from that trust. If that person is legally incapable of receiving it, my trustee may pay it to the guardian, parent or person having custody of that person, or may deposit the same in a savings fund in the name of that person, if a minor, payable to the minor upon attaining the age of majority or my trustee transfer the assets to an individual selected by my trustee to be the Custodian for such minor until the age of twenty-one years under the Uniform Transfers to Minors Act of Maryland. Upon any such payment, deposit or transfer under the provisions of this paragraph, the interests of all succeeding beneficiaries, whether vested or contingent, shall be terminated and my trustee shall be relieved of all duties in connection with such trust and shall not be required to account therefor in any court.

B.   All assets, if any, of my Estate at any time not finally distributable free of trust pursuant to one or more of the foregoing provisions of this Will shall be paid over and delivered by my trustee or personal representative, as the case may be, to The Johns Hopkins Hospital, Baltimore, Maryland.

ITEM TWELVETH

A.   Upon the death of any beneficiary hereunder, my trustee shall have full power to pay out of the principal of the trust from which the beneficiary was entitled or permitted, in the exercise of discretion herein granted, to receive income immediately prior to her or his death, before any other disposition of the trust provided for by this Will shall be made, such sum or sums as shall be necessary and proper, within the discretion of my trustee, to provide for any part or all of the funeral expenses (including the cost of a suitable marker for the grave) and the expenses of the last illness of the beneficiary, to the extent that the cash and other assets readily

- 13 -

reducible to cash in the estate of such beneficiary, as known to my trustee, shall be insufficient to satisfy the expenses.

B.　　Except as is elsewhere herein provided or permitted to the contrary, and subject to the provisions of the following paragraph, my trustee shall pay all amounts of income and principal payable hereunder to any person, into the hands of that person and not to any other person or entity whatsoever, whether claiming by her or his authority or otherwise. The payments shall not be subject to any assignment or order and may not be anticipated in any manner whatsoever. Neither the principal nor the income may be taken in execution by attachment or garnishment nor by any other legal or equitable proceeding whatsoever. However, deposit to the credit of the account of any person in a bank, trust company or other depositary shall be deemed to be the equivalent of payment into the hands of that person.

C.　　If any person entitled to payments of principal or income hereunder is under twenty-one years of age, or is incapacitated, mentally or physically, temporarily or permanently (and whether or not such person shall be so incapacitated shall be within the sound judgment of my trustee, which shall be binding upon all persons interested therein), then during the continuance of the trust as to that person, my trustee may make such payments of principal or income to the parent, guardian (with respect to the Marital Trust, only to the guardian of my Wife should she be disabled) or other individual or individuals who are, in the judgment of my trustee, in proper charge of the person, or my trustee, in its discretion, may expend, apply or transmit on her or his behalf any part or all of the principal or income for her or his continued maintenance, support, health, and education. In any such event, payments may be made, received and applied without the necessity of any accounting to or approval of any court, and all such payments made in good faith shall constitute a complete release and acquittance therefore of my trustee.

D.　　Anything in this Will to the contrary notwithstanding, and whether or not any reference is made in any other provision of this Will to the limitations imposed by this Paragraph D, neither my personal representative nor my trustee shall have or exercise any authority, power, or discretion over the Marital Share or the income thereof, or the property constituting the Marital Share, nor shall any payment or distribution by my personal representative or my trustee be limited or restricted by any provision of this Will that would in any way prevent my estate from receiving the benefit of the marital deduction as hereinbefore set forth.

- 14 -

E.   If my Wife shall die simultaneously with me or under such circumstances that it is impossible, or there is no sufficient proof, to determine who predeceased the other, she shall be deemed to have survived me and the provisions of this Will shall be construed upon that presumption, notwithstanding the provisions of any law establishing a different presumption of order of death.

F.   I hereby direct that my trustee, in its determination from time to time upon the exercise or non-exercise of the discretionary power granted to it to make payments from the principal of a trust or share thereof to or for the benefit of a beneficiary or one or more of a group of beneficiaries, may take into consideration the other income and assets readily reducible to cash reasonably available to the respective beneficiaries for the purposes for which the discretionary power is granted. In this connection, I authorize and empower my trustee to rely conclusively upon such information with respect to income and other financial resources as may, in its judgment, have been presented to it in good faith, whether by the beneficiary or on behalf of the beneficiary by another. I hereby admonish my trustee, however, that it is not my intent that the discretion herein granted shall be exercisable only upon the complete exhaustion of other financial resources of the beneficiaries hereof. If my trustee, after reasonable effort, is unable to obtain any such information, then it is authorized to make payments from the principal of the trust without regard to any other income and other financial resources of the beneficiary.

ITEM THIRTEENTH

A.   The powers and discretions hereinafter granted to my personal representative and to my trustee are in addition to, and not in derogation or limitation of, any other powers implied or necessary for the performance of their respective duties, and all such powers may be exercised by them, respectively, without previous application to or subsequent ratification by any Court.

B.   I authorize and empower my personal representative and my trustee, each respectively, in its sole and absolute discretion:

(1)   To invest, reinvest and change the investments of any trust and to keep the same invested in such stocks, common or preferred, common trust funds, bonds, mortgages, mutual funds, certificates of deposit (including certificates of deposit issued by the Corporate trustee), or other property, real or personal, and in such proportions, as it may consider advisable or proper, without being restricted as to the character of any investment by any statute or rule of law or court governing the investment of trust funds.

(2)   To retain any and all property which I may own at the time of my death Until such time as it may deem it desirable to sell or otherwise dispose of the same; provided,

- 15 -

however, any such property held as a part of the Marital Trust which is or becomes unproductive shall, if my Wife so directs, be sold or otherwise disposed of pursuant to the powers hereinbelow set forth.

(3) To sell (either at public or private sale), lease for such term or terms as it may deem desirable, irrespective of the possible termination of the trust, pledge, mortgage, transfer, exchange, partition, convert or otherwise dispose of, or grant options with respect to, any and all property, real or personal, at any time forming a part of my estate or of any trust, in such manner, at such time or times, for such purposes, for such prices and upon such terms, credit and conditions as it may deem desirable.

(4) To borrow money for any purposes connected with the protection, preservation or improvement of my estate or of any trust created, including for the purpose of exercising any outstanding stock options possessed by my estate or any trust created hereunder, whenever it shall deem such action advisable.

(5) To vote in person or by general or limited proxy, with or without power of substitution, with respect to any shares of stock or other securities held by it, and to consent, directly or through a committee or other agent, to the reorganization, consolidation, merger, dissolution or liquidation of any corporation in which my estate or any trust may have any interest, or to the sale, lease, pledge or mortgage of any property by or to any such corporation; and to make any payments and to take any step which it may deem necessary or proper to obtain the benefit of any such transaction.

(6) To administer my estate and the trusts hereunder in accordance with the provisions of any principal and income act in force and effect from time to time.

(7) To pay, compromise, compound, extend, modify, renew, adjust, submit to arbitration, sell or release any claims or demands of my estate or any trust hereunder against others or of others against my estate or against any such trust as it shall deem advisable, and to make any payments in connection therewith.

(8) To create reserves out of income to insure prompt payment of taxes or assessments, repairs and all other obligations, and to restore to income such reserves as may be unused.

(9) To advance money for the protection of the trust or trusts and for all expenses, losses and liabilities incurred in or about the execution or protection of any such trust or because of the holding or ownership of any property subject thereto. For all such advances, the trustee shall have a lien on the trust property and may reimburse itself with interest therefor out of the trust property.

(10) To exercise any outstanding stock options possessed by my estate or by any trust created hereunder.

(11) Subject to the provisions of Paragraph C hereof, to receive other property

- 16 -

of any type acceptable to the trustee, including, but not by way of limitation, life insurance proceeds, which may be devised, bequeathed, assigned, granted, conveyed or made payable to the trustee by me, my Wife, or by any other person, to be added to and administered in accordance with the then applicable provisions of the trust or trusts hereunder; provided, however, if more than one trust is then being administered hereunder, my Wife, by Will, or such other person, in the instrument of transfer, may specify, among which trust and in what proportions such property shall be allocated. If my Wife shall add investments of her own during her lifetime, such additions shall be allocated to the Marital Trust, and in addition to any other rights of withdrawal that may have been granted to her elsewhere in this Will, she shall at all times have the right to withdraw from the principal of the Marital Trust an amount equal to the value when received of all such additions she shall have made to it.

(12)   To make divisions or distributions of all or any part of my estate or of any trust hereby created in kind or in cash, or partly in kind and partly in cash, to cause any share, part or portion of my estate or any such trust to be composed of property different in kind from any other share, part or portion, and, in its discretion, to allocate particular assets or portions thereof or undivided interests therein to anyone or more of the beneficiaries hereunder taking into account the income tax bases of such assets as it shall deem to be for the best interests of the beneficiaries of my estate and of any trust hereby created. For the purpose of any such distribution, to select such securities or other property as it may deem suitable, and to place such valuation upon such securities or other property as it may determine. The decision of said personal representative or trustee shall be final and binding upon all parties in interest.

(13)   To execute, acknowledge and deliver any and all instruments in writing which my personal representative or my trustee may deem advisable to carry out any of the foregoing powers, including the power to indicate any division or distribution of my estate or of any trust by deeds or other writings or instruments recorded among the public records of any jurisdiction where any such property may be located. No party to any such instrument in writing signed by my personal representative or my trustee shall be bound to see to the application by it of any money or other consideration paid or delivered to it pursuant to the terms of such instrument.

(14)   To treat my entire trust estate, other than the Marital Trust, as a common fund for the purpose of investment, notwithstanding any provision herein for division thereof into shares or separate trusts.

(15)   To decide with absolute discretion whether disbursements by my personal representative shall be taken as estate tax or income tax deductions, and to elect annual accounting periods; all such decisions and elections shall be final and conclusive upon all persons interested hereunder whether or not the amount of their respective interests or shares are thereby affected.

(16)   To employ counsel in the administration of my estate.

(17)   To employ accountants, investment advisers and such other agents as my personal representative or my trustee deem advisable to assist it in the administration or

- 17 -

investment of my estate or any trusts, and my personal representative or my trustee may rely upon information or advice furnished by such agents. My personal representative or my trustee may charge the compensation of such accountants, investment advisers or other agents, in addition to other expenses and charges, against income or principal, or in part against both, as my personal representative or my trustee shall, in its discretion, determine.

(18)   In addition to all other powers and discretions hereinbefore or hereinafter granted to my personal representative and my trustee, I hereby expressly grant to and confer upon them full power, authority and discretion to retain as an investment hereunder any interest owned by me at the time of my death in any business enterprise or enterprises, whether conducted as proprietorship, partnership or corporation, for such period of time as my personal representative and/or trustee, in the exercise of its or their discretion, may deem to be advisable or proper, without any liability for any loss or depreciation in the value thereof; and I expressly authorize and empower my personal representative and/or trustee to continue, or to participate in the continuance of, the operation of any such business or businesses, for such time or times as my personal representative and/or trustee, in its or their judgment and discretion, may deem to be for the best interests of my estate and the trusts hereinbefore created, without any liability for loss or depreciation which may arise by reason of such continuation, with full power to keep and retain all the capital employed therein at the time of my death, to contribute such additional capital thereto from time to time as my personal representative and/or trustee may see fit, to employ such persons in such capacities (preferably persons employed therein at the time of my death), as it or they may deem advisable, to discharge any employees, to execute contracts, borrow money, extend credit, and in general to do and to perform any and all things incident to the operation and continuation of any interest in such business or businesses as fully and effectually as I could have done if I had continued to live and had remained the absolute owner thereof. My personal representative and my trustee shall also have full power to incorporate, or to participate in the incorporation of, any unincorporated business or businesses, and to receive and retain, as a part of my estate or any of the trusts hereinbefore created, the stock issued and representing my interest in such business or businesses, as a result of such incorporation, and any certificates issued by any partnership to evidence any interest in such partnership, for such period of time as my personal representative and/or trustee deems advisable or proper.

C.   (1)   If any life insurance proceeds or other funds or assets, including payments from any retirement plans, are payable directly to my trustee hereunder as beneficiary, I direct my trustee to collect such funds and make available to my personal representative such part of the funds as my personal representative, in its discretion, shall deem necessary or advisable for the payment of my funeral and administration expenses and death taxes, or to complete the funding of the Marital Share or any other bequest hereunder, without regard to the availability to my personal representative of any other assets. My personal representative shall, in any and all events, direct the allocation of such funds so that the Marital Share shall be funded to the full extent provided in this Will.

- 18 -

(2)   To the extent that my trustee shall have the right to exercise any option or election respecting the manner of payment of any funds or other assets which may be payable directly to the trustee as beneficiary, I direct that my trustee shall have the absolute discretion to exercise any such option or election in such manner as it shall deem advisable, regardless of the effect thereof on my estate, the trust estates created hereunder, or any beneficiary or other person interested therein, and the determination of my trustee in the exercise of any such option or election shall be final and binding on all persons interested therein.

D.   My personal representative and my trustee, while acting in good faith, shall not be liable or held responsible for any loss or depreciation in the value of my estate or of any trust created hereunder, but shall be liable only for loss resulting from its own willful default or gross negligence.

E.   I direct that all powers herein granted shall last beyond the termination of the trust or trusts herein created until a complete and final distribution of all assets held hereunder shall be made.

F.   I direct that if my trustee shall receive any payments from any so-called "qualified" pension or profit-sharing plan, my trustee shall have the absolute discretion to elect, in whole or in part, among an annuity option, installment method, lump-sum distribution or any other mode of settlement permitted under such qualified plan.

ITEM FOURTEENTH

A.   (1)   I nominate BANK OF AMERICA, N.A., and its successors, and LOWELL R. BOWEN to be my trustee of the trusts hereinbefore created. If LOWELL R. BOWEN is unable or unwilling to act, I appoint CHARLES T. BOWYER in his place, provided CHARLES T. BOWYER is an employee of the law firm of Miles & Stockbridge P.C. or its successor. If CHARLES T. BOWYER is unable or unwilling to act, I direct that the Board of Directors of Miles & Stockbridge or its successor shall have the right to designate a principal of that firm to act as personal co-trustee.

(2)   I direct that my individual co-trustee, by a written instrument filed among the records of the trust estate, shall have the continuing right to remove and to replace, and to successively remove and to replace, the Corporate co-trustee at any time acting hereunder.

(3)   Any trustee at any time acting hereunder shall have the right to resign at any time by giving thirty days notice to that effect to the then current adult income beneficiaries.

- 19 -

(4)   The trustee of any trust created hereunder shall have the right to move and remove the situs of the trust estate to any place within the United States of America.

B.   I appoint LOWELL R. BOWEN to be my personal representative. In the event that he shall fail to qualify or cease to act, I appoint CHARLES T. BOWYER, if he is in the employ of Miles & Stockbridge, P.C., to be my personal representative in his place or stead. If CHARLES T. BOWYER shall fail to qualify or cease to act, I direct that the Board of Directors of Miles & Stockbridge P.C. or its successor shall have the right to designate a principal of that firm to act as personal representative. It is a condition of each of these appointments that the allowable commissions of my personal representative shall not exceed 0.75% of the value of the property subject to administration.

C.   I direct that my personal representative be excused from bond.

D.   It is not my intention that the trusts hereby created shall be administered under the supervision of a court of equity, and in the event that my trustee shall at any time apply to any court for any purpose in connection with any such trust or the provisions of this my Will, it is my intention that such court shall have jurisdiction of the specific matter in question and shall not take jurisdiction over such trust or any other trusts unless requested so to do by my trustee.

E.   Any personal representative or personal co-trustee at any time or from time to time acting hereunder may be an employee, officer, director or stockholder of, or otherwise interested in, any corporation in the stock or other securities of which any part of my estate or of any trust hereunder may be invested, and may participate in the making of new investments in such stocks or other securities, and such co-personal representative or trustee shall be entitled to receive and retain, without accountability to anyone therefor, any compensation, emoluments or profits which she or he may derive from employment by, connection with, or interest in any such corporation.

F.   All powers (discretionary or otherwise) and all duties and immunities herein conferred or imposed upon the personal representative and upon the trustee shall be appurtenant to each respective office and shall devolve, respectively, upon any remaining or successor personal representative, and upon any surviving, remaining or successor trustees or trustee.

G.   My corporate co-trustee shall be entitled to receive commissions in accordance with its schedule of fees in effect from time to time and shall be entitled to receive reasonable additional compensation for services of any unusual nature, such as investigations relating to

- 20 -

payments to be made in the exercise of discretion conferred hereunder, and other unusual services of whatever nature not incidental to the normal management and administration of the trust estate.

IN WITNESS WHEREOF, I have hereunto subscribed my name and affixed my seal this ___ day of June, 2007.

_____(SEAL)

THOMAS L. CLANCY, JR.

INITIALED upon the margins of the first 20 pages, SIGNED, SEALED, PUBLISHED and DECLARED by the above-named Testator, THOMAS L. CLANCY, JR., as and for his Last Will, in the presence of us, who at his request, in his presence, and in the presence of each other, have hereunto subscribed our names as witnesses the day and year above-written.

NAME _Mary Beth Kijek_   NAME _Mary R. Muh_

ADDRESS _39185 Jocelyn Way_   ADDRESS _1525 Old Plum Point Road_

Mechanicsville, MD 20659   _Huntingtown, MD 20639_

<u>FIRST CODICIL TO</u>
<u>LAST WILL AND TESTAMENT OF</u>
<u>THOMAS L. CLANCY, JR.</u>

I, THOMAS L. CLANCY, JR., of Calvert County, Maryland, declare this to be the First Codicil to my Last Will and Testament executed by me on the 11th day of June, 2007 and referred to herein as "my Will."

I amend Paragraph A of ITEM TENTH of my Will by changing the period at the end of the paragraph to a semicolon and adding the following:

"provided, however, I direct that the amount of any gifts that I have made during my lifetime, individually or jointly with my Wife, to or for the benefit of the older child (or the descendants of the older child) in respect of whom the share is being created, shall be added to the value of the Non-Exempt Older Children's Residuary Trust at the time of its division into separate shares or trusts, and shall at that time be deducted from the respective share or trust to be set apart for that older child or for his or her descendants, if that older child is then deceased. For this purpose, only gifts reported on federal gift tax returns are to be counted."

In all other respects not inconsistent with this First Codicil, I ratify, reaffirm, and republish my Will.

IN WITNESS WHEREOF, I have hereunto subscribed my name and affixed my seal this 19th day of September, 2007.

_____ (SEAL)
THOMAS L. CLANCY, JR.

SIGNED, SEALED, PUBLISHED and DECLARED by THOMAS L. CLANCY, JR., the above-named Testatrix as and for a First Codicil to his Last Will and Testament dated June 11, 2007, in the presence of us, who at his request, in his presence, and in the presence of each other, have hereunto subscribed our names as witnesses.

NAME _Mary R. Mathis_   NAME _Robert Youndelman_
ADDRESS _1525 Old Plum Point Rd_ ADDRESS _18 Gay St._
Huntingtown, MD 20639   _New York, N.Y. 10014_

SECOND CODICIL TO
LAST WILL AND TESTAMENT OF
THOMAS L. CLANCY, JR.

I, THOMAS L. CLANCY, JR., of Baltimore City, Maryland, declare this to be the Second Codicil to my Last Will and Testament executed by me on the 11th day of June, 2007, as heretofore amended by the First Codicil executed by me on the 18th day of September, 2007, collectively referred to herein as "my Will."

I amend Paragraph B of ITEM EIGHTH of my Will by deleting therefrom the words "or my child or children by my Wife who are living from time to time," and the words "or their" and otherwise leaving said paragraph unchanged.

I amend Paragraph C of ITEM EIGHTH of my Will by deleting its text in its entirety and inserting in place thereof "[Intentionally omitted.]"

I amend Paragraph D of ITEM EIGHTH of my Will by deleting therefrom the words "or upon her remarriage, whichever event shall first occur," and otherwise leaving said paragraph unchanged.

I amend Paragraph D of ITEM TWELVETH of my Will by deleting the text thereof in its entirety and replacing it with the following:

> "D.   No asset or proceeds of any assets shall be included in the Marital Share or the Non-Exempt Family Residuary Trust as to which a marital deduction would not be allowed if included. Anything in this Will to the contrary notwithstanding, and whether or not any reference is made in any other provision of this Will to the limitations imposed by this Paragraph D, neither my personal representative nor my trustee shall have or exercise any authority, power or discretion over the Marital Share or the Non-Exempt Family Residuary Trust or the income thereof, or the property constituting the Marital Share or the Non-Exempt Family Residuary Trust, nor shall any payment or distribution by my personal representative or my trustee be limited or restricted by any provision of this Will, such that, in any such event, my estate would be prevented from receiving the benefit of the marital deduction as hereinbefore set forth. My Wife shall have the power at any time by written direction to compel my trustee to convert unproductive property held in the Marital Trust into income producing property. Likewise, my Wife shall have the power at any time by written direction to compel my trustee to convert unproductive property held in the Non-Exempt Family Residuary Trust into income producing property."

4851-1280-7188

I amend Paragraph A and Paragraph B of ITEM FOURTEENTH by deleting "Lowell R. Bowen" wherever such name shall appear and inserting in place thereof "J.W. Thompson Webb" and otherwise leaving such paragraphs unchanged.

In all other respects not inconsistent with this Second Codicil, I ratify, reaffirm and republish my Will.

IN WITNESS WHEREOF, I have hereunton subscribed my name and affixed by seal this 25ᵗʰ day of July, 2013.

(signature) (SEAL)
THOMAS L. CLANCY, JR.

SIGNED, SEALED, PUBLISHED and DECLARED by THOMAS L. CLANCY, JR., the above-named Testatrix as and for a Second Codicil to his Last Will and Testament dated June 11, 2007, as previously amended by First Codicil dated September 18, 2007, in the presence of us, who at his request, in his presence, and in the presence of each other, have hereunto subscribed our names as witnesses.

NAME: _(signature)_

ADDRESS: 104 St. John, Rd.

Baltimore, MD 21210

NAME: Monica Silafani

ADDRESS: 502 Westview Road

Bel Air, MD 21015

4851-1280-7188

CHAPTER 5

LAST WILLS OF NOTABLE INDIVIDUALS OF SOUND AND STAGE

We make a living by what we get;
we make a life by what we give.

WINSTON CHURCHILL

CLARK GABLE
February 1, 1901 — November 16, 1960

Clark Gable was a film actor from the 1930s to 1950s. He is best known for his role as Rhett Butler in the 1939 classic "Gone with the Wind," which earned him an Academy Award nomination for Best Actor. He also played the role of mutineer Fletcher Christian in the 1935 classic "Mutiny on the Bounty." His Last Will, which he signed on September 19, 1955, left all his property to his former wife, Josephine Dillon, and his current wife, Kathleen G. Gable.[74] He died of a heart attack on November 16, 1960 in Los Angeles, California, to the heartbreak of many ladies of his time.

---

74. *See below,* Fourth and Fifth sections, respectively, of the *Last Will and Testament of Clark Gable,* dated September 19, 1955.

LAST WILL AND TESTAMENT OF CLARK GABLE

I, CLARK GABLE, being of sound and disposing mind, and free from fraud, duress, menace or undue influence, do hereby make, declare and publish this, my Last Will and Testament.

FIRST: I hereby expressly revoke any and all former wills and Codicils thereto heretofore made by me.

SECOND: I hereby declare that I am married to Kathleen G. Gable and that I have no children.

THIRD: I direct that all of my just debts, expenses of last illness and expenses of burial be first paid.

FOURTH: I give, devise and bequeath to JOSEPHINE DILLON, my former wife, that certain real property situate in the County of Los Angeles, State of California, known as 12746 Landale, North Hollywood, California, and more particularly described as follows:

The West fifty (50) feet of the East one hundred (100) feet of Lot 9, Tract 5588, as per map recorded in Book 59, page 49, of Maps, in the office of the Recorder of said County.

FIFTH: All of the rest, residue and remainder of my estate, real, personal or mixed, I give, devise and bequeath to my beloved wife, KATHLEEN G. GABLE.

SIXTH: I direct that all succession, inheritance or other death taxes or duties (by whatever name called) imposed upon or in relation to any property owned by me at the time of my death or required to be included in my gross estate under the provisions of any tax law shall be paid out of the residue of my estate without any charge therefor against any specific bequest or devise hereunder or against any assets not included in my probate estate.

SEVENTH: I hereby generally and expressly disinherit each and all persons whomsoever claiming to be and who may be my heirs at law, and each and all persons whomsoever who, if I died intestate, would be entitled to any part of my estate, except those herein provided for. If any devisee, legatee or beneficiary under this Will, or any person claiming under or through any devisee, legatee or beneficiary, or any other person who, if I died wholly or partially intestate, would be entitled to share in my estate, shall in any manner whatsoever, directly or indirectly, contest this Will or attack or oppose, or in any manner seek to impair or invalidate any provision hereof, or shall endeavor to succeed to any part of my estate otherwise than through this Will, then in each of the above mentioned cases I hereby bequeath to such person or persons the sum of One ($1.00) Dollar only, and all other bequests, devises and interest in this Will given to such person or persons shall be forfeited and become a part of the residue of my estate.

EIGHTH: I hereby appoint my beloved wife, KATHLEEN G. GABLE, to serve as executrix of my estate, without bond.

IN WITNESS WHEREOF, I have hereunto set my hand this 19 day of September␣, 1955.

_____

CLARK GABLE

The foregoing instrument, consisting of three pages, including the page signed by the , was on the date hereof by the said CLARK GABLE, subscribed, published and declared to be his Last Will and Testament in the presence of us, and each of us, who at his request and in his presence, and in the presence of each other, have signed the same as witnesses thereto.

_____   Residing at _____

_____   Residing at _____

MARILYN MONROE
June 1, 1926 — August 5, 1962

It is hard to believe, but Marilyn Monroe's estate remained open until 2001 — almost 40 years! It was probated in the New York Surrogate Court, which finally declared the estate completely settled. The court ordered the transfer of the remaining assets of the estate to Marilyn Monroe L.L.C., a Delaware limited liability company managed by Anna Strasberg, the surviving spouse of the late method acting teacher Lee Strasberg (who taught Marilyn's acting lessons). Strasberg owned 75 percent of the company and the Anna Freud Centre owned 25 percent. In 2010, the L.L.C. was acquired by Authentic Brands Group and NECA for an estimated $50 million, which in turn formed a company named The Estate of Marilyn Monroe, L.L.C. The estate continues to generate significant earnings. In 2011-2012, it brought in $15 million in revenue, only behind the estates of Michael Jackson and Elvis Presley.

LAST WILL AND TESTAMENT OF MARILYN MONROE

I, MARILYN MONROE, do make, publish and declare this to be my Last Will and Testament.

FIRST: I hereby revoke all former Wills and Codicils by me made.

SECOND: I direct my Executor, hereinafter named, to pay all of my just debts, funeral expenses and testamentary charges as soon after my death as can conveniently be done.

THIRD: I direct that all succession, estate or inheritance taxes which may be levied against my estate and/or against any legacies and/or devises hereinafter set forth shall be paid out of my residuary estate.

FOURTH: (a) I give and bequeath to BERNICE MIRACLE, should she survive me, the sum of $10,000.00.

    (b) I give and bequeath to MAY REIS, should she survive me, the sum of $10,000.00.

    (c) I give and bequeath to NORMAN and HEDDA ROSTEN, or to the survivor of them, or if they should both predecease me, then to their daughter, PATRICIA ROSTEN, the sum of $5,000.00, it being my wish that such sum be used for the education of PATRICIA ROSTEN.

    (d) I give and bequeath all of my personal effects and clothing to LEE STRASBERG, or if he should predecease me, then to my Executor hereinafter named, it being my desire that he distribute these, in his sole discretion, among my friends, colleagues and those to whom I am devoted.

FIFTH: I give and bequeath to my Trustee, hereinafter named, the sum of $100,000.00, in Trust, for the following uses and purposes:

    (a) To hold, manage, invest and reinvest the said property and to receive and collect the income therefrom.

    (b) To pay the net income therefrom, together with such amounts of principal as shall be necessary to provide $5,000.00 per annum, in equal quarterly installments, for the maintenance and support of my mother, GLADYS BAKER, during her lifetime.

    (c) To pay the net income therefrom, together with such amounts of principal as shall be necessary to provide $2,500.00 per annum, in equal quarterly installments, for the maintenance and support of MRS. MICHAEL CHEKHOV during her lifetime.

(d) Upon the death of the survivor between my mother, GLADYS BAKER, and MRS. MICHAEL CHEKHOV to pay over the principal remaining in the Trust, together with any accumulated income, to DR. MARIANNE KRIS to be used by her for the furtherance of the work of such psychiatric institutions or groups as she shall elect.

SIXTH: All the rest, residue and remainder of my estate, both real and personal, of whatsoever nature and wheresoever situate, of which I shall die seized or possessed or to which I shall be in any way entitled, or over which I shall possess any power of appointment by Will at the time of my death, including any lapsed legacies, I give, devise and bequeath as follows:

(a) to MAY REIS the sum of $40,000.00 or 25% of the total remainder of my estate, whichever shall be the lesser,

(b) To DR. MARIANNE KRIS 25% of the balance thereof, to be used by her as set forth in ARTICLE FIFTH (d) of this my Last Will and Testament.

(c) To LEE STRASBERG the entire remaining balance.

SEVENTH: I nominate, constitute and appoint AARON R. FROSCH Executor of this my Last Will and Testament. In the event that he should die or fail to qualify, or resign or for any other reason be unable to act, I nominate, constitute and appoint L. ARNOLD WEISSBERGER in his place and stead.

EIGHTH: I nominate, constitute and appoint AARON R. FROSCH Trustee under this my Last Will and Testament. In the event he should die or fail to qualify, or resign or for any other reason be unable to act, I nominate, constitute and appoint L. Arnold Weissberger in his place and stead.

Marilyn Monroe (L.S.)

SIGNED, SEALED, PUBLISHED and DECLARED by MARILYN MONROE, the Testatrix above named, as and for her Last Will and Testament, in our presence and we, at her request and in her presence and in the presence of each other, have hereunto subscribed our names as witnesses this 14th day of January, One Thousand Nine Hundred Sixty-One

Aaron R. Frosch residing at 10 West 86th St. NYC

Louise H. White residing at 709 E. 56 St., New York, NY

ELVIS PRESLEY
January 8, 1935 — August 16, 1977

Photo by Ollie Atkins, White House photographer (1970)

Elvis Presley, one of the most popular singers of all time, died with a considerable fortune that he left to his family, primarily to his daughter, Lisa Marie, through a Testamentary Trust. His Last Will and Testament is particularly interesting because it makes use of Testamentary Trusts to provide for his family long after his death.

LAST WILL AND TESTAMENT OF ELVIS A. PRESLEY

I, Elvis A. Presley, a resident and citizen of Shelby County, Tennessee, being of sound mind and disposing memory, do hereby make, publish and declare this instrument to be my last will and testament, hereby revoking any and all wills and codicils by me at any time heretofore made.

Item I - Debts, Expenses and Taxes

I direct my Executor, hereinafter named, to pay all of my matured debts and my funeral expenses, as well as the costs and expenses of the administration of my estate, as soon after my death as practicable. I further direct that all estate, inheritance, transfer and succession taxes which are payable by reason under this will, be paid out of my residuary estate; and I hereby waive on behalf of my estate any right to recover from any person any part of such taxes so paid. My Executor, in his sole discretion, may pay from my domiciliary estate all or any portion of the costs of ancillary administration and similar proceedings in other jurisdictions.

Item II - Instruction Concerning Personal Property: Enjoyment in Specie

I anticipate that included as a part of my property and estate at the time of my death will be tangible personal property of various kinds, characters and values, including trophies and other items accumulated by me during my professional career. I hereby specifically instruct all concerned that my Executor, herein appointed, shall have complete freedom and discretion as to disposal of any and all such property so long as he shall act in good faith and in the best interest of my estate and my beneficiaries, and his discretion so exercised shall not be subject to question by anyone whomsoever.

I hereby expressly authorize my Executor and my Trustee, respectively and successively, to permit any beneficiary of any and all trusts created hereunder to enjoy in specie the use or benefit of any household goods, chattels, or other tangible personal property (exclusive of choses in action, cash, stocks, bonds or other securities) which either my Executor or my Trustees may receive in kind, and my Executor and my Trustees shall not be liable for any consumption, damage, injury to or loss of any tangible property so used, nor shall the beneficiaries of any trusts hereunder or their executors of administrators be liable for any consumption, damage, injury to or loss of any tangible personal property so used.

Item III - Real Estate

If I am the owner of any real estate at the time of my death, I instruct and empower my Executor and my Trustee (as the case may be) to hold such real estate for investment, or to sell same, or any portion therof, as my Executor or my Trustee (as the case may be) shall in his sole judgment determine to be for the best interest of my estate and the beneficiaries thereof.

Item IV - Residuary Trust

After payment of all debts, expenses and taxes as directed under Item I hereof, I give, devise, and bequeath all the rest, residue, and remainder of my estate, including all lapsed legacies and devices, and any property over which I have a power of appointment, to my Trustee, hereinafter named, in trust for the following purposes:

(a) The Trustees is directed to take, hold, manage, invest and reinvent the corpus of the trust and to collect the income therefrom in accordance with the rights, powers, duties, authority and discretion hereinafter set forth. The Trustee is directed to pay all the expenses, taxes and costs incurred in the management of the trust estate out of the income thereof.

(b) After payment of all expenses, taxes and costs incurred in the management of the expenses, taxes and costs incurred in the management of the trust estate, the Trustee is authorizes to accumulate the net income or to pay or apply so much of the net income and such portion of the principal at any time and from time to time to time for health, education, support, comfortable maintenance and welfare of: (1) My daughter, Lisa Marie Presley, and any other lawful issue I might have, (2) my grandmother, Minnie Mae Presley, (3) my father, Vernon E. Presley, and (4) such other relatives of mine living at the time of my death who in the absolute discretion of my Trustees are in need of emergency assistance for any of the above mentioned purposes and the Trustee is able to make such distribution without affecting the ability of the trust to meet the present needs of the first three numbered categories of beneficiaries herein mentioned or to meet the reasonably expected future needs of the first three classes of beneficiaries herein mentioned. Any decision of the Trustee as to whether or not distribution, to any of the persons described hereunder shall be final and conclusive and not subject to question by any legatee or beneficiary hereunder.

(c) Upon the death of my Father, Vernon E. Presley, the Trustee is instructed to make no further distributions to the fourth category of beneficiaries and such beneficiaries shall cease to have any interest whatsoever in this trust.

(d) Upon the death of both my said father and my said grandmother, the Trustee is directed to divide the Residuary Trust into separate and equal trusts, creating one such equal trust for each of my lawful children then surviving and one such equal trust for the living issue collectively, if any, of any deceased child of mine. The share, if any, for the issue of any such deceased child, shall immediately vest in such issue in equal shares but shall be subject to the provisions of Item V herein. Separate books and records shall be kept for each trust, but it shall not be necessary that a physical division of the assets be made as to each trust.

The Trustee may from time to time distribute the whole or any part of the net income or principal from each of the aforesaid trusts as the Trustee, in its uncontrolled discretion, considers necessary or desirable to provide for the comfortable support, education, maintenance, benefit and general welfare of each of my children. Such distributions may be made directly to such beneficiary or to the guardian of the person of such beneficiary and without repsonsibilty on my Trustee to see to the application of nay such distributions and in making such distributions, the Trustee shall take into account all other sources of funds known by the Trustee to be available for each respective beneficiary for such purpose.

(e) As each of my respective children attains the age of twenty-five (25) years and provided that both my father and my grandmother are deceased, the trust created hereunder for such child care terminate, and all the remainder of the assets then contained in said trust shall be distributed to such child so attaining the age of twenty-five (25) years outright and free of further trust.

(f) If any of my children for whose benefit a trust has been created hereunder should die before attaining the age of twenty- five (25) years, then the trust created for such a child shall terminate on his death, and all remaining assets then contained in said trust shall be distributed outright and free of further trust and in equal shares to the surviving issue of such deceased child but subject to the provisions of Item V herein; but if there be no such surviving issue, then to the brothers and sisters of such deceased child in equal shares, the issue of any other deceased child being entitled collectively to their deceased parent's share. Nevertheless, if any distribution otherwise becomes payable outright and free of trust under the provisions of this paragraph (f) of the Item IV of my will to a beneficiary for whom the Trustee is then administering a trust for the benefit of such beneficiary under provisions of this last will and testament, such distribution shall not be paid outright to such beneficiary but shall be added to and become a part of the trust so being administered for such beneficiary by the Trustee.

Item V - Distribution to Minor Children

If any share of corpus of any trust established under this will become distributable outright and free of trust to any beneficiary before said beneficiary has attained the age of eighteen (18) years, then said share shall immediately vest in said beneficiary, but the Trustee shall retain possession of such share during the period in which such beneficiary is under the age of eighteen (18) years, and, in the meantime, shall use and expend so much of the income and principal for the care, support, and education of such beneficiary, and any income not so expended with respect to each share so retained all the power and discretion had with respect to such trust generally.

Item VI - Alternate Distributees

In the event that all of my descendants should be deceased at any time prior to the time for the termination of the trusts provided for herein, then in such event all of my estate and all the assets of every trust to be created hereunder (as the case may be) shall then distributed outright in equal shares to my heirs at law per stripes.

Item VII - Unenforceable Provisions

If any provisions of this will are unenforceable, the remaining provisions shall, nevertheless, be carried into effect.

Item VIII - Life Insurance

If my estate is the beneficiary of any life insurance on my life at the time of my death, I direct that the proceeds therefrom will be used by my Executor in payment of the debts , expenses and taxes listed in Item I of this will, to the extent deemed advisable by the Executor. All such proceeds not so used are to be used by my Executor for the purpose of satisfying the devises and bequests contained in Item IV herein.

Item IX - Spendthrift Provision

I direct that the interest of any beneficiary in principal or income of any trust created hereunder shall not be subject to claims of creditors or others, nor to legal process, and may not be voluntarily or involuntarily alienated or encumbered except as herein provided. Any bequests contained herein for any female shall be for her sole and separate use, free from the debts, contracts and control of any husband she may ever have.

Item X - Proceeds From Personal Services

All sums paid after my death (either to my estate or to any of the trusts created hereunder) and resulting from personal services rendered by me during my lifetime, including, but not limited to, royalties of all nature, concerts, motion picture contracts, and personal appearances shall be considered to be income, notwithstanding the provisions of estate and trust law to the contrary.

Item XI - Executor and Trustee

I appoint as executor of this, my last will and testament, and as Trustee of every trust required to be created hereunder, my said father.

I hereby direct that my said father shall be entitled by his last will ant testament, duly probated, to appoint a successor Executor of my estate, as well as a successor Trustee or successor Trustees of all the trusts to be created under my last will and testament.

If, for any reason, my said father be unable to serve or to continue to serve as Executor and/or as Trustee, or if he be deceased and shall not have appointed a successor Executor or Trustee, by virtue of his last will and testament as stated -above, then I appoint National Bank of Commerce, Memphis, Tennessee, or its successor or the institution with which it may merge, as successor Executor and/ or as successor Trustee of all trusts required to be established hereunder.

None of the appointees named hereunder,including any appointment made by virtue of the last will and testament of my said father, shall be required to furnish any bond or security for performance of the respective fiduciary duties required hereunder, notwithstanding any rule of law to the contrary.

Item XII - Powers, Duties, Privileges and Immunities of the Trustee

Except as otherwise stated expressly to the contrary herein, I give and grant to the said Trustee (and to the duly appointed successor Trustee when acting as such) the power to do everything he deems advisable with respect to the administration of each trust required to be established under this, my last will and Testament, even though such powers would not be authorized or appropriate for the Trustee under statutory or other rules of law. By way of illustration and not in limitation of the generality of the foregoing grant of power and authority of the Trustee, I give and grant to him plenary power as follows:

(a) To exercise all those powers authorized to fiduciaries under the provisions of the Tennessee Code Annotated, Sections 35-616 to 35-618, inclusive, including any amendments thereto in effect at the time of my death, and the same are expressly referred to and incorporated herein by reference.

(b) Plenary power is granted to the Trustee, not only to relieve him from seeking judicial instruction, but to the extent that the Trustee deems it to be prudent, to encourage determinations freely to be made in favor of persons who are the current income beneficiaries. In such instances the rights of all subsequent beneficiaries are subordinate, and the Trustee shall not be answerable to any subsequent beneficiary for anything done or omitted in favor of a current income beneficiary may compel any such favorable or preferential treatment. Without in anywise minimizing or impairing the scope of this declaration of intent, it includes investment policy, exercise of discretionary power to pay or apply principal and income, and determination principal and income questions;

(c) It shall be lawful for the Trustee to apply any sum that is payable to or for the benefit of a minor (or any other person who in the Judgment of the Trustee, is incapable of making proper disposition thereof) by payments in discharge of the costs and expenses of educating, maintaining and supporting said beneficiary, or to make payment to anyone with whom said beneficiary resides or who has the care or custody of the beneficiary, temporarily or permanently, all without intervention of any guardian or like fiduciary. The receipt of anyone to whom payment is so authorized to be made shall be a complete discharge of the Trustees without obligation on his part to see to the further application hereto, and without regard to other resource that the beneficiary may have, or the duty of any other person to support the beneficiary;

(d) In Dealing with the Trustee, no grantee, pledge, vendee, mortgage, lessee or other transference of the trust properties, or any part therof, shall be bound to inquire with respect to the purpose or necessity of any such disposition or to see to the application of any consideration therefore paid to the Trustee.

Item XIII - Concerning the Trustee and the Executor

(a) If at any time the Trustee shall have reasonable doubt as to his power, authority or duty in the administration of any trust herein created, it shall be lawful for the Trustee to obtain the advice and counsel of reputable legal counsel without resorting to the courts for instructions; and the Trustee shall be fully absolved from all liability and damage or detriment to the various trust estates of any beneficiary thereunder by reason of anything done, suffered or omitted pursuant to advice of said counsel given and obtained in good faith, provided that nothing contained herein shall be construed to prohibit or prevent the Trustee in all proper cases from applying to a court of competent jurisdiction for instructions in the administration of the trust assets in lieu of obtaining advice of counsel.

(b) In managing, investing, and controlling the various trust estates, the Trustee shall exercise the judgment and care under the circumstances then prevailing, which men of prudence discretion and judgment exercise in the management of their own affairs, not in regard to speculation, but in regard to the permanent disposition of their funds, considering the probable income as well as the probable safety of their capital, and, in addition, the purchasing power of income distribution to beneficiaries.

(c) My Trustee (as well as my Executor) shall be entitled to reasonable and adequate and adequate compensation for the fiduciary services rendered by him.

(d) My Executor and his successor Executor and his successor Executor shall have the same rights, privileges, powers and immunities herein granted to my Trustee wherever appropriate.

(e) In referring to any fiduciary hereunder, for purposes of construction, masculine pronouns may include a corporate fiduciary and neutral pronouns may include an individual fiduciary.

Item XIV - Law Against Perpetuities

(a) Having in mind the rule against perpetuities, I direct that (notwithstanding anything contained to the contrary in this last will and testament) each trust created under this will (except such trust created under this will (except such trusts as have heretofore vested in compliance with such rule or law) shall end, unless sooner terminated under other provisions of this will, twenty-one (21) years after the death of the last survivor of such of the beneficiaries hereunder as are living at the time of my death; and thereupon that the property held in trust shall be distributed free of all trust to the persons then entitled to receive the income and/or principal therefrom, in the proportion in proportion in which they are then entitled to receive such income.

(b) Notwithstanding anything else contained in this will to the contrary, I direct that if any distribution under this will become payable to a person for whom the Trustee is then administering a trust created hereunder for the benefit of such person, such distribution shall be made to such trust and not to the beneficiary outright, and the funds so passing to such trust shall become a part thereof as corpus and be administered and distributed to the same extent and purpose as if such funds had been a part of such a trust at its inception.

Item XV - Payment of Estate and Inheritance Taxes

Notwithstanding the provisions of Item X herein, I authorize my Executor to use such sums received by my estate after my death and resulting from my personal services as identified in Item X as he deem necessary and advisable in order to pay the taxes referred to in Item I of my said will.

In WITNESS WHEREOF, I, the said ELVIS A. PRESLEY, do hereunto set my hand and seal in the presence of two (2) competent witnesses, and in their presence do publish and declare this instrument to be my Last Will and Testament, this 3rd day of March, 1977.

[Signed by Elvis A. Presley]
ELVIS A. PRESLEY

The foregoing instrument, consisting of this and eleven (11) preceding typewritten pages, was signed, sealed, published and declared by ELVIS A.PRESLEY, the Testator, to be his Last Will and Testament, in our presence, and we, at his request and in his presence and in the presence of each other, have hereunto subscribed our names as witnesses, this 3rd day of March, 1977, at Memphis, Tennessee.

[Signed by Ginger Alden]
Ginger Alden residing at 4152 Royal Crest Place

[Signed by Charles F. Hodge]
Charles F. Hodge residing at 3764 Elvis Presley Blvd.

[Signed by Ann Dewey Smith]
Ann Dewey Smith residing at 2237 Court Avenue.
State of Tennessee
County of Shelby

Ginger Alden, Charles F. Hodge, and Ann Dewey Smith, after being first duly sworn, make oath or affirm that the foregoing Last Will and Testament, in the sight and presence of us, the undersigned, who at his request and in his sight and presence, and in the sight and presence of each other, have subscribed our names as attesting witnesses on the 3rd day of March, 1977, and we further make oath or affirm that the Testator was of sound mind and disposing memory and not acting under fraud, menace or undue influence of any person, and was more than eighteen (18) years of age; and that each of the attesting witnesses is more than eighteen (18) years of age.

[Signed by Ginger Alden]
Ginger Alden

[Signed by Charles F. Hodge]
Charles F. Hodge

[Signed by Ann Dewey Smith]
Ann Dewey Smith

Sworn To And Subscribed before me this 3rd day of March, 1977.

Drayton Beecker Smith II Notary Public

My commission expires:

August 8, 1979

Admitted to probate and Ordered Recorded August 22, 1977

Joseph W. Evans, Judge

Recorded August 22, 1977

B.J. Dunavant, Clerk

By: Jan Scott, D.C.

JIM MORRISON
December 8, 1943 — July 3, 1971

Jim Morrison was the lead singer of The Doors, a radically popular rock band of the 1960s. Their iconic song "Light my Fire" is considered by many as one of the best rock-n-roll songs of all time. Many of The Doors' fans have made exceptions to testing the decibel limits of their hearing by cranking up the volume to "Light my Fire" while driving down the freeway, like many did along the I-405 Freeway corridor in southern California. Jim Morrison was an avid reader, and few know that he graduated with a bachelor's degree from the UCLA Film School with a degree in Theater Arts. He was found dead at 27 years old in Paris, France of an apparent drug overdose.

LAST WILL AND TESTAMENT OF JIM MORRISON

I, James D. Morrison, being of sound mind and disposing body, memory and understanding, and after considerations of all persons, the object of my bounty and with full knowledge of the nature and extent of my assets, do hereby make, publish and declare my Last Will and Testament, as follows:

FIRST: I declare that I am a resident of Los Angeles County, California; that I am unmarried and have no children.

SECOND: I direct the payment of all debts and expenses of last illness.

THIRD: I do hereby devise and bequeath each and every thing of value of which I may die possessed, including real property, personal property and mixed properties to PAMELA S. COURSON of Los Angeles County.

In the event the said PAMELA S. COURSON should predecease me, or fail to survive for a period of three months following the date of my death, then and in such event, the devise and bequest to her shall fail and the same is devised and bequeathed instead to my brother, ANDREW MORRISON of

Monterey, California, and to my sister, ANNE R. MORRISON of Coronado Beach, California, and to share and share alike; provided, however, further that in the event either of them should predecease me, then and in such event, the devise and bequest shall go to the other.

FOURTH: I do hereby appoint PAMELA S. COURSON and MAX FINK, jointly, Executors, or

Executor and Executrix, as the case may be, of my estate, giving to said persons, and each of them, full power of appointment of substitution in their place and stead by their Last Will and Testament, or otherwise.

In the event said PAMELA S. COURSON shall survive me and be living at the time of her appointment, then in such event, bond is hereby waived.

I subscribe my name to this Will this 12 day of February, 1969, at Beverly Hills, California.

Signed,
James D. Morrison

JAMES BROWN
May 3, 1933 — December 25, 2006

James Brown, Performing in Hamburg, Germany
Photo by Heinrich Klaffs/Licensed by www. creativecommons.org

The Godfather of Soul and Funk

James Brown created his Last Will in the year 2000. When he died on December 25, 2006, his estate plan was revealed. To the shock and disappointment of his relatives, he left his $100 million estate to a special trust to help poor and needy children. Brown's worldwide music empire included copyrights to over 800 songs and the rights to his image. His Last Will, with a charitable Testamentary Trust was carefully drafted by very competent legal minds. The trust left most of Brown's assets to the "I Feel Good" Trust, an educational charity established to benefit South Carolina and Georgia students in need. It was a very generous gift by James Brown who understood the stark difficulty of growing up in poverty in the South.

Matters were not going to remain smooth for long with the Brown Estate. Litigation promptly erupted between and among family members and blood relatives, and against the $100 million plus fortune Brown left to the special trust to help the needy. Unfortunately, even with a well-constructed estate plan, litigation tied up the estate for years. The litigation has tied up the distribution of any funds to the stated beneficiaries designated personally by James Brown in his Last Will and Charitable Testamentary Trust.

Although James Brown had a valid Will in place when he died on December 25, 2006, he failed to update it. His existing Will did not reflect his most recent marriage, and it did not mention his youngest child, James Brown II. As for family, James Brown officially had fathered at least nine children at the time of his death. He also had three ex-wives, and a woman who may or may not have been his widow. This person, Ms. Tomi Rae Hynie, was technically still married to another man when she tied the knot with James Brown (although her marriage to the other man was purportedly later annulled). Ms. Hynie also had a child named James Brown II, but the child's lineage to James Brown as the father had not been determined through DNA analysis. So, although Brown was married to Ms. Hynie for five years until he died, all the while never updating his Will or Testamentary Trust during those five years of marriage, some relatives raised the argument that maybe James Brown did not want to include Hynie or his new son in his Will.

Then, in early 2009, the legal wrangling over the estate seemed to be reaching a possible resolution, guided in large part by the legal intervention of the South Carolina Attorney General's Office. This is very unusual to see state government getting involved. In a private probate setting, does the state's Attorney General have standing to intervene? The involvement by Attorney General Henry McMaster included brokering the settlement in 2009 among the interested parties. What was the state's stake in James Brown's Will? In the settlement agreement, the South Carolina Attorney General and the family struck a settlement deal, giving the family a 50 percent share in the estate. The deal seemed odd for a state Attorney General to override the wishes of a Decedent under his Will, and to otherwise cut a deal with different relatives to restructure the distribution of funds in contravention of the designations by the Decedent, James Brown. But it soon became more apparent by many that the Attorney General's intervention to strike a deal was purportedly done to gain political favor among African-American voters. The James Brown Estate and the story swirling around about his wealth and his generous intentions were big news in the South. But in the deal, the charitable trust was effectively cut out of 50 percent of the wealth that James Brown had gifted to it. That 50 percent portion taken from the trust was split between Ms. Hynie, as the surviving spouse, and the children. Specifically, Ms. Hynie would receive one-fourth of the Brown estate, and the other one-fourth would be split equally among all the children, including James Brown II (Ms. Hynie's son).

The tentative settlement was appealed by two of Brown's former trustees, who had been removed from administering the charitable Trust by the probate court's decision to approve the settlement. The former trustees argued that Brown's intent was clear. He wanted his assets to fund a Trust for needy children, and that the Trust and the Trust estate was never found to be invalid.

So how could a post-mortem agreement trump the intent of the Testator? In February 2013, the South Carolina Supreme Court agreed, and overturned the 2009 settlement that split up the multimillion-dollar estate of James Brown. The Court stated that the former Attorney General could not rule over what James Brown wanted to do with his assets.[75] So, the South Carolina Supreme Court voided the state's settlement due to "*the*

---

75. Wilson v. Dallas, 743 S.E. 2d 746 (2013). The case originally dealt with and was captioned as: In re The Estate of James Brown and The James Brown 2000 Irrevocable Trust u/a/d August 1, 2000. Regarding the parties, Alan Wilson is the named Plaintiff in the appellate cases. He was the Attorney General of South Carolina at the time, who had intervened in the probated estate. Albert H. Dallas, the named Defendant in the appellate cases, was one of the purported Trustees of the James Brown 2000 Irrevocable Trust. It is quite remarkable that it had to take the highest court in South Carolina to literally scold an Attorney General that even in his official capacity, he could not just intervene into a probated case (no legitimate party in standing), and attempt to rule (settle with parties) against the wishes of a decedent concerning the disposition of his own assets as documented in a legitimate and legal Last Will and Testamentary Trust.

government's unprecedented encroachment into estate administration…"[76] and remanded the case to the Aiken County Circuit Court, with the idea that the parties abide by the terms of the original Will. By February 2015, the Aiken County Circuit Court ruled that Tomi Rae Hynie was James Brown legitimate wife. Therefore, she was entitled to a portion of the estate. The court additionally ruled that James Brown was of sound mind when he made his Will before dying of heart failure on Christmas Day 2006, at age 73. That meant, essentially, that his Last Will and charitable Trust were valid instruments to be followed by the Brown estate. Immediately, the South Carolina Supreme Court took the unusual step in staying all further actions of the Circuit Court while the Supreme Court evaluated the case.[77] Since the death of James Brown in 2006, his estate continues to remain hung up in the courts even though his Will and Charitable "I Feel Good" Irrevocable Trust are legitimate and clearly show James Brown's intent to dedicate most of his assets to charity.[78] As of mid-2018, the matter remains stayed.

---

76. Id. at 768 (Concurring opinion)
77. *See,* "SC Supreme Court Freezes James Brown estate case," The Associated Press (Updated Feb 27, 2015)
78. *See below,* Will of James Brown, dated Aug. 1, 2000.

LAST WILL
OF
JAMES BROWN

H. Dewain Herring, Esquire
Law Offices of H. Dewain Herring, LLC
3612 Landmark Dr., Suite A
Columbia, South Carolina 29204

LAST WILL AND TESTAMENT
OF
JAMES BROWN

Introductory Clause

ITEM I

General Bequest of Personal and Household Effects With a Mandatory Memorandum

ITEM II

Pour-Over Gift to Trustee of Testator's Inter Vivos Trust

ITEM III

Alternate Provision to Incorporate Trust by Reference if Pour-Over is Invalid

ITEM IV

Naming the Personal Representative, Personal Representative Succession, Personal
Representative's Fees and Other Matters
Naming Individuals as Personal Representative
Individual Personal Representatives Succession
Fee Schedule for Individual Personal Representative
Personal Representative Voting Rights

ITEM V

Definition of Personal Representative

ITEM VI

Powers for Personal Representative

ITEM VII

Definition of Words Relating to the Internal Revenue Code

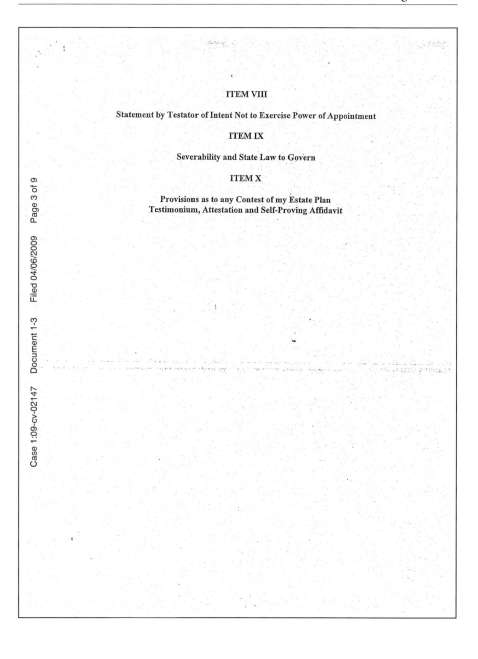

ITEM VIII

Statement by Testator of Intent Not to Exercise Power of Appointment

ITEM IX

Severability and State Law to Govern

ITEM X

Provisions as to any Contest of my Estate Plan
Testimonium, Attestation and Self-Proving Affidavit

LAST WILL AND TESTAMENT
OF
JAMES BROWN

Introductory Clause. I, *James Brown*, also known as "The Godfather of Soul", a resident of and domiciled in the Community of Beech Island, County of Aiken and State of South Carolina, do hereby make, publish and declare this to be my Last Will and Testament, hereby revoking all Wills and Codicils at any time heretofore made by me.

I have six living children: *Deanna J. Brown Thomas*; *Yamma N. Brown*; *Vanisha Brown*; *Daryl J. Brown*; *Larry Brown*; and *Terry Brown*. These named children and any of their legitimate issue who shall also be lineage issue of mine shall be the entire class that I acknowledge to be my heirs and issue. Except as otherwise provided in this Will and corresponding instruments, I have intentionally failed to provide for any other relatives or other persons, whether claiming, or to claim, to be an heir of mine or not. Such failure is intentional and not occasioned by accident or mistake.

ITEM I

General Bequest of Personal and Household Effects With a Mandatory Memorandum. I give and bequeath all my personal and household effects of every kind including but not limited to furniture, appliances, furnishings, pictures, silverware, china, glass, books, jewelry, wearing apparel, boats, automobiles, and other vehicles, and all policies of fire, burglary, property damage, and other insurance on or in connection with the use of this property, as follows:

(1) I may leave written memoranda disposing of certain items of my tangible personal property. Any such item of tangible personal property shall pass according to the terms of such memoranda in existence at the time of my death. If no such written memoranda is found or identified by my Personal Representative within ninety (90) days after my Personal Representative's qualification, it shall be conclusively presumed that there is no such memoranda and any subsequently discovered memoranda shall be ineffective. Any property given and devised to a beneficiary who is not living at the time of my death and for whom no effective alternate provision has been made shall pass according to the provisions of the following paragraph, and not pursuant to any anti-lapse statute.

(2) In default of such memoranda, or to the extent such memoranda do not completely or effectively dispose of such property, I give and bequeath the rest of my personal and household effects of every kind to my children surviving me in approximately equal shares; provided, however, the issue of a deceased child surviving me shall take per stirpes the share their parent would have taken had he or she survived me. If my issue do not agree to the division of the property among themselves, my Personal Representative shall make such division among

Last Will and Testament of James Brown
c:\6010.1\last will J. Brown FNL2

them, the decision of my Personal Representative to be in all respects binding upon my issue. If any beneficiary hereunder is a minor, my Personal Representative may distribute such minor's share to such minor or for such minor's use to any person with whom such minor is residing or who has the care or control of such minor without further responsibility and the receipt of the person to whom it is distributed shall be a complete discharge of my Personal Representative. The cost of packing and shipping such property shall be charged against my estate as an expense of administration.

ITEM II

Pour-Over Gift to Trustee of Testator's Inter Vivos Trust. I give, devise and bequeath all the rest, residue and remainder of my property of every kind and description (including lapsed legacies and devises), wherever situate and whether acquired before or after the execution of this Will, to *Alford A. Bradley, Albert H. Dallas, David G. Cannon* as Trustee(s) under that certain Irrevocable Trust Agreement between me as Grantor and *Alford A. Bradley, Albert H. Dallas, David G. Cannon* as Trustee(s) executed prior to or of even date with the execution of this Will. My Trustees shall add the property bequeathed and devised by this Item to the principal of the above Trust and shall hold, administer and distribute the property in accordance with the provisions of the Irrevocable Trust Agreement including any amendments made solely by the Trustee(s), if any had to be made to carry out the terms of said Trust.

ITEM III

Alternate Provision to Incorporate Trust by Reference if Pour-Over is Invalid. In the event for any reason the bequest and devise above is ineffective and invalid, then I hereby give, devise and bequeath the rest, residue and remainder of my property of every kind and description (including lapsed legacies and devises), wherever situate and whether acquired before or after the execution of this Will, to *Alford A. Bradley, Albert H. Dallas, David G. Cannon* as Trustee(s) to be held, administered and distributed in accordance with the provisions of that certain Trust Agreement between me as Grantor and *Alford A. Bradley, Albert H. Dallas, David G. Cannon* as Trustee(s) executed prior to or of even date with the execution of this Will, which Irrevocable Trust Agreement is hereby incorporated by reference and made a part hereof the same as if the entire Trust Agreement were set forth herein, including any amendments thereto made solely by the Trustee(s), if any had to be made to carry out the terms of said Trust.

ITEM IV

Naming the Personal Representative, Personal Representative Succession, Personal Representative's Fees and Other Matters. The provisions for naming the Personal Representative, Personal Representative succession, Personal Representative's fees and other matters are set forth below:

(1)   **Naming Individuals as Personal Representative.** I hereby nominate, constitute and appoint as Personal Representatives of this my Last Will and Testament *Alford A. Bradley, Albert H. Dallas, David G. Cannon*, and direct that they shall serve without bond.

(2)   **Individual Personal Representatives Succession.** If any of the three (3) individual Personal Representative should fail to qualify as Personal Representative hereunder, dies, or for any reason should cease to act in such capacity, the remaining Personal Representative(s) shall continue to serve and shall elect and/or appoint another Representative so that at all times there are three (3) individual Personal Representative(s) serving. If the Personal Representatives are unable to come to such agreement as to a successor then they are obligated to seek the advise of the Advisory Board Members set out in that certain Advisory Board document signed and dated of even date with this Will, if there is a then recognized Board in effect. If the Advisory Board is unable to persuade the remaining Personal Representative(s) to reach an election or appointment, then, absent an agreement the court having jurisdiction over this Will shall then appoint the remaining individual Personal Representative who shall also serve without bond.

(3)   **Fee Schedule for Individual Personal Representative.** For its services as Personal Representative, the individual Personal Representative shall receive reasonable compensation for the services rendered and reimbursement for reasonable expenses.

(4)   **Personal Representative Voting Rights.** If there is more than one Personal Representative serving, then the vote of the Personal Representatives for any action hereunder must be by majority action of the Personal Representatives.

ITEM V

Definition of Personal Representative. Whenever the word "Personal Representative" or any modifying or substituted pronoun therefor is used in this my Will, such words and respective pronouns shall include both the singular and the plural, the masculine, feminine and neuter gender thereof, and shall apply equally to the Personal Representative named herein and to any successor or substitute Personal Representative acting hereunder, and such successor or substitute Personal Representative shall possess all the rights, powers and duties, authority and responsibility conferred upon the Personal Representative originally named herein.

Last Will and Testament of James Brown
c:\6010.1\last will J. Brown FNL2

ITEM VI

Powers for Personal Representative. By way of illustration and not of limitation and in addition to any inherent, implied or statutory powers granted to Personal Representatives generally, my Personal Representative is specifically authorized and empowered with respect to any property, real or personal, at any time held under any provision of this my Will: to allot, allocate between principal and income, assign, borrow, buy, care for, collect, compromise claims, contract with respect to, continue any business of mine, convey, convert, deal with, dispose of, enter into, exchange, hold, improve, incorporate any business of mine, invest, lease, loan, manage, mortgage, grant and exercise options with respect to, take possession of, pledge, receive, release, repair, sell, sue for, to make distributions or divisions in cash or in kind or partly in each without regard to the income tax basis of such asset, and in general, to exercise all the powers in the management of my Estate which any individual could exercise in the management of similar property owned in his or her own right, upon such terms and conditions as to my Personal Representative may seem best, and to execute and deliver any and all instruments and to do all acts which my Personal Representative may deem proper or necessary to carry out the purposes of this my Will, without being limited in any way by the specific grants of power made, and without the necessity of a court order.

ITEM VII

Definition of Words Relating to the Internal Revenue Code. As used herein, the words "gross estate," "adjusted gross estate," "taxable estate," "unified credit," "state death tax credit," "maximum marital deduction," "marital deduction," "pass," and any other word or words which from the context in which it or they are used refer to the Internal Revenue Code shall have the same meaning as such words have for the purposes of applying the Internal Revenue Code to my estate. For purposes of this Will, my "available generation-skipping transfer exemption" means the generation-skipping transfer tax exemption provided in section 2631 of the Internal Revenue Code of 1986, as amended, in effect at the time of my death reduced by the aggregate of (1) the amount, if any, of my exemption allocated to lifetime transfers of mine by me or by operation of law, and (2) the amount, if any, I have specifically allocated to other property of my gross estate for federal estate tax purposes. For purposes of this Will if at the time of my death I have made gifts with an inclusion ratio of greater than zero for which the gift tax return due date has not expired (including extensions) and I have not yet filed a return, it shall be deemed that my generation-skipping transfer exemption has been allocated to these transfers to the extent necessary (and possible) to exempt the transfer(s) from generation-skipping transfer tax. Reference to sections of the Internal Revenue Code and to the Internal Revenue Code shall refer to the Internal Revenue Code amended to the date of my death.

Last Will and Testament of James Brown
e:\6010.1\last will J. Brown FNL2

ITEM VIII

Statement by Testator of Intent Not to Exercise Power of Appointment. I hereby refrain from exercising any power of appointment that I may have at the time of my death.

ITEM IX

Severability and State Law to Govern. If any part of this Will shall be invalid, illegal or inoperative for any reason, it is my intention that the remaining parts, so far as possible and reasonable, shall be effective and fully operative. Regardless of the situs of execution of this Will, it is acknowledged that it is deemed to have been executed in conformity with and shall be construed, regulated and governed by and in accordance with the laws of the State of South Carolina.

ITEM X

Provisions as to any Contest of My Estate Plan. Should any beneficiary under this Will or my Irrevocable Trust, and as amended, dated prior to or of even date with this Will and as referred to herein, become an adverse party in a proceeding for the probate of my Will or in any manner contest the validity of my Irrevocable Trust, such beneficiary shall forfeit his or her entire interest thereunder and such interest shall pass to such other beneficiaries as would be entitled to take as if such beneficiary predeceased me. Furthermore, any person not provided for in this Will, my Irrevocable Trust or other such instrument, whether or not claiming to be a beneficiary or party in interest, shall not have standing or be qualified to contest, claim an interest in or otherwise dispute the disposition of my estate, as I herewith disclaim and disinherit any such persons. Any such alleged claim shall be considered an affront to my wishes and shall be challenged as such by my fiduciaries.

END OF PAGE
SEE NEXT PAGE FOR EXECUTION

Testimonium, Attestation and Self-Proving Affidavit. I, *James Brown*, the Testator, sign my name to this instrument this ___/___ day of __AUGUST_____, 2000, and being first duly sworn, do hereby declare to the undersigned authority that I sign and execute this instrument as my Last Will and that I sign it willingly (or willingly direct another to sign for me), that I execute it as my free and voluntary act for the purposes therein expressed, and that I am eighteen years of age or older, of sound mind (with the capacity to understand the nature of my act, to know my property, and to remember and recollect the natural objects of my bounty), and under no constraint or undue influence.

_____(Seal)
James Brown, Testator

We, the witnesses, sign our names to this instrument, being first duly sworn, and do hereby declare to the undersigned authority that the Testator signs and executes this instrument as his last will and that he signs it willingly (or willingly directs another to sign for him), and that each of us, in the presence and hearing of the Testator, and in the presence of each other, hereby signs this will as witness to the Testator's signing, and that to the best of our knowledge the Testator is eighteen years of age or older, of sound mind (with the capacity to understand the nature of his act, to know his property, and to remember and recollect the natural objects of his bounty), and under no constraint or undue influence.

_____(Seal)
(Witness)

_____(Seal)
(Witness)

The State of _South Carolina_ GEORGIA ___)
County of _Aiken 784_ RICHMOND ___)   Probate

Subscribed, sworn to, and acknowledged before me by *James Brown*, the Testator, and subscribed and sworn to before me by the above signed witnesses, this _1st_ day of _August_____, 2000.

_____(Seal)

Notary Public for __S C_____

My Commission Expires: __3/17/2010__

Last Will and Testament of James Brown
e:\6010.1\last will J. Brown FNL2

ANNA NICOLE SMITH
November 28, 1976 — February 8, 2007

> *Death is not the end. There remains the litigation over the estate.*
>
> UNKNOWN

Anna Nicole Smith (born Vickie Lynn Hogan, then later assuming the name Vickie Lynn Marshall after her marriage to oil tycoon J. Howard Marshall) left her entire estate to Howard Stern to be held in trust for the benefit of her son, Daniel Wayne Smith. Unfortunately, her son predeceased her. Moreover, Anna Nicole Smith's Last Will and Testament made no provision for other heirs.[79]

Ms. Smith was still attempting to gain the estate of her late husband when she died in 2007. She met her wealthy 87-year-old husband, J. Howard Marshall, in 1991 at a Houston, Texas strip club. Mr. Marshall was an oil tycoon billionaire. Ms. Smith was 24 years old at the time and was employed as a nude dancer at the strip club called Gigi's Cabaret. After a lap dance from Ms. Smith, a romance began that soon turned into marriage, notwithstanding the 63-year age difference. Mr. Marshall died just 13 months later. Despite the new marriage, however, Mr. Marshall's Will did not pass any assets to Ms. Smith. So, she went to court demanding a portion of his $1.6 billion estate on multiple grounds, including tortious interference with an expected inheritance by Mr. Marshall's son. The litigation was substantial, with each higher or different court seemingly contradicting the decisions establishing the division of assets. Up until the U.S. Supreme Court, they included:[80]

---

79. *See below*, Last Will and Testament of Vicki Lynn Marshall, dated Jul. 30, 2001.
80. Biography.com, "Anna Nicole Smith Biography," A&E Television Networks, Apr. 2, 2014, Updated Apr. 27, 2017, URL: https://www.biography.com/people/anna-nicole-smith-183547

- The Bankruptcy Court awarding Ms. Smith $474 million.

- The Federal District Court vacating the Bankruptcy Court's decision and ruling that she was entitled to only $88 million.

- The Texas Probate Court subsequently ruling that Ms. Smith was entitled to nothing.

- The 9th Circuit Court of Appeals vacating the Federal District Court decision, declaring that only the Texas Probate Court had jurisdiction. [81]

Finally, the U.S. Supreme Court got involved in the case. In *Marshall v. Marshall*, 547 U.S. 293 (2006), Ms. Smith prevailed by unanimous decision in the argument that federal courts had jurisdiction over her claim. But five years later, in *Stern v. Marshall*, 564 U.S. 462 (2011), the U.S. Supreme Court, in a narrow 5 to 4 decision, ruled that she was not entitled to the court recoveries that had been previously awarded to her by a lower court. Finally, after two decades of contentious litigation, a ruling in July 2015 by the Court of Appeals for the First District in Houston ended the chance for any recovery by Ms. Smith's estate.[82]

Anna Nicole Smith bore a daughter in 2007, named Danielynn, but then Ms. Smith died just five months later of a drug overdose at age 39.[83] She also lost her 20-year-old son to a drug overdose while he was visiting her in the hospital in September 2006.[84]

---

81. Marshall v. Marshall, 392 F. 3d 1118 (9th Cir. 2004).
82. Fisher, D. (2015, July 14). Court Ruling Likely Ends Anna Nicole Smith Estate's Fight For Marshall Family Millions. Retrieved April 21, 2017, from, https://www.forbes.com/sites/danielfisher/2015/07/14/texas-appeals-court-reverses-sanctions-against-anna-nicole-smith-estate/#54b4ea691a7e
83. "Anna Nicole Smith Dies at 39," Abby Goodnough and Margalit Fox, The New York Times (Feb. 8, 2007).
84. "Anna Nicole Smith's Adult Son Dies in Bahamas," Associated Press (Sept. 12, 2006).

Ms. Smith's Last Will was created in July 2001. It named her son Daniel as the sole beneficiary of her estate, and specifically excluded other children from any inheritance. After her daughter, Danielynn, was born in 2007, Ms. Smith failed to update her Last Will to eliminate the disinheritance of later-born children, which included Danielynn (*See,* Article 1 of her Will below regarding "Family Declarations and Statutory Disinheritance." The Will named Howard K. Stern as the Executor.[85]

A petition to probate Ms. Smith's Will was filed in Los Angeles County Superior Court in 2007. It indicated personal property valued at $10,000 and real property valued at $1.8 million (with a $1.1 million mortgage) at the time of death. The petition for probate listed Larry Birkhead as a party in interest to Ms. Smith's estate. He was Ms. Smith's former boyfriend. Mr. Larry Birkhead subsequently presented the court with the results of a paternity test, which evidenced that he was the real father of Danielynn, and not Mr. Stern. Therefore, the court awarded the entire estate of Anna Nicole Smith to her surviving daughter, Danielynn, with Mr. Birkhead appointed by the court as guardian for Danielynn.[86] It was fortunate to see in this case that a paternity test overcame the disinheritance clause in Ms. Smith's Will, affording baby Danielynn the rights to her mother's estate.

---

85. See below, Last Will and Testament of Vicki Lynn Marshall, dated Jul. 30, 2001.
86. Hall, S. (2007, June 19). Stern and Birkhead Work Together for Anna Nicole. Retrieved June 18, 2017, from, https://www.eonline.com/news/55436/stern-and-birkhead-work-together-for-anna-nicole

LAST WILL AND TESTAMENT OF VICKIE LYNN MARSHALL

I, VICKIE LYNN MARSHALL, also known as Vickie Lynn Smith, and Vickie Lynn Hogan, and Anna Nicole Smith, a resident of Los Angeles County, California, declare that this is my Will. I revoke all prior Wills and Codicils. I hereby dispose of all property that I am entitled to dispose of by Will and exercise all general powers of appointment that I am entitled to exercise. I have not entered into a contract to make or not revoke a Will.

1.

ARTICLE I

FAMILY DECLARATIONS AND STATUTORY DISINHERITANCE

I am unmarried. I have one child DANIEL WAYNE SMITH. I have no predeceased children nor predeceased children leaving issue.

Except as otherwise provided in this Will, I have intentionally omitted to provide for my spouse and other heirs, including future spouses and children and other descendants now living and those hereafter born or adopted, as well as existing and future stepchildren and foster children.

* END OF ARTICLE *

2.

ARTICLE II

DISPOSITION OF ESTATE

All of the property of my estate (the "residue"), after payment of any taxes or other expenses of my estate as provided below, including property subject to a power of appointment exercised hereby, shall be distributed to HOWARD STERN, ESQ., to hold in trust for my child under such terms as he and a court of competent jurisdiction may declare, such that my children are distributed sufficient sums for the health, education, and support according to their accustomed manner of living from either the income or principal of the trust until age twenty-five; and are at that time given one-third of all of the income of the trust and one-third of the principal of the trust as then constituted; and at thirty are given one-half of the income from the trust and one-half of the principal of the trust as then constituted; and at thirty-five are given all of the principal of the trust. If, in the discretion of the Trustee, the amount remaining in the Trust is too small to efficiently administer, he may give all of the corpus of the Trust to my child at once.

* END OF ARTICLE *

3.

ARTICLE III

PROVISIONS REGARDING EXECUTORS

3.1 Nomination of Executor.

I nominate as Executor and as successor Executors of this Will those named below. Each successor Executor shall serve in the order and priority designated if the prior designated Executor fails to qualify or ceases to act.

First:
HOWARD STERN, ESQ.

Second:
RON RALE, ESQ.

Third:
ERIC JAMES LUND, ESQ.

Fourth:
Wells Fargo Bank (Sandra K. Von

Paul) or its successors by merger, consolidation, or otherwise.

3.2 Power to Nominate Executor.

If all of the foregoing Executors are unable or unwilling to act, the majority of the adult beneficiaries under this Will shall have the power to designate as successor Executor any corporate fiduciary having assets under management of at least Two Hundred Fifty Million Dollars ($250,000,000). Such designation shall be filed with the court in which this Will is probated.

3.3. Waiver of Bond.

I request that no bond be required of any Executor nominated above, including nonresidents, whether such Executor is acting alone or together with another.

3.4. Powers of Executor.

My Executor shall have the following powers in addition to all powers now or hereafter conferred by law, and except as otherwise expressly provided, shall have the broadest and most absolute permissible discretion in exercising all powers. I intend and direct that the probate court uphold any action taken by my Executor, absent clear and convincing evidence of bad faith or gross negligence.

3.4.1. Independent Administration.

My Executor may administer my estate with full authority under the California Independent Administration of Estates Act.

3.4.2. Tax Elections and Decisions.

My Executor may value my gross estate for federal estate tax purposes as of the date of my death or any permissible alternate valuation date, my claim any items of expense as income or estate

3.4.3. Disclaimers.

My Executor may disclaim all or any portion of any bequest, devise or trust interest provided for me under any Will or Trust. In particular, I authorize and encourage my Executor to try to obtain overall tax savings, even though this may change the ultimate recipients of the property that is disclaimed.

3.4.4. Limitations on Tax Elections and Decisions.

No person serving as Executor for federal tax purposes, hereunder or pursuant to the terms of the Trust, shall have authority to make or participate in any tax election or decision if the power to do so would result in his or her having a general power of appointment (for federal gift and estate tax purposes) over property with respect to which he or she would (or might) not otherwise have such a general power, and in such event such authority shall pass to the next successor fiduciary who is not so disqualified.

3.4.5. Management and Administrative Powers of Executor.

Subject to any express limitation stated elsewhere in this will, I hereby grant to my Executor all administrative powers that may legally be granted to an Executor under California law as of the date of my death, including, without limitation and to the extent that I am permitted to do so by California law. Without limiting any of the foregoing, I specifically provide that my Executor shall have the broadest and most unrestricted powers to sell, lease or retain any property, make investments, make tax elections and tax oriented decisions, defer distributions, retain professional advisors and compensate them from my estate, or continue or restructure any business. I also direct that my Executor obtain court approval only as my Executor deems appropriate or if such approval is required by law despite any provision in a Will purporting to eliminate the need for such approval, it being my desire that, whenever possible, my Executor rely on Notices of Proposed Action or Waivers of Notice and Consents, unless my Executor desires court approval.

3.5. Resignation of Executor.

My Executor may resign at any time (a) by filing a written instrument with the court having jurisdiction over my estate, or (b) by giving written notice to all successor Executors.

3.6. Successor Executors.

All authority, titles and powers of the original Executor shall automatically pass to a successor Executor. A successor Executor may accept as correct or contest any accounting made by any predecessor Executor; provided that a successor Executor shall be obligated to inquire into the propriety of any act or omission of a predecessor if so requested in writing by a Trustee of the Trust, any Protector of the Trust, or any adult beneficiary or the guardian of a minor beneficiary of the Trust within ninety (90) days of the date that the successor is appointed.

3.7. Liability of Executor.

No Executor, other than a corporate Executor, shall be liable to any person interested in my estate for any act or default of my Executor or any other person, or for any obligation of my estate, unless it results from my Executor's own bad faith, willful misconduct, or gross negligence. My estate shall indemnify my Executor from any liability with respect to which my Executor is held harmless pursuant to the preceding sentence. I specifically indemnify my Executor, including any corporate Executor, from any personal liability for any clean-up costs relating to property held in my estate that contains toxic substances, and direct that any such clean-up costs be paid from my estate in proportion to its interest in the toxic property. Furthermore, if my Executor suspects that property held in my estate may present toxic clean-up problems, my Executor may obtain an environmental assessment, and my estate shall pay for such assessment. Prior to appointment, a nominated Executor may obtain court authority for such assessment, and be reimbursed from the residue of my estate therefor. Such assessment shall also be obtained before any purchase of any property by my estate if my Executor suspects toxic contamination, the cost of such assessment to be paid from my estate.

3.8. Executor's Authority to Transfer to Trust.

I hereby authorize my Executor (or the person nominated to serve as Executor even if no Letters Testamentary are issued) to transfer to the Trustee of the Trust any asset and to execute any document in connection with any such transfer to the extent necessary or appropriate to carry out any assignment of assets to the Trust.

3.9. Co-Executors.

If more than one person is serving as Executor, one Executor acting alone may transfer securities and execute all documents in connection therewith; open accounts with one or more bank and savings and loan associations; authorize deposit or withdrawal of funds to or from accounts; and sign checks. Transfer agents, corporations and financial institutions dealing with a single Executor as provided in the preceding sentence shall have no liability as a consequence of dealing with only one Executor. My Executor may delegate any ministerial duties to any Co-Executor.

* END OF ARTICLE *

4.

ARTICLE IV

GENERAL PROVISIONS

4.1 No Interest.

No interest shall be paid on any gift hereunder, except to the extent necessary to qualify for the marital deduction.

4.2. Life Insurance Policies.

4.2.1. Collection of Proceeds.

Upon the death of any person insured under a policy of insurance payable to my Executor, my Executor may exercise any option provided in the policy, and receive all sums due under the terms of the policy. To facilitate receipt of such sums, my Executor may execute receipts and other instruments, and compromise disputed claims; provided, however, that if payment of a claim is contested, my Executor shall not be obligated to take any action for collection until my Executor has been personally indemnified to my Executor's satisfaction against any liability or expense, including attorney's fees; provided, further, that my Executor may use any funds in my Executor's hands to pay the expenses, including attorney's fees, to collect the proceeds of a policy, and may reimburse himself, herself or itself for advances made for this purpose. No insurance company shall have any obligation to inquire into the application of the proceeds of any policy. Upon payment to my Executor of the amounts due under a policy, an insurance company shall be relieved of all further liability thereunder.

4.3. Construction.

4.3.1. Number and Gender.

In all matters of interpretation, the masculine, feminine and neuter shall each include the other, as the context indicates, and the singular shall include the plural and vice versa.

4.3.2. Headings.

The headings in this Will are inserted for convenient reference and shall be ignored in interpreting this Will.

4.3.3. Severability of Provisions.

If any provision hereof is unenforceable, the remaining provisions shall remain in full effect.

4.4. Governing Law.

The validity, interpretation, and administration of this Will shall be governed by the laws of the State of California in force from time to time.

* END OF ARTICLE *

5.

ARTICLE V

TAXES AND OTHER EXPENSES OF MY ESTATE

5.1. Payment from Trust.

All federal estate and other death taxes imposed and all expenses and charges incidental thereto, shall be payable by the Executor out of the residue of the estate, without charge against or reimbursement from any beneficiary; but excluding the taxes referred to in the following subsections 5.1.1. through 5.1.13 below, which shall be paid as provided below.

The foregoing taxes excluded from payment from the Residuary Amount shall be charged against and paid from the property and interests with respect to which such taxes are imposed, or by the recipients or owners of such property and interests within thirty (30) days after a written demand from the Trustee, as the Trustee deems appropriate. Except as otherwise provided above with respect to certain of the taxes imposed by the Code, the amounts to be paid pursuant to the preceding sentence shall be computed on a pro-rata basis based on the ratio of (a) the value for federal estate tax purposes of the property and interests with respect to which such taxes are imposed, to (b) the value of the my taxable Estate for federal estate tax purposes, multiplied by (c) the sum of the total estate and other death taxes payable, i.e (a/b) x c. Notwithstanding the foregoing, none of the taxes listed in Subsections 5.1.1 through 5.1.13 above shall be payable (directly or indirectly) by or from a gift to or in trust for the Survivor if the effect of such payment would be to cause an increase in the overall death taxes payable by reason of my death nor shall any such taxes be payable (directly or indirectly) by or from a gift to any charitable entity if the effect of such payment would be to reduce the charitable deduction allowable to my Estate.

5..1..2. Any additional taxes under Section 2032A(c) of the Code, which shall be paid or bonded by the recipients of the property subject to special use valuation as provided in Section 2032A(c)(5);

5..1..2. Any tax under Section 2036 of the Code caused by my retaining any interest subject to Section 2036 of the Code, which shall be paid as provided in Section 2207B of the Code;

5..1..3. Any taxes under Section 2039 of the Code;

5..1..4. Any tax under Section 2041 of the Code caused by my possession of a general power of appointment not validly exercised by me during my lifetime or in this Will, imposed upon or in relation to any property or interest therein included in my gross estate for federal estate tax purposes, which shall be paid as provided in Section 2207 of the Code;

5..1..5. Any tax under Section 2042 of the Code with respect to any policy of insurance if the Deceased Trustor did not possess the right to change the beneficiary of such policy on the date of my death, which shall be paid as provided in Section 2206 of the Code;

5..1..6. Any taxes under Section 2056A(b) of the Code, which shall be computed and paid as provided in Section 2056A(b) of the Code;

5..1..7. Any taxes caused by failure to make a full election under Section 2056(b)(7) of the Code with respect to any portion of the Marital Gift. Such taxes shall be paid from the portion of the Marital Gift as to which such election is not made or from any separate Trust created to hold such portion;

5..1..8. Any generation-skipping transfer taxes under Section 2601 et seq. of the Code, which shall be computed as provided in Section 2601 et seq. of the Code and be paid as provided in Section 2603 of the Code;

5..1..9. Any taxes under Section 2701 et seq. of the Code;

5..1..10. Any tax under Section 4980A(d) of the Code.

5..1..11. Any tax caused by my possession of a vested reversion or remainder interest that has been deferred under Section 6163 of the Code; and,

5..1..12. Any state death tax imposed on property subject to the taxes described in Subsections 5.1.1. through 5.1.13 above.

ARTICLE VI

NO CONTEST; DISINHERITANCE

6.1. Contestants Disinherited.

If any legal heir of mine, any person claiming under any such heir, or any other person, in any manner, directly or indirectly, contests or attacks this Will or the Trust or any of the provisions of said instruments, or conspires with or assists anyone in any such contest, or pursues any creditor's claim that my Executor reasonably deems to constitute a contest, any share or interest in my estate or the Trust is revoked and shall be disposed of as if the contesting beneficiary had predeceased me without descendants, and shall augment proportionately the shares of my estate passing to or in trust for my beneficiaries who have not participated in such acts. This Article shall not apply to a disclaimer. Expenses to resist a contest or other attack of any nature shall be paid from my estate as expenses of administration.

6.2. General Disinheritance.

Except as otherwise provided herein and in the Trust, I have intentionally omitted to provide for any of my heirs, or persons claiming to be my heirs, whether or not known to me.

* END OF ARTICLE *

7.

ARTICLE VII

OFFICE OF GUARDIAN

7.1. Nomination of Guardian of the Person.

I nominate HOWARD STERN as guardian and successor guardian of the person of my minor child DANIEL WAYNE SMITH:

Any such nominee who is a resident of a state other than California may, at the nominee's election, file a petition for appointment in such other state and/or in California. I request that any court having jurisdiction permit the guardian to change the residence and domicile of my minor children to the jurisdiction where the guardian resides.

I give the guardian of the person of my minor children the same authority as a parent having legal custody and authorize the guardian to exercise such authority without need for notice, hearing, court authorization, instructions, approval or confirmation in the same manner as a parent having legal custody. I request that no bond be required because of the grant of these independent powers.

7.2. Waiver of Bond.

I request that no bond be required of any guardian nominated above.

* END OF ARTICLE *

Signature Clause. I subscribe my name to this Will at Los Angeles, California, on this ___30th____ day of _____July_____, 2001.

_____/S/ Vicki Lynn Marshall_____

VICKI LYNN MARSHALL

CHAPTER 6

Famous Early Wills

If we lose love and self-respect for each other,
[then] this is how we finally die.

Maya Angelou

Thomas Jefferson
April 13, 1743 — July 4, 1826

Thomas Jefferson was the third president of the United States (1801–1809) and the principal author of the Declaration of Independence. As seen below, the Last Will and Testament of Thomas Jefferson created a Testamentary Trust for his daughter, Martha Randolph, and provided for the freedom of several, but not all, of his slaves. Sally Hemming, and her children were apparently some of the few slaves who were freed under Jefferson's Will. Although it was publicized during Jefferson's presidential candidacy that Hemming's children were fathered by Thomas Jefferson, that fact was not officially confirmed by the Jefferson lineage of family members until DNA testing was conducted in the 1990s — over 200 years after the fact. Historically, Sally Hemming had accompanied Jefferson to France when Jefferson served as the Minister to France from 1784 to 1789 on behalf of the newly formed United States of America.[87]

Unfortunately, the Jefferson estate was insolvent after Jefferson died.[88] Jefferson had a very large plantation estate with as many as 300 slaves working on it at one time. Jefferson apparently spent beyond his means to sustain a large farm, and his way of life. When his heirs took over, they were compelled to pay substantial estate debts, which drained the estate of its assets. The Estate had to liquidate most of the personal property items, and sell Monticello, including the surrounding 500 acres of land. Most notably, the Estate sold the remaining 130 slaves to pay creditors of the estate.[89] They were not set free.

LAST WILL AND TESTAMENT OF THOMAS JEFFERSON

I Thomas Jefferson of Monticello in Albemarle, being of sound mind and in my ordinary state of health, make my Last Will and testament in manner and form as follows.

I give to my grandson Francis Eppes, son of my dear deceased daughter Mary Eppes, in fee simple, all that part of my lands at Poplar Forest lying West of the following lines, to wit, Beginning at Radford's upper corner near the double branches of Bear creek and the public road, & running thence in a straight line to the fork of my private road, near the barn, thence along that private road (as it was changed in 1817) to it's crossing of the main branch of North Tomahawk creek, and, from that crossing, in a direct line over the main ridge which divides the North and South Tomahawk, to the South Tomahawk, at the confluence of two branches where the old road to the Waterlick crossed it, and from that confluence up the Northernmost branch (which separates McDaniel's and Perry's fields) to it's source, & thence by the shortest line to my Western boundary. and having, in a former correspondence with my deceased son in law John W. Eppes contemplated laying off for him with remainder to my grandson Francis, a certain portion

---

87. "Jefferson-Hemings Resources," The Jefferson Monticello, https://www.monticello.org/site/plantation-and-slavery/jefferson-hemings-resources

88. Herbert, S. (1995). *Principal and Interest: Thomas Jefferson and the Problem of Debt* (p. 14). University of Virginia Press

89. Lucia, S. (1993). Jefferson Legacies. Those Who Labor for My Happiness: Thomas Jefferson and His Slaves (pp 147-180). University of Virginia Press.

in the Southern part of my lands in Bedford and Campbell, which I afterwards found to be generally more indifferent than I had supposed, & therefore determined to change it's location for the better; now to remove all doubt, if any could arise on a purpose merely voluntary & unexecuted, I hereby declare that what I have herein given to my sd grandson Francis is instead of and not additional to what I have formerly contemplated.

I subject all my other property to the payment of my debts in the first place.

Considering the insolvent state of affairs of my friend & son in law Thomas Mann Randolph, and that what will remain of my property will be the only resource against the want in which his family would otherwise be left, it must be his wish, as it is my duty, to guard that resource against all liability for his debts, engagements or purposes whatsoever, and to preclude the rights, powers and authorities over it which might result to him by operation of law, and which might, independantly of his will, bring it within the power of his creditors, I do hereby devise and bequeath all the residue of my property real and personal, in possession or in action, whether held in my own right, or in that of my dear deceased wife, according to the powers vested in me by deed of settlement for that purpose, to my grandson Thomas J. Randolph, & my friends Nicholas P. Trist, and Alexander Garrett & their heirs during the life of my sd son in law Thomas M. Randolph, to be held & administered by them, in trust, for the sole and separate use and behoof of my dear daughter Martha Randolph and her heirs. and, aware of the nice and difficult distinctions of the law in these cases, I will further explain by saying that I understand and intend the effect of these limitation to be, that the legal estate and actual occupation shall be vested in my said trustees, and held by them in base fee, determinable on the death of my sd son in law, and the remainder during the same time be vested in my sd daughter and her heirs, and of course disposable by her last will, and that at the death of my sd son in law, the particular estate of sd trustees shall be determined and the remainder, in legal estate, possession and use become vested in my sd daughter and her heirs, in absolute property for ever.

In consequence of the variety and indescribableness of the articles of property within the house at Monticello, and the difficulty of inventorying and appraising them separately and specifically, and its inutility, I dispense with having them inventoried and appraised; and it is my will that my executors be not held to give any security for the administration of my estate. I appoint my grandson Thomas Jefferson Randolph my sole executor during his life, and after his death, I constitute executors my friends Nicholas P. Trist and Alexander Garrett joining to them my daughter Martha Randolph after the death of my sd son in law Thomas M. Randolph.

Lastly I revoke all former wills by me heretofore made; and in Witness that this is my will, I have written the whole with my own hand on two pages, and have subscribed my name to each of them this 16th day of March one Thousand eight hundred and twenty six. Th: Jefferson

I Thomas Jefferson of Monticello in Albemarle make and add the following Codicil to my will, controuling the same so far as it's provisions go.

I recommend to my daughter, Martha Randolph, the maintenance and care of my well-beloved sister Anne Scott Marks, and trust confidently that from affection to her, as well as for my sake, she will never let her want a comfort.

I have made no specific provision for the comfortable maintenance of my son in law Thomas M. Randolph, because of the difficulty and uncertainty of devising terms which shall vest any beneficial interest in him which the law will not transfer to the benefit of his creditors to the destitution of my daughter and her family and disablement of her to supply him: whereas property placed under the executive right of my daughter and her independant will, as if she were a femme sole, considering the relations in which she stands both to him and his children, will be a certain resource against want for all.

I give to my friend James Madison of Montpellier my gold-mounted walking staff of animal horn, as a token of the cordial and affectionate friendship which for nearly now an half century, has united us in the same principles and pursuits of what we have deemed for the greatest good of our country.

I give to the University of Virginia my library, except such particular books only, and of the same edition, as it may already possess, when this legacy shall take effect. The rest of my said library remaining after those given to the University shall have been taken out, I give to my two grandsons in law Nicholas P. Trist and Joseph Coolidge.

To my grandson Thomas Jefferson Randolph I give my silver watch in preference of the golden one, because of it's superior excellence. my papers of business going of course to him, as my executor, all others of a literary or other character I give to him as of his own property.

I give a gold watch to each of my grand children who shall not have already received one from me, to be purchased and delivered by my executor, to my grandsons at the age of 21. and grand-daughters at that of sixteen.

I give to my good, affectionate, and faithful servant Burwell his freedom, and the sum of three hundred Dollars to buy necessaries to commence his trade of painter and glazier, or to use otherwise as he pleases. I give also to my good servants John Hemings and Joe Fosset their freedom at the end of one year after my death: and to each of them respectively all the tools of their respective shops or callings: and it is my will that a comfortable log house be built for each of the three servants so emancipated on some part of my lands convenient to them with respect to the residence of their wives, and to Charlottesville and the University, where they will be mostly employed, and reasonably convenient also to the interest of the proprietor of the lands; of which houses I give the use of one, with a curtilage of an acre to each, during his life or personal occupation thereof.

I give also to John Hemings the services of his two apprentices, Madison and Eston Hemings, until their respective ages of twenty one years, at which period respectively, I give them their freedom. and I humbly and earnestly request of the legislature of Virginia a confirmation of the bequest of freedom to these servants, with permission to remain in this state where their families and connections are, as an additional instance of the favor, of which I have recieved so many other manifestations, in the course of my life, and for which I now give them my last, solemn, and dutiful thanks.

In testimony that this is a Codicil to my will of yesterday's date, and that it is to modify so far the provisions of that will, I have written it all with my own hand, in two pages, to each of which I subscribe my name this 17th day of March one thousand eight hundred and twenty six. Th: Jefferson

———————————————

[The following text is included only in the court copy of the will.]

At a court held for Albemarle County the 7th of August 1826.

This instrument of writing purporting to be the last will and testament of Thomas Jefferson Deceased was produced into court and the hand writing of the testator proved by the oath of Valentine W. Southall and ordered to be recorded.

Teste: Alexander Garrett CC

ALFRED BERNHARD NOBEL
October 21, 1833 — December 10, 1896

"If I come up with 300 ideas in a year, and only one of them is useful, I am content."

ALFRED NOBEL

Reprinted by permission
Copyright © The Nobel Foundation
The Nobel Prize medal is a registered trademark of the Nobel Foundation

Alfred Bernhard Nobel was a Swedish chemist, engineer, industrialist, and inventor. He was born in Stockholm, Sweden in 1833. At age 9, he moved with his family to Saint Petersburg, Russia, where his

202 THE INDIVIDUAL'S GUIDEBOOK TO WILLS AND ESTATES

father began manufacturing machine tools and making explosives.[90] For a time, the family business prospered making military equipment, especially during the Crimean War in the mid-1850s. When he turned 17, Nobel went to Paris, France to study chemistry. A year later, he moved to the United States to work under the direction of John Ericsson, who developed the screw propeller for ships and built the ironclad submarine *Monitor*. Alfred Nobel worked in the United States for four years before returning to Saint Petersburg, Russia to work in his father's munitions factory. Nobel moved back to Sweden in 1859 after the family business hit hard times. He built a laboratory on his family property and continued experimenting with explosives.[91]

Nobel found a way to keep nitroglycerin from being so volatile by mixing it with silica, a porous siliceous earth.[92] In combination with his own invention of the blasting cap as a safe means in setting off high explosives, he developed dynamite, which he coined from the Greek word dynamis, meaning power.[93] Dynamite was immensely more explosive than using just regular gunpowder. It was dynamite that allowed humankind to tunnel through and move mountains and break up the earth to mine great masses of coal, iron ore, and other minerals.[94] The momentum behind the great industrial revolution of the world was due in large part to Nobel's discovery. And Alfred Nobel grew very rich from it.

On the other hand, dynamite also killed and injured life in vast numbers never seen before. Even Nobel's younger brother, Emil, and others, died

90. Ringertz, N. (n.d.). Alfred Nobel — His Life and Work. Retrieved September 22, 2017, https://www.nobelprize.org/alfred-nobel/alfred-nobel-his-life-and-work/
91. Alfred Nobel Biography. (2014, April 2). Retrieved November 12, 2017, https://www.biography.com/people/alfred-nobel-9424195
92. Alfred Nobel. (2014). Retrieved November 28, 2017, http://famouschemists.org/alfred-nobel/
93. Mining Hall of Fame. (n.d.). Retrieved March 16, 2017, from https://www.mininghalloffame.org/inductee/nobel
94. Ringertz, N. (2016, November 22). Alfred Nobel: His Life and Work. Retrieved June 18, 2017, from https://www.nobelprize.org/alfred-nobel/alfred-nobel-his-life-and-work/

in Nobel's factories experimenting with dynamite in the mid-1860s.[95] It became so dangerous that the authorities forced him to experiment with taming the volatility of nitroglycerine on a barge anchored on a lake outside the Stockholm city limits.[96] But Emil's death had a dramatic impact on Alfred Nobel, which drove him on a passionate quest to develop a safer explosive. And it was in 1867 that he combined the absorbent texture of silica with nitroglycerin to make dynamite.[97]

Then, in 1888, when his other brother Ludvig died, some newspapers erroneously thought that it was Alfred Nobel who died instead. And one French newspaper speciously published an obituary saying that "the merchant of death is dead."[98] Nobel worried how history would remember his legacy. Although he invented dynamite, which truly helped the industrial world to grow immensely, it also killed a lot of people. This conflict likely tugged at his soul…probably so much so, that it could have logically moved him to redraft a new Will, which he did in 1895, only a year prior to his death. In his Last Will, he made dramatic changes in his gifts to his family, providing very limited bequests and annuities to relatives and certain others, and gave the vast residue of his estate to fund five (now six)[99] Nobel prizes. He signed his Last Will on November 27, 1895, in Paris, France (*See below*, his Last Will, one translated into English, and his original Will, in Swedish).

---

95. "Nobel, Alfred." Encyclopedia of Modern Europe: Europe 1789-1914: Encyclopedia of the Age of Industry and Empire. Retrieved August 03, 2017 from Encyclopedia.com: https://www.encyclopedia.com/history/encyclopedias-almanacs-transcripts-and-maps/nobel-alfred-0

96. Alfred Nobel — His Life and Work, NobelPrize.org. Nobel Media AB 2018, (n.d.). Retrieved August 17, 2018, https://www.nobelprize.org/alfred-nobel/alfred-nobel-his-life-and-work

97. Alfred Nobel Biography. (2014, April 2). Retrieved May 18, 2017, from https://www.biography.com/people/alfred-nobel-9424195

98. Schultz, C. (2013, October 9). Blame Sloppy Journalism for the Nobel Prizes. Retrieved April 4, 2017, https://www.smithsonianmag.com/smart-news/blame-sloppy-journalism-for-the-nobel-prizes-1172688/

99. The Nobel Prize was originally awarded in the areas of Chemistry, Literature, Peace, Physics and Medicine (or Physiology. Later, in 1968, the Nobel Prize Committee created a 6th award in the area of Economics. Today, these annual awards are known to be the most prestigious academic honors to receive in the world.

Nobel suffered from heart disease during the last years of his life. The irony of it all is that the medical prescription for treating his heart condition consisted of taking small doses of nitroglycerin. Mr. Alfred Bernhard Nobel died at the age of 63 in San Remo, Italy on December 10, 1896, following a stroke.[100]

Nobel did not approve of inherited wealth. He thought wealthy families should provide their children with a first-class education and enough funding to cover a basic living standard. All other accumulated wealth should be redirected back into society in some helpful way.[101]

When Alfred Nobel died in December 1896, many were surprised to hear that he dedicated his wealth to a private foundation to honor "…those who, during the preceding year, shall have conferred the greatest benefit to mankind…" The wealth was to be invested in "safe securities" and the interest earned to be conferred upon the winners of the annual prizes awarded. At the time when Nobel died, he held one of the world's largest private fortunes.[102]

Despite having a validly written Will, Nobel's post-mortem estate was stalled by various relatives fighting to gain a bigger piece of the estate. Further, an effort was initiated by some of Nobel's disinherited relatives to have Nobel's Last Will declared totally invalid. Additionally, Nobel's charitable foundation attracted the attention of the Swedish government and King Oscar II of Sweden.[103]

King Oscar II held that the family claims should not be cast aside on the whimsical ideas of an aged person who wants to give his fortune away as prize

100. Alfred Nobel. (2016, October 9). Retrieved March 17, 2018, www.famousscientists. org/alfred-nobel/
101. Ibid.
102. The Last Will of Alfred Bernhard Nobel, Paris, France, 18 Nov 1895.
103. Alfred Nobel's Will. (n.d.). Retrieved August 20, 2017, from https://www.nobel-peaceprize.org/History/Alfred-Nobel-s-will
Norwegian Nobel Institute

money. But after extended meetings between the Swedish government and the Executors Ragnar Sohlman and Rudolf Lilljequist, a resolution was worked out where Alfred Nobel's vision would come true. On June 29, 1900, King Oscar II approved the statutes of the newly established Nobel Foundation.[104]

On December 10, 1901, the first Nobel Prizes were awarded in Stockholm and Oslo. And it was not until 2015 that a copy of Mr. Nobel's Last Will was made public. Viewed below are copies of Nobel's Last Will, one in a typed version, and the other consisting of photographs of Nobel's actual Last Will.

Mr. Nobel is honorably noted by the entire world for the distinguished Nobel Prize awards which are given out each year. Nobel started an annual world ritual, beginning in 1901, awarding a highest honor and most distinguished award to those in the world who have greatly benefited humankind in their respective fields of physics, chemistry, physiology (or medicine), literature, and peace. In 1968, the Nobel Prize Committee created a 6th award in the area of economics.

LAST WILL OF ALFRED BERNHARD NOBEL

I, the undersigned, Alfred Bernhard Nobel, do hereby, after mature deliberation, declare the following to be my last Will and Testament with respect to such property as may be left by me at the time of my death:

To my nephews, Hjalmar and Ludvig Nobel, the sons of my brother Robert Nobel, I bequeath the sum of Two Hundred Thousand Crowns each;

To my nephew Emanuel Nobel, the sum of Three Hundred Thousand, and to my niece Mina Nobel, One Hundred Thousand Crowns;

To my brother Robert Nobel's daughters, Ingeborg and Tyra, the sum of One Hundred Thousand Crowns each;

Miss Olga Boettger, at present staying with Mrs Brand, 10 Rue St Florentin, Paris, will receive One Hundred Thousand Francs;

Mrs Sofie Kapy von Kapivar, whose address is known to the Anglo-Oesterreichische Bank in Vienna, is hereby entitled to an annuity of 6000 Florins Ö.W. which is paid to her by the said Bank, and to this end I have deposited in this Bank the amount of 150,000 Fl. in Hungarian State Bonds;

---

104. Id.

Mr Alarik Liedbeck, presently living at 26 Sturegatan, Stockholm, will receive One Hundred Thousand Crowns;

Miss Elise Antun, presently living at 32 Rue de Lubeck, Paris, is entitled to an annuity of Two Thousand Five Hundred Francs. In addition, Forty Eight Thousand Francs owned by her are at present in my custody, and shall be refunded;

Mr Alfred Hammond, Waterford, Texas, U.S.A. will receive Ten Thousand Dollars;

The Misses Emy and Marie Winkelmann, Potsdamerstrasse, 51, Berlin, will receive Fifty Thousand Marks each;

Mrs Gaucher, 2 bis Boulevard du Viaduc, Nimes, France will receive One Hundred Thousand Francs;

My servants, Auguste Oswald and his wife Alphonse Tournand, employed in my laboratory at San Remo, will each receive an annuity of One Thousand Francs;

My former servant, Joseph Girardot, 5, Place St. Laurent, Châlons sur Saône, is entitled to an annuity of Five Hundred Francs, and my former gardener, Jean Lecof, at present with Mrs Desoutter, receveur Curaliste, Mesnil, Aubry pour Ecouen, S.& O., France, will receive an annuity of Three Hundred Francs;

Mr Georges Fehrenbach, 2, Rue Compiègne, Paris, is entitled to an annual pension of Five Thousand Francs from January 1, 1896 to January 1, 1899, when the said pension shall discontinue;

A sum of Twenty Thousand Crowns each, which has been placed in my custody, is the property of my brother's children, Hjalmar, Ludvig, Ingeborg and Tyra, and shall be repaid to them.

The whole of my remaining realizable estate shall be dealt with in the following way: the capital, invested in safe securities by my executors, shall constitute a fund, the interest on which shall be annually distributed in the form of prizes to those who, during the preceding year, shall have conferred the greatest benefit to mankind. The said interest shall be divided into five equal parts, which shall be apportioned as follows: one part to the person who shall have made the most important discovery or invention within the field of physics; one part to the person who shall have made the most important chemical discovery or improvement; one part to the person who shall have made the most important discovery within the domain of physiology or medicine; one part to the person who shall have produced in the field of literature the most outstanding work in an ideal direction; and one part to the person who shall have done the most or the best work for fraternity between nations, for the abolition or reduction of standing armies and for the holding and promotion of peace congresses. The prizes for physics and chemistry shall be awarded by the Swedish Academy of Sciences; that for physiological or medical work by the Caroline Institute in Stockholm; that for literature by the Academy in Stockholm, and that for champions of peace by a committee of five persons to be elected by the Norwegian Storting. It is my express wish that in awarding the prizes no consideration whatever shall be given to the nationality of the candidates, but that the most worthy shall receive the prize, whether he be a Scandinavian or not.

As Executors of my testamentary dispositions, I hereby appoint Mr Ragnar Sohlman, resident at Bofors, Värmland, and Mr Rudolf Lilljequist, 31 Malmskillnadsgatan, Stockholm, and at Bengtsfors near Uddevalla. To compensate for their pains and attention, I grant to Mr Ragnar Sohlman, who will presumably have to devote most time to this matter, One Hundred Thousand Crowns, and to Mr Rudolf Lilljequist, Fifty Thousand Crowns;

At the present time, my property consists in part of real estate in Paris and San Remo, and in part of securities deposited as follows: with The Union Bank of Scotland Ltd in Glasgow and London, Le Crédit Lyonnais, Comptoir National d'Escompte, and with Alphen Messin & Co. in Paris; with the stockbroker M.V. Peter of Banque Transatlantique, also in Paris; with Direction der Disconto Gesellschaft and Joseph Goldschmidt & Cie, Berlin; with the Russian Central Bank, and with Mr Emanuel Nobel in Petersburg; with Skandinaviska Kredit Aktiebolaget in Gothenburg and Stockholm, and in my strong-box at 59, Avenue Malakoff, Paris; further to this are accounts receivable, patents, patent fees or so-called royalties etc. in connection with which my Executors will find full information in my papers and books.

This Will and Testament is up to now the only one valid, and revokes all my previous testamentary dispositions, should any such exist after my death.

Finally, it is my express wish that following my death my veins shall be opened, and when this has been done and competent Doctors have confirmed clear signs of death, my remains shall be cremated in a so-called crematorium.

Alfred Bernhard Nobel   *Paris, 27 November, 1895*

That Mr Alfred Bernhard Nobel, being of sound mind, has of his own free will declared the above to be his Last Will and Testament, and that he has signed the same, we have, in his presence and the presence of each other, hereunto subscribed our names as witnesses:

Sigurd Ehrenborg
former Lieutenant
Paris: 84 Boulevard Haussmann

R. W. Strehlenert
Civil Engineer
4, Passage Caroline

Thos Nordenfelt
Constructor
8, Rue Auber, Paris

Leonard Hwass
Civil Engineer[105]

---

105. English Translation by Jeffrey Ganellen 2018

In its original Swedish language, the handwritten format hereby follows of the:

LAST WILL OF ALFRED BERNHARD NOBEL

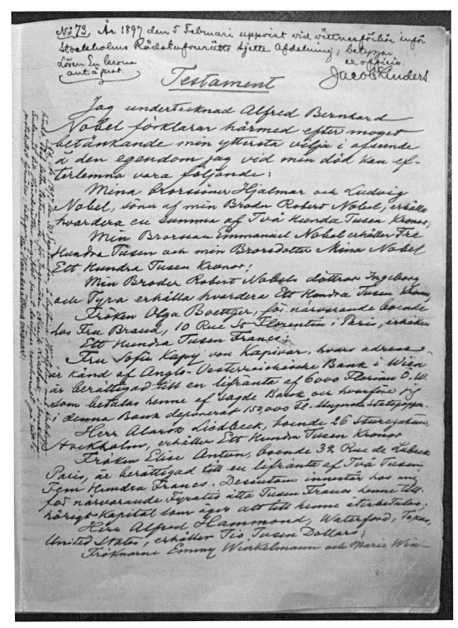

1 (of 4) The first page of Alfred Nobel's Last Will, dated 27 November, 1895.
Copyright © The Nobel Foundation

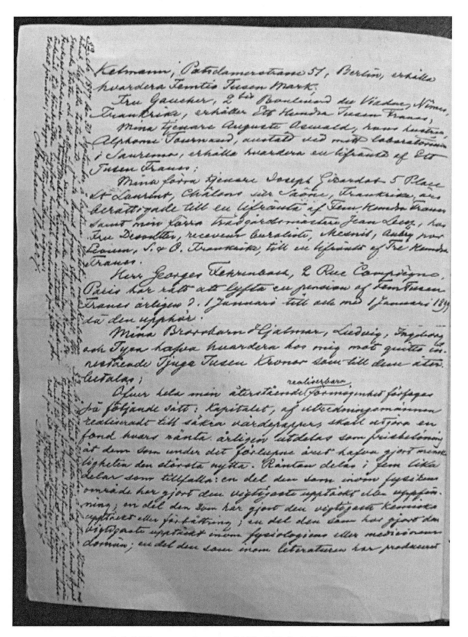

2 (of 4) The second page of Alfred Nobel's Last Will.
Copyright © The Nobel Foundation

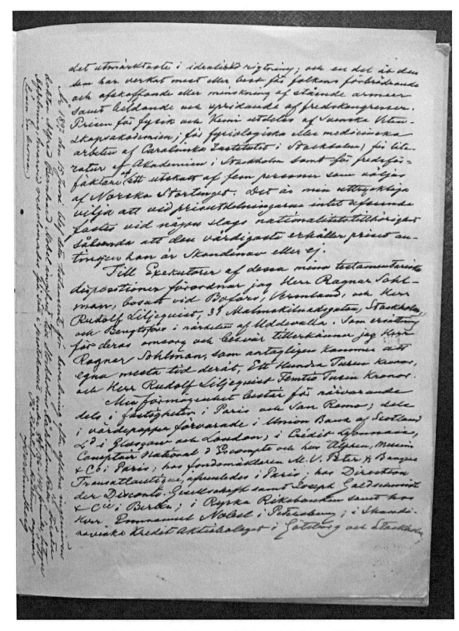

3 (of 4) The third page of Alfred Nobel's Last Will.
Copyright © The Nobel Foundation

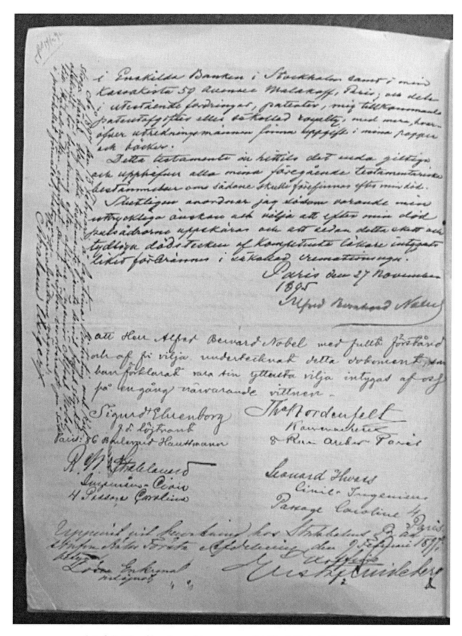

4 (of 4) The fourth and last page of Alfred Nobel's Last Will.
Copyright © The Nobel Foundation

All four pages above are copies of the original Last Will of Alfred Bernhard Nobel, which are reprinted by permission of The Nobel Foundation

CHAPTER 7

Legal Reference Charts: Comparative Laws Around the U.S. on Probate, Trusts, Digital Estate Planning, and Estate Taxation

Probate and Trust Laws in the 50 States and District of Columbia

The following listing shows the respective probate[106] and trust[107] laws of each state and the District of Columbia as of January 1, 2018.

State Probate Statutes

Alabama   Title 43 Wills and Decedents' Estates
                           Chapter 2 Administration of Estates
                           Chapter 8 Probate Code
                           Article 3 Intestate Succession

---

106. Everplans. (n.d.). State-by-state probate laws. Retrieved June 5, 2017, from https://www.everplans.com/articles/state-by-state-probate-laws
107. Updates and revisions of probate and trust laws made by the author. Disclaimer: provided as general information and reference only. Speak to an estate and trust attorney regarding specific advice.

Alaska	Title 13 Decedents' Estates, Guardianships, Transfers, and Trusts Title 13 Chapter 16 Probate of Wills and Administration
Arizona	Title 14 Trusts, Estates and Protective Proceedings Title 14 Chapter 2 Intestate Succession and Wills Title 14 Chapter 3 Probate of Wills and Administration
Arkansas	Title 28 Wills, Estates, and Fiduciary Relationships Title 28 Subtitle 2 Descent and Distribution Title 28 Subtitle 3 Wills
California	California Probate Code, Division 6, Part 1-Wills (Sections 6100-6390) Part 2-Intestate Succession (Sections 6400-6455)
Colorado	Title 15 Probate, Trusts, and Fiduciaries Title 15, Art. 10-16: Colorado Probate Code
Connecticut	Title 45 Probate Courts and Procedure
Delaware	Title 12 Decedents' Estates and Fiduciary Relations Title 12 Part II Wills Title 12 Part III Descent and Distribution
District of Columbia	Division III: Title 18 Wills Division III: Title 19. Descent, Distribution, and Trusts: Chapter 1. Rights of Surviving Spouse or Domestic Partner, and Children Chapter 3. Intestate' Estates Division III: Title 20. Probate and Administration
Florida	Title XLII Estates and Trusts Title XLII Chapter 732 Part I: Intestate Succession Title XLII Chapter 732 Part V: Wills

Georgia	Title 53 Wills, Trusts, and Administration of Estates Title 53 Chapters 2 through 4: Wills, Probate, and Descent and Distribution
Hawaii	Title 30A Uniform Probate Code
Idaho	Title 15 Uniform Probate Code Title 15 Chapter 2 Intestate Succession — Wills Title 15 Chapter 3 Probate of Wills and Administration Title 15 Chapter 7 Trust Administration
Illinois	Chapter 755 Estates Chapter 760 Trusts and Fiduciaries
Indiana	Title 29 Probate Title 30 Trusts and Fiduciaries
Iowa	Title XV Chapter 633 Probate Code Title XV Chapter 634 Private Foundations and Charitable Trusts Title XV Chapter 635 Administration of Small Estates Title XV Chapter 636 Sureties-Fiduciaries-Trusts-Investments
Kansas	Chapter 59 Probate Code
Kentucky	Chapter 140 Inheritance and Estate Taxes Chapter 386 Administration of Trusts - Investments Chapter 391 Descent and Distribution Chapter 394 Wills Chapter 395 Personal Representatives Chapter 396 Claims Against Decedents' Estates
Louisiana	Book III, Title I Of Successions Uniform Probate Law
Maine	Title 18 Decedents' Estates and Fiduciary Relations Title 18A Probate Code

Maryland	Titles 1 to16 Estates and Trusts
Massachusetts	MGL Part II, Title II, Chapter 190B: Article II Intestacy (Descent and Distribution) Wills, and Donative Transfers Article III Probate of Wills and Administration
Michigan	Chapters 701 to 713 Probate Code
Minnesota	Chapters 524-532 Estates of Decedents; Guardianships
Mississippi	Title 91 Trusts and Estates
Missouri	Title XXXI, Chapters 456-475 Trusts and Estates of Decedents
Montana	Title 72 Estates, Trusts and Fiduciary Relationships
Nebraska	Chapter 30 Decedents' Estates; Protection of Persons and Property
Nevada	Title 12 Wills and Estates of Deceased Persons Title 13 Guardianships; Conservatorships; Trusts
New Hampshire	Title LVI Probate Courts and Decedents' Estates
New Jersey	Titles 3A and 3B Administration of Estates — Decedents and Others
New Mexico	Chapter 45 Uniform Probate Code Chapter 46 Fiduciaries and Trusts
New York	Chapter 17-B Estates, Powers and Trusts
North Carolina	Chapter 41 Estates Chapter 47 Probate and Registration
North Dakota	Title 30.1 Uniform Probate Code

Ohio   Title XXI Courts - Probate - Juvenile

Oklahoma   Title 58 Probate Procedure
                        Title 84 Wills and Succession

Oregon   Chapter 111 Probate Law
                        Chapter 112 Intestate Succession and Wills
                        Chapter 113 Initiation of Estate Proceedings
                        Chapter 114 Administration of Estates
                        Chapter 115 Claims, Actions, and Suits Against
                        Estates

Pennsylvania   Title 20 Decedents, Estates and Fiduciaries

Rhode Island   Title 33 Probate Practice and Procedure

South Dakota   Title 29A Uniform Probate Code
                        Title 55 Fiduciaries and Trusts

South Carolina   Title 21 Estates, Trusts, Guardians and Fiduciaries
                        Title 62 Probate Code

Tennessee   Title 30 Administration of Estates
                        Title 31 Descent and Distribution
                        Title 32 Wills
                        Title 35 Fiduciaries and Trust Estates

Texas   Texas Probate Code
                        Texas Probate Code Chapter V Estates of
                        Decedents
                        Texas Probate Code Chapter IV Execution and
                        Revocation of Wills
                        Texas Probate Code Chapter XIII Guardianship

Utah   Title 22 Fiduciaries and Trusts
                        Title 75 Uniform Probate Code

Vermont   Title 14 Decedents' Estates and Fiduciary Relations

Virginia	Title 64.2 Wills, Trusts and Fiduciaries
	Chapter 2 Descent and Distribution
	Chapter 4 Wills
	Chapter 5 Persona Representative and
	Administration of Estates
Washington	Title 11 Probate and Trust Law
	Chapter 11.04 Descent and Distribution
	Chapter 11.12 Wills
West Virginia	Chapter 41 Wills
	Chapter 42 Descent and Distribution
	Chapter 44 Administration of Estates and Trusts
Wisconsin	Chapter 701 Trusts
	Chapter 853 Wills
	Chapters 851 to 882 Probate
Wyoming	Title 2 Wills, Decedents' Estates and Probate Code
	Title 2 Chapter 2 Probate Court
	Title 2 Chapter 6 Wills
	Title 2 Chapter 7 Administration of Estates

DIGITAL ESTATE PLANNING LAWS AROUND THE UNITED STATES

It is the expected norm for the average individual to have one or more email accounts, social media accounts, and even blogs. Today, most everyone uses an operating system or digital medium to communicate with others, buy merchandise, and to do practically everything else via a computing system. IDs and passwords are how many of us access our lives and livelihood. In response, more and more states are enacting digital estate-planning laws to override challenges that are otherwise blocked or challenged by third-party merchants who claim that digital information on its site is owned by them, and not by the individual customer, including the confidential ID and password created. That has challenged, if not prevented, even Executors or Trustees from having access to discover a Decedent's sources and assets. The same goes for a guardian or Attorney-in-fact under a Durable Power of Attorney finding information for an incapacitated individual. For example, the terms-of-service agreements (TOSA) used by many companies (generally known as Custodians) that store digital assets (e.g., Google, Facebook, or Yahoo) provide that an individual's account is non-transferable and terminates at death. The digital estate-planning laws enacted by the states essentially override the TOSA and allow authorized fiduciaries to access accounts by typically serving a request and proof of authority on a Custodian.

Digital estate planning laws are very new. Most of them are less than five years old, with most states enacting such laws from 2016 to 2018. A good handful of states still have no digital access laws on the books. Nevertheless, it becomes critical to be sure that your digital Custodian does not close the door on your fiduciaries. The way to be sure is to include assent language authorizing fiduciaries to access accounts, IDs and passwords that you want disclosed should you become incapacitated or die. This assures that your wishes are honored, especially if state digital statutes require that such affirmative language be required in a Last Will, Trust, Durable Power of Attorney, or other legitimate record. For example, look at Virginia's recently enacted digital estate planning laws in the chart below. A custodian can otherwise deny access, even under the access laws, unless the Decedent or incapacitated person has language in an estate-planning document authorizing access to his or her digital account(s). For Virginians, that can be tough, if not completely frustrating, especially if most residents have no estate planning documents prepared. For sample language, please refer to the Durable Power of Attorney sample document in Chapter 3. It includes a paragraph on Digital Information authorizing the Attorney-in-fact to access the Principal's digital information.[108] You may or may not want everything accessed. Therefore, it is important to culture the language to your wishes. The chart that follows is a compilation of the latest and newest dig-

---

108. *See,* Paragraph 3(B)(xiii) "Digital Information." Durable Power of Attorney sample document in Chapter 3.

ital estate planning laws[109] enacted in most of the 50 United States. Even though it covers laws enacted up to January 1, 2019, it is listed as general information only. Specific and updated laws must be separately researched or advised through one's own estate planning counsel.

The following listing[110] shows the respective digital estate planning laws of each state and the District of Columbia:[111]

---

109. A large majority of U.S. states have recently enacted legislation that provides a Decedent's family (or Executor) the right to access and manage the Decedent's digital assets. Many of the digital access laws started in 2016, after the Uniform Law Commission promulgated the *Revised Uniform Fiduciary Access to Digital Assets Act* in 2015 ("Act"). The Act allows Executors, Trustees, or other persons appointed by the court ("Conservator" or "Fiduciary") to have full access to the Decedent's digital assets. While these laws are quite new, they are needed to overcome the obstacles presented by merchants with their terms of service agreement and privacy policy that prevent legitimate access to individual accounts. A continued challenge still to be met includes access to individual accounts that have complex addresses and privacy 'black holes' dealing with virtual currencies (i.e., crypto-currencies) and blockchain technologies. States are always trying to legally keep up with the issues presented by the fast-moving world of technology.

110. Special thanks to www.Everplans.com for allowing the use of the above digital estate-planning chart, with revisions made on the latest laws through January 2019. Although the author does not endorse any one legacy account custodian, he does encourage readers to properly prepare and store their valued financial and estate-planning information. Everplans is an entity that has developed an important new niche in an estate-planning portfolio, also known as legacy accounts, where individuals can find a secure digital archive to store valuable personal and family information, including estate planning documents, critical accounts and passwords, medical information, and other important family details. This archive becomes a tremendous and valuable resource for heirs.

111. Everplans. (2018, August 5). State-by-state Digital Estate Planning Laws. Retrieved March 2, 2019, from https://www.everplans.com/articles/state-by-state-digital-estate-planning-laws

Alabama

Law: HB 138 Revised Uniform Fiduciary Access to Digital Assets Act

Description: This law authorizes a Decedent's personal representative or trustee to access and manage digital assets and electronic communications.

Status: Effective January 1, 2018

Alaska

Law: HB 108 Revised Uniform Fiduciary Access to Digital Assets Act

Description: This law authorizes a Decedent's personal representative or trustee to access and manage digital assets and electronic communications.

Status: Effective October 31, 2017

Arizona

Law: SB 1413 Revised Uniform Fiduciary Access to Digital Assets Act

Description: This law authorizes a Decedent's personal representative or trustee to access and manage digital assets and electronic communications.

Status: Effective August 8, 2016

Arkansas

Law: HB2253 Revised Uniform Fiduciary Access to Digital Assets Act

Description: This law authorizes a Decedent's personal representative or trustee to access and manage digital assets and electronic communications.

Status: Approved on April 4, 2017, and became known as "Act 866"

California

Law: AB-691 Revised Uniform Fiduciary Access to Digital Assets Act

Description: This law authorizes a Decedent's personal representative or trustee to access and manage digital assets and electronic communications.

Status: Approved on September 24, 2016

Colorado

Law: SB 16-088 Revised Uniform Fiduciary Access to Digital Assets Act

Description: This law authorizes a Decedent's personal representative or trustee to access and manage digital assets and electronic communications.

Status: Approved on April 7, 2016

Connecticut

Law: SB 262 Public Act No. 05-136

Description: Executors may access email accounts. The state requires a death certificate and documentation of the Executor's appointment before the estate's representative can see the deceased person's emails or social networking accounts.

Status: Effective October 1, 2005

Delaware

Law: HB 345 Fiduciary Access to Digital Assets and Digital Accounts

Description: This act specifically authorizes fiduciaries to access and control the digital assets and digital accounts of an incapacitated person, principal under a personal power of attorney, decedents or settlors, and beneficiaries of trusts."

Status: Effective August 12, 2014

Florida

Law: SB 494, Chapter 740 Florida Fiduciary Access to Digital Assets Act

Description: This law grants fiduciaries legal authority over the Decedent's digital assets and accounts, and grants a guardian the right to access a ward's digital assets under certain circumstances.

Status: Effective July 1, 2016

Georgia

Law: SB 301 Revised Uniform Fiduciary Access to Digital Assets Act

Description: This law authorizes a Decedent's personal representative or trustee to access and manage digital assets and electronic communications.

Status: Effective July 1, 2018

Hawaii

Law: SB2298 Revised Uniform Fiduciary Access to Digital Assets Act

Description: This law authorizes a Decedent's personal representative or trustee to access and manage digital assets and electronic communications.

Status: Effective July 1, 2016

Idaho

Law: SB 1303 Revised Uniform Fiduciary Access to Digital Assets Act

Description: This law authorizes a Decedent's personal representative or trustee to access and manage digital assets and electronic communications.

Status: Effective July 1, 2016

Illinois

Law: HB 4648 Revised Uniform Fiduciary Access to Digital Assets Act

Description: This law authorizes a Decedent's personal representative or trustee to access and manage digital assets and electronic communications.

Status: Effective August 12, 2016

Indiana

Law: SB 253 Revised Uniform Fiduciary Access to Digital Assets Act

Description: This law authorizes a decedent's personal representative or trustee to access and manage digital assets and electronic communications.

Status: Effective March 23, 2016

Iowa

Law: SF 333 Revised Uniform Fiduciary Access to Digital Assets Act

Description: The act authorizes access to digital assets by fiduciaries, including a Personal Representative, conservator, guardian, authorized agent, or trustee.

Status: Effective April 20, 2017

Kansas

Law: SB 63 Revised Uniform Fiduciary Access to Digital Assets Act

Description: The act authorizes access to digital assets by a fiduciary acting under a Last Will or Power of Attorney executed before, on, or after July 1, 2017; a personal representative acting for a Decedent who died before, on, or after July 1, 2017; a guardianship or conservatorship proceeding commenced before, on, or after July 1, 2017; and a trustee acting under a trust created before, on, or after July 1, 2017.

Status: Effective July 1, 2017

Kentucky

No legislation enacted.

Louisiana

No legislation enacted.

Maine

Law: LD 846 Revised Uniform Fiduciary Access to Digital Assets Act

Description: The act establishes procedures, standards and legal responsibilities to ensure the proper management and protection of digital assets and communications, consistent with federal requirements.

Status: Effective July 1, 2018

Maryland

Law: SB239/HB507 Maryland Fiduciary Access to Digital Assets Act

Description: This law authorizes a Decedent's personal representative or trustee to access and manage digital assets and electronic communications.

Status: Effective October 1, 2016

Massachusetts

No legislation enacted.

Status: HD 3489 Revised Uniform Fiduciary Access to Digital Assets Act was introduced to the House Committee on the Judiciary and was concurred by the State Senate on January 22, 2019.

The pending legislation lists January 1, 2020 as the tentative effective date

Michigan

Law: HB 5034 The Fiduciary Access To Digital Assets Act

Description: Provides for fiduciary access to digital assets; the law treats digital information, including social media and website accounts, to be treated like other assets after an owner dies.

Status: Effective June 27, 2016

Minnesota

Law: Minnesota Statutes Chapter 521A Revised Uniform Fiduciary Access to Digital Assets Act

Description: This law authorizes a Decedent's personal representative or trustee to access and manage digital assets and electronic communications.

Status: Effective August 1, 2016

Mississippi

Law: HB 489 Revised Uniform Fiduciary Access to Digital Assets Act

Description: This law authorizes a Decedent's personal representative or trustee to access and manage digital assets and electronic communications.

Status: Effective July 1, 2017

Missouri

Law: HB 1250 Revised Uniform Fiduciary Access to Digital Assets Act

Description: This law authorizes a Decedent's personal representative or trustee to access and manage digital assets and electronic communications.

Status: Effective August 28, 2018

Montana

Law: SB 118 Revised Uniform Fiduciary Access to Digital Assets Act

Description: This law authorizes a Decedent's personal representative or trustee to access and manage digital assets and electronic communications.

Status: Effective October 1, 2017

Nebraska

Law: LB 829 Revised Uniform Fiduciary Access to Digital Assets Act

Description: This law authorizes a Decedent's personal representative or trustee to access and manage digital assets and electronic communications.

Status: Effective January 1, 2017

Nevada

Law: SB 131

Description: This law establishes provisions governing the termination of a Decedent's accounts on electronic mail, social networking, messaging and other web-based services.

Status: Effective October 1, 2013

New Hampshire

No legislation enacted.

Status: SB 147 Revised Uniform Fiduciary Access to Digital Assets Act has been recently introduced in the New Hampshire legislature.

New Jersey

Law: SB 2527 Uniform Fiduciary Access to Digital Assets Act

Description: The act provides executors, trustees, guardians, and power of attorney holders ("fiduciaries") with the ability to access and control digital assets belonging to decedents, beneficiaries and wards.

Status: Effective December 12, 2017

New Mexico

Law: SB 60 Revised Uniform Fiduciary Access to Digital Assets Act

Description: This law authorizes a Decedent's Personal Representative or trustee to access and manage digital assets and electronic communications.

Status: Effective January 1, 2018

New York

Law: AB A9910A

Description: This law provides for the administration of digital assets; authorizes a user to use an online tool to direct the Custodian to disclose or not to disclose some or all of the user's digital assets, including the content of electronic communications; provides that this law does not impair the rights of a custodian or a user under a terms-of-service agreement to access and use digital assets of the user; and provides for a procedure for disclosing digital assets.

Status: Effective September 29, 2016

North Carolina

Law: SB 805 Fiduciary Access to Digital Assets

Description: This law authorizes a Decedent's personal representative or trustee to access and manage digital assets and electronic communications.

Status: Effective June 30, 2016

North Dakota

No legislation enacted.

Ohio

Law: HB 432 Revised Uniform Fiduciary Access to Digital Assets Act

Description: This law authorizes for continued access or control over a deceased or incapacitated person's electronic communications and any other digital asset to which the individual has an interest.

Status: Effective April 6, 2017

Oklahoma

Law: HB 2800

Description: An act relating to probate procedure; authorizing an Executor or administrator to have control of certain social networking, micro-blogging or e-mail accounts of the deceased; Effectively, Oklahoma law gives your Executor authority only over related email accounts (Okla. Stat. tit. 58, § 269).

Status: Further legislation has been introduced to revise and broaden the authorities under the limited digital estate-planning laws on the books.

Oregon

Law: SB 1554 Revised Uniform Fiduciary Access to Digital Assets Act

Description: "Allows a fiduciary, such as a Personal Representative, trustee or conservator, to access certain digital content within certain limits. It permits entities that hold electronic data to allow users to specify their wishes in the event they become inactive or when the entity receives a request for information. (If a user specifies, that trumps all other instructions, including a will.) The measure also permits fiduciaries to obtain a catalogue of digital communications, and sets forth a number of protocols for them, to cover a variety of situations, such as: when users consent to disclosure, or refuse, or fail to specify; or when disclosure has been ordered by a court."[112]

Status: Effective January 1, 2017

Pennsylvania

No legislation enacted.

Rhode Island

Law: Title 33: Probate practice and procedure, Chapter 33-27: Access to Decedents' Electronic Mail Accounts Act, Section 33-27-3

Description: Executors may access *only* email and social networking accounts. The state may require a death certificate and documentation of the Executor's appointment before the estate's representative can see the deceased person's emails or social networking accounts.

Status: Effective May 1, 2007

South Carolina

Law: SB 908 South Carolina Uniform Fiduciary Access To Digital Assets Act

Description: This law authorizes a Decedent's Personal Representative or trustee to access and manage digital assets and electronic communications.

Status: Effective June 3, 2016

---

112. Oregon's Summary of Legislation. (2016). SB 1554 Revised Uniform Fiduciary Access to Digital Assets Act.

South Dakota

Law: HB1080 Uniform Fiduciary Access to Digital Assets Act

Description: This law authorizes a Decedent's Personal Representative or trustee to access and manage digital assets and electronic communications.

Status: Effective July 1, 2017

Tennessee

Law: SB 326 Uniform Fiduciary Access To Digital Assets Act

Description: This law authorizes a Decedent's Personal Representative or trustee to access and manage digital assets and electronic communications.

Status: Effective July 1, 2016

Texas

Law: SB 1193 Revised Uniform Fiduciary Access to Digital Assets Act

Description: This law authorizes a Decedent's Personal Representative or trustee to access and manage digital assets and electronic communications.

Status: Effective September 1, 2017

Utah

Law: HB 13 Uniform Fiduciary Access to Digital Assets Act

Description: This law authorizes a Decedent's Personal Representative or trustee to access and manage digital assets and electronic communications.

Status: Effective on May 9, 2017

Vermont

Law: HB 152 (Act 13) Uniform Fiduciary Access to Digital Assets Act

Description: This law authorizes a Decedent's Personal Representative or trustee to access and manage digital assets and electronic communications.

Status: Effective on July 1, 2017

Virginia

Law: Uniform Fiduciary Access to Digital Assets Act,

Description: The law, known as the Digital Assets Act, is codified as Virginia Code §§ 64.2-116 through 64.2-132 (the "Digital Assets Act"). The Digital Assets Act will permit a fiduciary — the Executor or Administrator of an estate, the trustee of a trust, the guardian and conservator of an incapacitated person, and the agent under a power of attorney — to manage the principal's digital assets such as computer files, web domains, and virtual currency. *But take note that the law will restrict a fiduciary's access to electronic communications such as email and text messages (the "content of an electronic communication") and social media accounts, unless the original user specifically consented to such access in a Will, trust, power of attorney, or other record.*

Status: Effective July 1, 2017

Washington

Law: SB 5029 Revised Uniform Fiduciary Access to Digital Assets Act

Description: This provides a process for a digital asset custodian to disclose digital asset information when requested by a fiduciary who needs access to the information to fulfill fiduciary duties.

Status: Effective June 9, 2016

Washington, D.C. (District of Columbia)

No legislation enacted.

West Virginia

Law: SB 102 Uniform Fiduciary Access to Digital Assets Act

Description: This law provides that an agent under a power of attorney may exercise authority over the content of electronic communications sent or received by the principal, as well as other digital assets, and sets forth a procedure for disclosing digital assets by a custodian (such as Google, Facebook or Yahoo).

Status: Effective on June 5, 2018

Wisconsin

Law: AB 695 Revised Uniform Fiduciary Access to Digital Assets Act

Description: This provides a process for a digital asset custodian to disclose digital asset information when requested by a fiduciary who needs access to the information to fulfill fiduciary duties.

Status: Effective April 1, 2016 **Wyoming**

Law: SF0034 Uniform Fiduciary Access to Digital Assets Act

Description: This provides a process for a digital asset custodian to disclose digital asset information when requested by a fiduciary who needs access to the information to fulfill fiduciary duties.

Status: Effective July 1, 2016

STATE ESTATE TAX AND INHERITANCE TAX CHART

The following listing[113] shows the respective state estate tax rates and exemption amounts, where applicable, as of January 1, 2018, for the 50 United States and the District of Columbia. For reference, there are 13 states, plus the District of Columbia, that impose an estate tax and six states that have an inheritance tax. Maryland is the only state with both an estate tax and an inheritance tax. Washington state's top estate tax rate of 20 percent is the highest in the nation.

Alabama: No estate tax or inheritance tax

---

113. Walczak, J. (2017, June 27). State Inheritance and Estate Taxes. Retrieved November 18, 2017, from https://taxfoundation.org/state-inheritance-estate-taxes-economic-implications/

Alaska: No estate tax or inheritance tax

Arizona: No estate tax or inheritance tax

Arkansas: No estate tax or inheritance tax

California: No estate tax or inheritance tax

Colorado: No estate tax or inheritance tax

Connecticut: Nine estate tax-rate brackets, ranging from 7.2-12 percent *(exemption threshold: $2 million)*[114]

Delaware: 20 estate tax-rate brackets, with rates ranging from 0.8-16.0 percent *(exemption threshold matches the federal exemption limit, which is $11.2 million as of Jan. 1, 2018)*[115]

District of Columbia (Washington, D.C.): 11 estate tax-rate brackets with rates ranging from 6.4-16 percent[116] *(exemption limit threshold = federal threshold, beginning Jan. 1, 2018, which is $11.2 million)*

Florida: No estate tax or inheritance tax

Georgia: No estate tax or inheritance tax

Hawaii: Five estate tax-rate brackets, ranging from 0.8-16 percent *(Hawaii has a unique exemption limit, combining a $1 million exemption, plus the current $11.2 million federal exemption, which means that no estate tax is owed on the first $12.2 million of the gross estate)*[117]

Idaho: No estate tax or inheritance tax

---

114. C.G.S.A. § 12-391
115. 30 Del.C. § 1501 *et seq.*
116. D.C. Code §47-3702. Tax on transfer of taxable estate of residents
117. HRS § 236E-1 *et seq.*

Illinois: 20 estate tax rate brackets, ranging from 0.8-16 percent *(exemption threshold: $4 million)*[118]

Indiana: No estate tax or inheritance tax

Iowa: Inheritance tax rates range from 0 percent for lineal heirs, and from 5-15 percent for all others[119]

Kansas: No estate tax or inheritance tax

Kentucky: Inheritance tax rates range from 0 percent for lineal heirs, and from 4-16 percent for all others[120]

Louisiana: No estate tax or inheritance tax

Maine: Three estate tax-rate brackets ranging from 8-12 percent[121] *(exemption threshold: lowered from the matching federal estate tax exemption limit of $5.45 million, down to $1 million on post-mortem estates on or after January 1, 2018)*[122]

Maryland: 20 estate tax-rate brackets, with rates ranging from 0.8-16 percent *(exemption threshold: $3 million)*[123]; 0-10 percent inheritance tax rates: 0 percent for lineal heirs, 10 percent for all others[124]

Massachusetts: 20 estate tax-rate brackets, with rates ranging from 0.8-16 percent[125] *(exemption threshold: $1 million)*[126]

---

118. 35 ILCS 405/3
119. I.C.A. § 450.2
120. KRS § 140.010
121. Sec. 3. 36 MRSA §4103, sub-§1-A
122. Sec. 1. 36 MRSA §4102, sub-§5
123. MD Code, Estates & Trusts–General, § 7-302 *et seq.*
124. MD Code, Tax — General, § 7-203
125. MGL Pt 1, Title IX, ch. 65C, §2.
126. This is a cliff threshold tax, or a reversion tax. Specifically, Massachusetts has a $1 million exemption limit on its estate tax. Simply, if a resident's gross estate after

Michigan: No estate tax or inheritance tax

Minnesota: Six estate tax-rate brackets, with rates ranging from 12-16 percent [127] *(current 2018 exemption limit is $2,400,000, with annual structured increases that rise to $3 million by Jan. 1, 2020)*[128]

Mississippi: No estate tax or inheritance tax

Missouri: No estate tax or inheritance tax

Montana: No estate tax or inheritance tax

Nebraska: Inheritance tax rates range from 0-1 percent for lineal heirs[129], and from 13-18 percent for all others[130].

Nevada: No estate tax or inheritance tax

New Hampshire: No estate tax or inheritance tax

---

death is below $1 million, then zero estate tax is due. But, if a resident's gross estate is above $1 million, the exemption limit is *eliminated* and the estate taxes are calculated using the *entire* amount of the gross estate to arrive at the respective Massachusetts' estate tax.

127. M.S.A. § 291.01 *et seq.*
128. H.F.No. 1, Laws of Minnesota 2017, 1st Spec. Sess.
129. R.R.S. Neb. §77-2003: property passing to decedent's spouse shall not be subject to any inheritance tax; R.R.S. Neb. §77-2004: property passing to decedent's children, parents, grandparents, siblings or any lineal descendants are "Class 1 beneficiaries" who shall pay an inheritance tax rate of one percent.
130. R.R.S. Neb. §77-2005-property valued over fifteen thousand dollars and passing to "Class 2 beneficiaries" such as an uncle, aunt, niece or nephew shall pay an inheritance tax rate of 13 percent; R.R.S. Neb §77-2006: property valued over ten thousand dollars and passing to "Class 3 beneficiaries" that include all other lineal descendants shall pay an inheritance tax rate of 18 percent.

New Jersey: No estate tax after January *1, 2018*; inheritance tax rates range from 0 percent for lineal heirs, and from 11-16 percent for all others[131]

New Mexico: No estate tax or inheritance tax

New York: 14 estate tax-rate brackets, with rates ranging from 5-16 percent. The "cliff threshold" limit = $5.250 million.[132]

North Carolina: No estate tax or inheritance tax

North Dakota: No estate tax or inheritance tax

Ohio: No estate tax or inheritance tax

Oklahoma: No estate tax or inheritance tax

Oregon: 10 estate tax-rate brackets, with rates ranging from 10-16 percent[133] *(exemption threshold: $1 million)*

Pennsylvania: No estate tax; inheritance tax rates are 4.5 percent for lineal heirs, 12 percent for siblings, and 15 percent for all others[134]

Rhode Island: 20 estate tax-rate brackets, with rates ranging from 0.8-16 percent[135] *(exemption threshold: $1.5 million)*

---

131. *New Jersey Inheritance tax rate table:* https://www.state.nj.us/treasury/taxation/inheritance-estate/tax-rates.shtml
132. (New Jersey Administrative Code [NJAC] §18:26-1.1). So, no estate tax assessed if the gross estate is valued under the threshold limit of $5.250 million. But those estates valued over the threshold (cliff) limit are assessed an estate tax for the *entire* amount of the gross estate rather than only above the exemption limit. Massachusetts also has a cliff threshold aspect on its estate tax.
133. O.R.S. § 118.010.
134. 72 P.S. § 9106
135. RI Gen L § 44-22-1.1(a)(4) (2014); *see also,* Estate tax schedule, p. 23, Form RI-100A Estate Tax Return.

South Carolina: No estate tax or inheritance tax

South Dakota: No estate tax or inheritance tax

Tennessee: No estate tax or inheritance tax

Texas: No estate tax or inheritance tax

Utah: No estate tax or inheritance tax

Vermont: The only state with a flat state estate tax of 16 percent of a net estate[136] *(exemption threshold: $2.75 million)*

Virginia: No estate tax or inheritance tax

Washington: Eight estate tax-rate brackets with rates ranging from 10-20 percent[137] *(exemption threshold: $2.193 million as of Jan 1, 2018)*

West Virginia: No estate tax or inheritance tax

Wisconsin: No estate tax or inheritance tax

Wyoming: No estate tax or inheritance tax

136. 32 V.S.A. § 7442a
137. RCW 83.100.040

EPILOGUE

LESSONS LEARNED

There is no death, only a change of worlds.

CHIEF SEALTH[138]

We can learn a lot from the experiences of others, especially in estate planning. And what takes place in the post-mortem estate depends on what rules control the action. Either there is a script to legally guide the estate, such as a Will or Living Trust, or both, or state law takes control in an intestate estate where there is no Will in deciding how one's worldly possessions get split up.

In an intestate estate, the closest lineal or legal heirs to the Decedent inherit the assets. Most often, they are the spouse and children. Depending on which state law has jurisdiction, there are varying degrees as to what percentages and what properties are inherited by the spouse, the children, or both. Some states may provide all the properties to the surviving spouse, while other states divide the assets between the surviving spouse and Decedent's children. So, each state has varying percentages and circumstances regarding the division of assets among lineal heirs. Also, property divisions will differ, especially when comparing the nine community property states and one community property jurisdiction (See Footnote 33), versus the non-community property states. Further, state laws might distinguish be-

---

138. Northwest Native American Chief and namesake of modern-day Seattle, Washington

tween jointly owned assets versus separate property assets regarding asset division. (See Chapter 7 for a general legal reference of the intestate laws in your state). An estate planning attorney will know the nuances and strategic differences that your state has codified regarding the division of estate assets, as well as laws handling the care of any minor children after the Decedent dies.

The many legal uncertainties dealing with intestate succession should make it quite foreseeable to anyone about the wider range of risks to which heirs are exposed if a Decedent fails to script a Last Will. One notable example of a fallout for not having a Will is that stepchildren, cousins (if too far down the lineal ladder of bequests), friends, charities, pets or animals, and other non-lineal persons or entities, are left out of the intestate estate. *They get nothing.* The Testator in a Last Will, however, can pick and choose what charities or individuals will inherit his or her assets, who will care for any minor children, take care of any animals and pets, and virtually anything else designated by the Testator.

The legal venue for a Decedent's estate is the county of the state where he or she was a resident at the time of death. In an intestacy, the next of kin would generally petition the probate court for a "Letters of Administration" ("Letters") to become the Administrator or Executor of the estate.[139] The Executor would then obtain a court-certified copy of the Letters to be able to collect assets, obtain a Tax Identification Number from the Internal Revenue Service, open an estate bank account, operate any existing business operation, and all other tasks in behalf of the Decedent's estate.

What potentially can go wrong in a post-mortem estate in which Decedent dies without a valid Will or estate plan? With an estate lacking a Last Will or Trust, parties are sure to jump in and claim a piece of the estate.

---

139. The courts will generally award the Executor position to the closest next-of-kin, such as the surviving spouse. This exclusivity period is generally codified to last only for a certain period, like 40 days, or two months, before other parties would be able to petition the court to open probate proceedings in the case and serve as the Administrator or Executor of the estate.

Contests and possible appeals can be anticipated. Legal and accounting costs can be significant. Moreover, the intestate probate case likely has to otherwise provide notice to the likely heirs and the creditors of the Executor's action with a hearing for court approval *each* time an Executor's task is needed to advance the probate. And it can be costly. They can include notices for hearings to open estate accounts, sell real or personal property, enter into contracts, distribute property to heirs, hire professionals like an attorney, accountant or real estate broker, and authorize the reasonableness of fees of professionals. And the list can go on. But under a Last Will with non-intervention powers, the Executor, without objection from a party in interest, is able to conduct the administration of the estate without needing to seek court approval each time an action is undertaken.

All the while, the inherent uncertainty of issues needing to be resolved in an intestate estate can start to unnerve the patience of potential heirs. And the longer the case remains open, the more the nerves will likely become frayed. With this frictional scenario, heirs are either thinking how to gain the estate assets or else figuring out how to keep others from unfairly taking advantage of them. A gnawing suspicion grows. Unfortunately, the bumpy scene can sap the hallowed time that otherwise should be dedicated to sharing warm memories of the beloved Decedent. So, if intestacy creates family infighting over a Decedent's assets, it is going to crowd out the heart-warming moments otherwise expected in the mourning of a loved one. Attitudes change, and the love is lost, all from the negative consequences that can be caused by an intestate estate.

Even the celebrity estates described in the book tell stories about events not uncommon to what we all experience in real life. If we fail to plan, then our post-mortem estate can expect to face the consequences of added litigation, asset distributions to unintended heirs, general heartache among family and friends, and the likelihood of bad blood entering previously happy, life-long relationships going forward. We saw examples in Chapter 1 about people like Howard Hughes, Kurt Cobain, and Steve McNair who left estates without any Last Will or Trust. Heartache and expensive litigation were evident in all of them.

So, having no Last Will prepared, right now, is really no good. You have to prepare, or else you expose your estate to many unwarranted risks, including pitting family members against each other. We know that mortality is a certainty, but it can be fraught with unpredictability. Something can happen to you next year, next week, or even tomorrow. The uncertainty tells all of us that, most times, death is a surprise. So, don't plan around it; prepare a Last Will with it in mind.

We should take note of some of the Last Wills of celebrities listed in the book. Elvis Presley, for example, created an excellent Last Will, within which it established a Testamentary Trust that sprung to life upon his death. He preserved the great majority of his assets, providing for his beloved father until his death, then having the bulk of his estate remain in trust for his daughter, Lisa Marie Presley. The trust, and subsidiary trusts, carefully accounted for his assets, including copyrights, his likeness, and trademarks. It also preserved assets for Lisa Marie until she had the understanding (and the assistance of good legal counsel) to take control over her late father's estate. Royalties generated by Elvis Presley's likeness, copyrights, and trademarks are known to bring in between $35 million to $50 million annually![140]

And compare Elvis' estate to the intestate estate of Howard Hughes. Contests erupted attempting to validate competing Wills allegedly written by Hughes. The Nevada courts finally determined that Hughes had no valid Will. With no valid Last Will, many alleged heirs, up to 400 of them, came out to claim a share of the estate. In the end, the court split up the vast fortune of the Hughes estate among 22 cousins who qualified as lineal heirs. The estate was valued in the billions of dollars when Hughes died in 1976. The innumerable meetings and hearings to resolve all the estate and financial issues cost the Hughes estate tens of millions of dollars in fees and costs to various attorneys, accountants, and other professionals.

---

140. Greenburg, Z. (2017, October 30). The Top Earning Dead Celebrities of 2017. Retrieved December 14, 2017, https://www.forbes.com/sites/zackomalleygreenburg/2017/10/30/the-top-earning-dead-celebrities-of-2017/#34c7d69241f5

Did Howard Hughes really want to otherwise give his fortune to these "court-qualified" individuals? He likely never met most of them! Although Hughes lived a reclusive life, he was known to be a charitable individual. During his lifetime, he contributed generously to start charitable research and medical foundations, like the Hughes Medical Institute. Using particular types of Trusts, charitable donations are used to deduct against taxes owed, which, in turn, help to lower or eliminate estate taxes, especially in larger estates. Wealthier individuals have similar Trusts set up to control and handle their financial estate after death. A common example is seen in the television credits that are shown at the end of various PBS (Public Broadcasting Service) broadcasts, which highlight individual or charitable trusts who have donated to PBS. These estates are examples of entities generally set up to shelter very wealthy estates from estate taxes, or to provide charitable gift-giving to society after death. For Howard Hughes, he was known to be the richest individual in the world at the time he died in 1976. It is still a wonder what he really wanted to do with his financial empire. We, unfortunately, will never know. For having no valid Will, or accompanying Trusts, for an estate with such tremendous wealth, was truly a preventable misfortune. The IRS was the major creditor in the Hughes estate, taking close to half his fortune for estate taxes. Most if not all of the estate taxes paid to IRS could have otherwise gone to qualified charitable institutions if Howard Hughes had constructed a valid Last Will, accompanied with a Trust or Trusts directing how the funds would be endowed.

Preparing a Last Will needs attention to organization and to the proper division of assets to designated heirs. The language has to be clearly understood so that every heir reads the same language the same way. Constructing a Last Will starts by piecing it together, section by section; like modular housing. It isn't hard to do. The ease in completing a Will is like working on it like a step-by-step construction effort.

Most mistakes in a Last Will can be avoided. Experience has shown that the most common mistakes primarily center on vague and ambiguous language. If a phrase, a sentence, or paragraph can possibly derive more than one meaning (ambiguous language), or is otherwise confusing (vague language), then a revision is in order. The language should ripple in resonance with the body of the Will. Clearly spell out who will inherit the estate assets and how the assets will be distributed among the heirs. Sometimes imagining how the different heirs would read the language can bring perspective and better understanding to how to shape the writing.

Take note that a Last Will is a farewell letter — a final notice to the world. So, make it count. Ideally, have someone else review one's estate planning; a trusted friend or spouse is good. Have an estate-planning attorney make sure it is legally sufficient as well as grammatically well written.

Take reference to how Chief Justice Warren Burger wrote his own Last Will (See Chapter 4), which probably was not the best thing to do. Moreover, given the sparse language comprising the document, the Chief Justice probably took a quick pen to it and likely had no one review it. In his Last Will, he identified his heirs, appointed a personal representative, and distributed assets of his estate, using fewer than 100 words. And even with the additional closing language, and signatures of the witnesses and the Testator, the entire Will was still just a page in length. As a result, the very short Will left too much to interpretation regarding the vague and ambiguous language concerning the disposition of estate assets. The contests interpreting the Will turned out to become very expensive. A good portion of the estate was consumed by the litigation, arguing how the estate's assets were to be classified and distributed. Another significant portion went to pay for estate taxes.[141]

More and more court contests interpreting portions of Last Wills are occuring on a regular basis across our country. Poorly-drafted Last Wills and Trusts can lead to arguments in the interpretation of language that sadly result in expensive legal contests among heirs. For so many reasons, getting a Last Will done is very important, but getting it done correctly, in the way you desire it, is most important. Language in a Last Will that could be interpreted as vague or ambiguous is generally due to a lack of clear under-

---

141. *See,* "Warren Burger's Will: A Fool for a Lawyer," Ellen Warren, Chicago Tribune (Nov. 5, 1995); http://articles.chicagotribune.com/1995-11-05/news/9511050250_1_chief-justice-warren-burger-watchful-supreme-court

standing, either in understanding the laws or understanding how to write well. So, poor language in a Last Will can cause a lot of anguish, hardship, and heartache, unfortunately for all sides. Given the volatility that can occur in a post-mortem estate, if details about organization and asset dispositions are poorly explained (through a bad or out-of-date Last Will) or unexplained (by failing to include the proper language, or having no Last Will), then completing a solid Last Will becomes ever more pressing.

In the future, the lack of planning will continue to ensnarl estates. Courts will be very busy, and attorneys and accountants, on both sides, will be paid to straighten out the issues. So, plan instead, and provide for the smooth transition of wealth through proper estate planning. Look for language that brings clarity and an easy read. Some of the most serene moments for family and friends are shared after one dies. They are very sentimental and special, intended to find a calming joy in the peaceful thoughts shared by everyone else still alive.

Having a solid Last Will in place will keep others from usurping or undermining the intent of the Decedent. A common example that occurs more often than one expects is where the surviving spouse (mom or dad) has a valid Will, and the family assets are equitably divided among the children. Later in life, the surviving spouse becomes infirm, and unable to live independently. One or more of the children decide to remain home, whether by need or choice, and care for the parent during the last years of life. In turn, those children may later hold the conviction that the house is theirs, or mostly theirs, related to the years caring for the parent.

Another example is with personal property assets. Heirs may claim that the surviving parent gave him or her a particular asset, such as an art piece, a family heirloom, or the rosewood table. Any number of contests can arise over personal property items unless enough specificity regarding the distribution of personal property assets are clearly identified in an attachment to the Will called a Tangible Personal Property List. It details selected personal property items and to whom they are to be given. Also, the Testator can determine a system where heirs can divide personal property items, such as going in turn or in sequence in choosing them. As much as possible, let the Last Will dictate the proper division of the estate, and not the more passionate voice of one or more of the children (or other heirs) who may mistakenly believe that they are in control by virtue of possession, or by exhibiting a stronger character over that of the other heirs.

If the Decedent has a Last Will, most often, the heirs are resigned to follow it under the protection of the court. Only in a small number of cases is the Decedent's entire Last Will challenged by way of a Will contest to invalidate the Will. In those challenged cases, the first approach by a potential heir who feels inequitably served is to invalidate a Will by legal insufficiency or technicality, such as the lack of signatures of proper witnesses present when the Decedent signed the Will, or else by questioning the Decedent's capacity at the time the Will was written. Incapacity contests are generally based either on the mental capacity of the Decedent at the time he or she signed the Will (did the Decedent know what was being signed and recognize what assets were being given to whom?) or a claim that the Decedent was under duress or undue influence (usually by a close relative) at the time the Will was drafted (did the Decedent want or desire to give estate assets away in the amounts and to the particular individuals or entities as designated in the Will, or was he or she coerced to do so?), or both.

Lastly, we have seen the average value of individual estates become richer over time. The subsequent consideration for such estates is determining whether the value of the *gross estate* obligates the payment of Federal or State estate taxes, or both. The United States Congress recently overhauled its tax structure for estates, which takes effect beginning in calendar year 2018.[142] Essentially, federal estate tax exemption limits were doubled for individuals from approximately $5,490,000 in 2017 to $11,180,000 million in 2018, with subsequent years through 2025 indexed for inflation.[143] So, that means that the federal estate tax exemption limit for married couples for 2018 has doubled to $22.4 million! But there is a sunset provision where Congress made these federal estate tax provisions temporary, lasting

---

142. Tax Cuts and Jobs Act of 2017, Pub. L. 115-97 (Dec. 22, 2017).
143. 26 U.S. Code Section 2010(c)(3)(C)-Unified Credit against tax imposed; *see also,* https://www.irs.gov/businesses/small-businesses-self-employed/estate-tax

from calendar years 2018 through 2025. Absent any further Congressional action, that means the exemption amount will revert back to the original $5 million base set in 2011.[144]

The new federal estate tax exemption limits will allow over 99 percent of post-mortem estates to avoid paying federal estate taxes. Going forward, it is estimated that only two-tenths of 1 percent of estates will pay federal estate taxes. Yet many more estates will be subject to state estate taxes. Specifically, there are 13 states, plus the District of Columbia, that impose state estate taxes. Furthermore, six states additionally charge state inheritance taxes. Only Maryland charges both an inheritance tax and an estate tax. An estate tax is imposed on the estate of a Decedent for the transfer of bequests to heirs if the value of the gross estate exceeds the state exemption limit. An inheritance tax is generally imposed on the recipient of inherited funds from a Decedent's estate. In Maryland, however, the personal representative of a Decedent's estate is required to pay the inheritance tax, not to mention the estate tax.[145] As is similar with federal estate taxes, both state estate and inheritance taxes have exemption limits or exclusion amounts, which means that no tax is due unless the taxable amount exceeds a certain dollar or percentage limit of the gross estate. These amounts vary among the applicable states, which are highlighted in the State Estate Tax and Inheritance Tax Chart in Chapter 7. The chart shows how state estate taxes can affect individual estates with relatively low levels of comparative wealth. Meaning, more estates are having to pay state estate taxes. In the State of Washington, for example, if your gross estate goes above the applicable exclusion amount of $2,193,000 (as of January 1, 2018), be prepared to pay a Washington state estate tax of 15 percent (after subtracting the applicable exclusion amount and any applicable tax deductions). And when looking at the State Estate Tax and Inheritance Tax Chart, although Washington estate taxes start at 10 percent for a Decedent's gross estate valued from $0

---

144. Ebeling, A. (2017, December 21). Final Tax Bill Includes Huge Estate Tax Win For The Rich: The $22.4 Million Exemption. Retrieved March 12, 2018, https://www. forbes.com/sites/ashleaebeling/2017/12/21/final-tax-bill-includes-huge-estate-tax-win-for-the-rich-the-22-4-million-exemption/#358c4b4b1d54

145. MD Est & Trusts Code § 7-307.

up to $1,000,000.00 and then steps up to 14 percent for gross estates valued above $1,000,000.00 and up to $2,000,000.00, no individual estates in those gross-estate ranges would pay any state estate tax in Washington because of the applicable exclusion amount, which is annually indexed for inflation.[146] Similarly, look at your state to see whether it has an estate tax and what its applicable exclusion amount or exemption threshold it imposes under law. Washington state does not have an inheritance tax, but its top-tier estate tax rate is 20 percent, making it the highest state estate tax rate in the nation.

Wealthier individuals with federal or state estate tax considerations should especially consider the assistance of specialized estate-planning counsel whose practices also include protecting wealthier estates from state and federal estate taxes. They should be able to advise you what option or options to consider in your state. Spousal Protection Trusts, Credit Shelter Trusts, or Charitable Trusts are just some examples of ways to legally lessen, prevent, or avoid paying federal or state estate taxes, or both. This book does not cover details about structuring estate plans for wealthy estates focusing on state and federal estate tax protections.

Overall, it is always best to take the time to be careful and thorough in understanding your own estate documents. If court battles can occur in estates among high net-worth individuals, it can certainly happen to anyone, including you. So, do not hastily complete your own Last Will or have your cousin, who happens to be a divorce or patent attorney, write one for you. Instead, it is best to find a qualified estate-planning attorney through good referrals, through your local county bar association's lawyer referral service, or searching reputable estate planning networks.

Lastly, there looms a great social and financial dilemma over the American landscape concerning the enormous transfers of wealth taking place over the next 30 years. Assets will be moving down to and from the baby boomers, and down to the Generation X class and the millennials. But with over

---

146. RCW 83.100.040, Estate Tax Imposed-Amount of Tax; *see also,* https://dor.wa.gov/find-taxes-rates/other-taxes/estate-tax-tables.

65 percent of Americans still without any estate plan in place, and another 7-10 percent needing structural revisions to existing estate documents, we remain at a standstill. At this stage, it is a national crisis to be this unprepared. There are so many of us with no Last Will, no Trust; or even a Durable Power of Attorney for healthcare or financial management. Now it's time to change those statistics.

BIBLIOGRAPHY

Beyer, G. (1999). Wills, Trusts and Estates, "Reasons Most People Die Intestate." Aspen Law & Business.

Havens, J., & Schervish, P. (2014). National Wealth Transfer and Potential for Philanthropy Technical Report. *Center on Wealth and Philanthropy;* Boston College.

(2016, June). Demystifying the Last Will and Testament-Survey of Americans Without Wills. *The U.S. Legal Wills Blog:* . Retrieved September 8, 2017, from https://www.uslegalwills.com/blog/americans-without-wills/

Rev. Code of Wa, ch. 11.04.015(1)(b) - Descent and distribution of real and personal estate. 1 Oct 1974.

Molon, A. (2014, April 5). Inside Kurt Cobain's $450M Empire. Retrieved May 22, 2018, from, https://www.cnbc.com/2014/04/04/kurt-cobain-and-the-big-business-of-dead-celebs.html

Martin, P. (2010, April 7). Lincoln's Missing Bodyguard. Retrieved October 22, 2016, from, https://www.smithsonianmag.com/history/lincolns-missing-bodyguard-12932069/

Staff, L. (2017, July 25). The Messy Afterlife of Jimi Hendrix, from http://www.legacy.com/news/celebrity-deaths/article/the-messy-afterlife-of-jimi-hendrix

Leiber, N. (2018, May 3). How Criminals Steal $37 Billion a Year from America's Elderly. *Bloomberg News.*

25 U.S. Code § 2206 - Descent and distribution, *as amended* (The statute discusses the non-testamentary disposition of assets of Native American land and certain other federally-governed properties, and the rules governing descent of estate assets regarding the devise or descent of trust or restricted property not disposed otherwise by a valid Will).

Civil Rights Act of 1964, Pub.L. 88-352, 78 Stat. 241 (1964).

Alexander, B. (2004, September 15). Judge Settles Family Feud Over Jimi Hendrix's Estate.). Retrieved May 18, 2017, from, https://www.nytimes.com/2004/09/25/us/judge-settles-long-family-feud-over-jimi-hendrixs-estate.html

NCV Newswire. (2017, March 16). Jimi Hendrix Estate Sues Andrew Pitsicalis and Leon Hendrix. New Cannabis Ventures.

L.L.C., H. (2017, March 16). Hendrix Sues Serial Infringer Andrew Pitsicalis. Retrieved September 19, 2017, from https://www.prnewswire.com/news-releases/hendrix-sues-serial-infringer-andrew-pitsicalis-300424994.html

Tn. Stat. Descent and Distribution, Tit. 31, Ch. 2, §104(a)(2) (2017).

(2013, December 10). Steve McNair and the Perils of Dying Without a Will. Retrieved August 22, 2017, from, www.familyarchivalsolutions.com/steve-mcnair-perils-dying-without-a-will/

Rev. Code of Wa, ch. 26.04.020(4)-Prohibited Marriages. Referendum Measure No. 74, Approved 6 Nov 2012.

Connell v. Francisco, 127 Wn. 2d. 339; 898 P.2d 831 (1995).

(n.d.). How to Appoint a Guardian for Your Children. Retrieved June 18, 2017, from https://www.lawdepot.com/law-library/estate-articles/how-to-appoint-a-guardian-for-your-children/

26 U.S. Code § 664. Charitable remainder trusts.

26 U.S. Code § 2518. Disclaimers.

26 CFR § 25.2518-2. Requirements for a qualified disclaimer.

Tax Cuts and Jobs Act of 2017, Pub. L. 115-97 (Dec. 22, 2017); 26 U.S. Code Section 2010(c)(3)-Unified Credit against tax imposed.

Inflation Adjustments Under Recently Enacted Tax Law, IR-2018-94 (April 13, 2018).

Gleckman, H. (2017, December 6). Only 1,700 Estates Would Owe Estate Tax in 2018. Retrieved December 14, 2018, https://www. taxpolicycenter.org/taxvox/only-1700-estates-would-owe-estate-tax-2018-under-tcja

How Many People Pay the Estate Tax? (n.d.). Retrieved October 4, 2018, https://www.taxpolicycenter.org/briefing-book/how-many-people-pay-estate-tax

Rev. Code of Wa. ch. 11.88.010(1)(c). Legal Determination of Incapacity.

Rev. Code of Wa. ch. 11.40.020(1). Notice to Creditors-Manner-Filings-Publication

Rev. Code of Wa. ch. 11.40.051(1). Claims Against Decedent-Time limits

The Rules of Professional Conduct of Washington State, RPC 1.14 *Client with Diminished Capacity.*

Health Insurance Portability and Accountability Act. Pub. L. No. 104-191 (1996).

"Living in a Committed Intimate Relationship? Planning for Unmarried Couples," *Real Property, Probate & Trust Newsletter,* Washington State Bar Association (Fall 2016).

Theprobatelawyerblog.com/Aug 30, 2016; Andy & Danielle Mayoras/ http://www.probatelawyerblog.com/2016/08/tom-clancy-estate-battle-ends-but-valuable-lesson-remains.html

The fight over the Estate of James Brown

Wilson v. Dallas, 743 S.E. 2d 746 (2013)

"SC Supreme Court Freezes James Brown estate case," The Associated Press (Updated Feb 27, 2015).

Fisher, D. (2015, July 14). Court Ruling Likely Ends Anna Nicole Smith Estate's Fight For Marshall Family Millions. Retrieved April 21, 2017, from, https://www.forbes.com/sites/danielfisher/2015/07/14/texas-appeals-court-reverses-sanctions-against-anna-nicole-smith-estate/#54b4ea691a7e

"Anna Nicole Smith Dies at 39," Abby Goodnough and Margalit Fox, The New York Times (Feb. 8, 2007).

"Anna Nicole Smith's Adult Son Dies in Bahamas," Associated Press (Sept. 12, 2006).

Biography.com, "Anna Nicole Smith Biography," A&E Television Networks, Apr. 2, 2014, Updated Apr. 27, 2017, URL: https://www.biography.com/people/anna-nicole-smith-183547

Anna Nicole Smith, aka Vickie Lynn Marshall

https://www.scrogginlaw.com/Celebrities-Article-FINAL-11-20-2016.PDF

http://www.probatelawyerblog.com/anna-nicole-smith/

http://www.celebchannel.net/anna-nicole-smith

Marshall v. Marshall, 547 U.S. 293 (2006)

Stern v. Marshall, 564 U.S. 462 (2011)

https://www.eonline.com/news/55436/stern-and-birkhead-work-together-for-anna-nicole

"Anna Nicole Smith Dies at 39," Abby Goodnough and Margalit Fox, The New York Times (Feb. 8, 2007).

"Anna Nicole Smith's Adult Son Dies in Bahamas," Associated Press (Sept. 12, 2006).

Hall, S. (2007, June 19). Stern and Birkhead Work Together for Anna Nicole. Retrieved June 18, 2017, from, https://www.eonline.com/news/55436/stern-and-birkhead-work-together-for-anna-nicole

"Jefferson-Hemings Resources," The Jefferson Monticello, https://www.monticello.org/site/plantation-and-slavery/jefferson-hemings-resources

Herbert, S. (1995). *Principal and Interest: Thomas Jefferson and the Problem of Debt* (p. 14). University of Virginia Press.

Lucia, S. (1993). *Those Who Labor for My Happiness: Thomas Jefferson and His Slaves* (pp 147-180). University of Virginia Press.

The fight over the Estate of Leona Helmsley

Affidavit of Carl Lekic filed in the Estate of Leona Helmsley

Helmsley, Leona, Queen of Mean," Inmate Aid, from, https://www.inmateaid.com/famous-inmates/helmsley-leona-queen-of-mean

uk.reuters.com, NY judge trims dog's $12 million inheritance

NY judge trims dog's $12 million inheritance. (2008, June 16). Retrieved April/May, 2017, from, https://uk.reuters.com/article/oukoe-uk-helmsley-dog-idUKN1634773920080617

Alfred Nobel — His Life and Work. NobelPrize.org. Nobel Media AB 2018.

https://www.nobelprize.org/alfred-nobel/alfred-nobel-his-life-and-work/

Encyclopedia of Modern Europe: Europe 1789–1914: Encyclopedia of the Age of Industry and Empire, "Alfred Nobel", Thomson Gale (2006).

Alfred Nobel. (2014). Retrieved November 28, 2017, http://famouschemists.org/alfred-nobel/

Schultz, C. (2013, October 9). Blame Sloppy Journalism for the Nobel Prizes. Retrieved April 4, 2017, https://www.smithsonianmag.com/smart-news/blame-sloppy-journalism-for-the-nobel-prizes-1172688/

Alfred Nobel's Will. (n.d.). Retrieved August 20, 2017, from https://www. nobelpeaceprize.org/History/Alfred-Nobel-s-will

Norwegian Nobel Institute

The Last Will of Alfred Bernhard Nobel, Paris, France, 18 Nov 1895.

Alfred Nobel-Other Reference Sources

https://www.nobelpeaceprize.org/History/Alfred-Nobel-s-will
https://www.biography.com/people/alfred-nobel-9424195
https://www.famousscientists.org/alfred-nobel/
http://famouschemists.org/alfred-nobel/
https://www.mininghalloffame.org/inductee/nobel

Greenburg, Z. (2017, October 30). The Top Earning Dead Celebrities of 2017. Retrieved December 14, 2017, https://www.forbes.com/sites/ zackomalleygreenburg/2017/10/30/the-top-earning-dead-celebrities- of-2017/#34c7d69241f5

Tax Cuts and Jobs Act of 2017, Pub. L. 115-97 (Dec. 22, 2017).

Ebeling, A. (2017, December 21). Final Tax Bill Includes Huge Estate Tax Win For The Rich: The $22.4 Million Exemption. Retrieved March 12, 2018, from, https://www.forbes.com/sites/ashleaebeling/2017/12/21/ final-tax-bill-includes-huge-estate-tax-win-for-the-rich-the-22-4- million-exemption/#358c4b4b1d54

Walczak, J. (2017, June 27). State Inheritance and Estate Taxes. Retrieved November 18, 2017, from https://taxfoundation.org/state-inheritance- estate-taxes-economic-implications/

Everplans. (2018, August 5). State-by-state Digital Estate Planning Laws. Retrieved March 2, 2019, from https://www.everplans.com/articles/ state-by-state-digital-estate-planning-laws

Special Thanks to the *The Nobel Foundation* for permission to include a true copy of the original Last Will of Alfred Nobel. The full text of Alfred Nobel´s Will can be found at:

http://www.nobelprize.org/alfred_nobel/will/will-full.html

Special thanks to the *Internet Legal Research Group* (ILRG) for providing a sample blank Last Will as a reference sample. The ILRG provides a categorized index of select web sites, as well as thousands legal forms and documents online.

https://www.irlg.com/

PR Newswire/March 16, 2017-Legacy Recordings and Experience Hendrix LLC (Mar 16, 2017).

Special Thanks to *The Tax Foundation,* www.taxfoundation.org, for use of its informational format of the State Estate and Inheritance Tax Chart, included with updates to reflect changes in various State laws.

"Warren Burger's Will: A Fool for a Lawyer," Ellen Warren, Chicago Tribune (Nov. 5, 1995); http://articles.chicagotribune.com/1995-11-05/news/9511050250_1_chief-justice-warren-burger-watchful-supreme-court

26 U.S. Code § 2010(c)(3) - Unified credit against tax imposed.

https://www.irs.gov/businesses/small-businesses-self-employed/estate-tax

https://www.forbes.com/sites/ashleaebeling/2017/12/21/final-tax-bill-includes-huge-estate-tax-win-for-the-rich-the-22-4-million-exemption/#491df0a81d54

RCW 83.100.040, Washington State Estate Tax Imposed-Amount of Tax.; see also, https://dor.wa.gov/find-taxes-rates/other-taxes/estate-tax-tables.

Washington State estate tax tables and exclusion amounts:

https://dor.wa.gov/find-taxes-rates/other-taxes/estate-tax-tables

ABOUT THE AUTHOR

Edward Melillo has been practicing law since 1995. He is semi-retired from his regular law practice, with only a few select clients. When available, he holds private seminars to assist others with their estate plans. Mr. Melillo served as editor-in-chief of the Washington State Bar Association's Elder Law Newsletter and has served on the boards of various non-profit organizations in the greater Puget Sound area of Washington State. He has provided pro-bono services over the years to clients in physical dire straits or in financial need, helping set up their Last Wills, Trusts, and Durable Powers of Attorney for health and financial management and/or Health Care Directives.

Over the years, we have adopted a number of dogs from rescues and shelters. First there was Bear and after he passed, Ginger and Scout. Now, we have Kira, another rescue. They have brought immense joy and love not just into our lives, but into the lives of all who met them.

We want you to know a portion of the profits of this book will be donated in Bear, Ginger and Scout's memory to local animal shelters, parks, conservation organizations, and other individuals and nonprofit organizations in need of assistance.

– Douglas & Sherri Brown,
President & Vice-President of Atlantic Publishing